Praise for *Innovation Engine: Driving Execution for Breakthrough Results*

Innovation Engine will help you build a climate and culture of innovation. A must-read for every serious executive desiring innovation as a daily habit in their organization and to drive innovation execution.

—Vijay Govindarajan, author of *New York Times* and *Wall Street Journal* best-seller, *Reverse Innovation*

Innovation Engine is one of the best books on "how to" on innovation—a must-read for every IT executive, leader and manager.

—Sukumar Rajagopal, Chief Information Officer and Head of Innovation, Cognizant Technology Solutions

Today's economic pressures, political uncertainty, and rapid change continue to intensify the competitive environment. To remain viable in this environment, companies and their leaders must strike a balance between solving for the immediate needs of a dynamic market and pursuing an innovation strategy that is forward-thinking and positions them one step ahead of the competition and their customers' need. This is an excellent book that offers unique insights and acts as a practical guide for institutions to execute for the future through innovation while solving for market needs for today.

—George Castineiras, Senior Vice President, Prudential Retirement

Innovation is highly pursued, desired, and, oh-so-often, bemoaned as lacking in large organizations. In this impressive book, Jatin has pulled together a comprehensive approach to innovation—in itself innovative—clearly laying out the path from ideation to implementation. He has considered virtually every aspect of the organization—from individuals, to teams, to approach—in this passionately argued text. Well done!

—Hari Mahadevan, Former Executive Officer, Rosetta

Innovation Engine is a thought-provoking and useful read for anyone seriously committed to competing to win.

—Rose Mihaly, Senior Vice President, Chief Administrative Officer, HLIkk (The Hartford, Tokyo, Japan)

Jatin brings out the secret ingredients that make innovative businesses tick—people, culture, and execution. Essential reading for business leaders looking for nuggets to make innovation happen and stick into their business operation.

—Sundara Nagarajan, Technical Director, NetApp

Jatin makes a strong argument to embed *Innovation Engine* into your corporate strategy to balance the short-term financial drivers of the business if the corporation is to achieve long-term success in a highly competitive environment. It is well worth the read.

—Bob Hedinger, Executive Vice President, Marketing, Sales and Business Development, Bell Labs and Skynet

Jatin is an impactful catalyst for innovation in organizations. This book captures the secret ingredients that have made him a successful innovation consultant.

—Rishikesha T. Krishnan, Professor of Corporate Strategy, Indian Institute of Management Bangalore, India, and author of *From Jugaad to Systematic Innovation: The Challenge for India*

Innovation Engine

Innovation Engine

Driving Execution for Breakthrough Results

JATIN DESAI

WILEY

Library of Congress Cataloging-in-Publication Data
Desai, Jatin.
  Innovation engine : driving execution for breakthrough results / Jatin Desai.
    pages cm
  Includes bibliographical references and index.
  ISBN 978-1-118-35503-9 (cloth); ISBN 978-1-118-42027-0 (ebk);
ISBN 978-1-118-64718-9 (ebk); ISBN 978-1-118-41688-4 (ebk)
  1. Technological innovations—Management.   2. Diffusion of innovations—Management.
3. New products.   4. Strategic planning.   I. Title.
  HD45.D366 2013
  658.4′063—dc23

Printed in the United States of America

10 9 8 7 6 5 4 3 2 1

To my parents,
Kalpana and Harshad Desai,
and to my eternal father, Sri Sathya Sai Baba.
I thank them for allowing me to exist and experience the life of Love.
I am nothing without them.
With loving gratitude,
—Jatin

Contents

Preface

Innovation Engine is about the process of innovation execution for organizations of any type and any shape. It will balance theory and practice with real-life case studies to support the practice.

This book is not about convincing you to embrace innovation as a strategy. It will not create a business case for leaders who are ill prepared for the new fundamentals driven by globalization and automation. The evolution of twenty-first-century intelligent organizations has already started. There are plenty of experts who have spent their entire life researching and telling us about how big bureaucratic organizations are the thing of the past. Today, in the middle of the Knowledge Era, leaders cannot afford the time and tardiness for a ten-year strategic plan to produce results, learn from someone else's emerging business models, or wait for the corporate office to make a decision. Today, the new norm is a swifter and more flexible organizational climate with faster decisions, a broader context, a larger tool bag, empathy for all stakeholders, and deep passion toward the vision. This book's goal is not to convince you to adopt this new norm.

Innovation Engine is about how to *prepare* and *grow* your organization in a hyperdynamic and globally connected environment—through foresight and strategic innovation.

It is designed for three groups of readers:

1. C-Suite. Executives interested in building a climate and culture of innovation
2. Management. Those responsible for implementing and driving an *innovation program*
3. Corporate innovators (intrapreneurs). Individuals looking to invent and commercialize their ideas to make a difference through the principles and practices of innovation

There are over 150 different product development and innovation management methods in the marketplace. Unfortunately, most are not effective. Some narrowly focus on only *one* of the following:

- Product development
- Research and development

- Technology
- Ideation through creativity

These methods no longer work because they solve for only one symptom related to growth.

Great companies have figured out a new *rhythm for growth*—purposefully harvesting a cultural balance between performance (left brain) and exploration (right brain). This balance is hard work and requires sacrifice with risk tolerance. These high performers unequivocally not only fulfill current customer desires but also analyze and address the emerging desires of the same customers and adjacent markets.

Most organizations have been very innovative, and in fact, that is probably how they got started. The founders most likely had an idea and a vision. They probably sacrificed all that they had—took on the personal risk, sacrificed their personal lives, and, with conviction and courage, jumped in. As these nimble start-ups grow to be multinationals, however, they forget their roots and the values that gave birth to them. This book will help mature, fast-growing organizations rewire their DNA to include innovation as a capability, a competence, and a strategic tool for moving forward. It will help you create your own *Innovation Engine* for continuous growth.

Acknowledgments

The material in this book is derived largely from our global experience using and teaching the DeSai body of knowledge over the last twenty-five years. This knowledge is based on walking the talk—working with clients of every size and every shape in just about every industry we can think of.

In that sense, I am deeply indebted to all the DeSai practitioners past and present, the plethora of client groups with whom they have worked, and the thousands (a guess) with whom I have worked personally since my father and I started our firm back in 1983.

When you write a first book, it is difficult to acknowledge only a few people since many of the broad ideas and suggestions took shape over one's entire life. Therefore, at the outset, I want to thank my family members, school teachers, family friends, mentors, professional colleagues, customers, suppliers, community activists, and many other life-journey men and women who have touched my heart and shaped my mind. Please accept my deepest gratitude for being part of my life. If you know me, you have helped me.

More specifically, I want to acknowledge the hard work of Wendy Kolanz for tirelessly providing the research and editing support during the development of this book; Cathy Swody and colleagues at Learning Research Institute, for providing assistance with original research that shaped the important framework for this book; and heartfelt gratitude to Larry Gregory and Tim Maurer, for their input and feedback during the development of each chapter.

I am very grateful to all the corporate executives, innovators, and intrapreneurs who gave their time, shared their stories and expertise, which helped shape the insights and ideas, including Juan Andrade of The ACE Group, George Castineiras of Prudential Retirement; Sukumar Rajagopal and Elilanban Neehivanan of Cognizant; Tom Maddison and Denise Fletcher of Xerox; Bob Hedinger, when with AT&T; Murali Muraleedharan of Tata Consulting; Kris Gopalakrishnan of Infosys; C. J. Marr, when with Alegent Health; Hari Mahdevan of Rosetta; Mark Wright, when with Bristol-Myers Squibb; Jagdish Vasishtha of Kinetic Glue; Shyam Ramamurthy of Yahoo; N. Balaji of Axis Bank; S.C. Bhargava, S. A. Kulkarni and Anand Kurien of Larsen & Toubro; Kapil Mehan, Arun Leslie George, and Parvez Shaikh of Coromandel International; and Randy Voss, when with Whirlpool.

I am particularly thankful for the important contribution and involvement of Rose Mihaly, John Madigan, Cheryl Chester, and Lon Smith, when with The Hartford Financial Services; Sundara Nagarajan, Daryl Conner of Conner Partners, Padma Thiruvengadam, when with Pfizer; Pradip Desai, when with Tata Consulting; Sairam Tadigadapa of Capital One; and Dan Brown, William Miller, Alain Rostain, Lokesh Venkataswamy, and Mukund Amin.

When I was conceiving this book, it was Dan Roberts of Ouellette Associates who encouraged me to speak to my acquisitions editor, Tim Burgard, at John Wiley & Sons. I thank you both for your guidance and support in helping to bring this book to the world. Additionally I would like to thank the rest of the team at Wiley: Stacey Rivera, Natasha Andrews-Noel, and Andrew Wheeler.

Importantly, I want to express a special gratitude to my wife, Anjali, and my sister, Falguni. They say behind every man there is a great woman who is the beacon of light. In my case, these two ladies have been shining the light of hope and strength every day of my life. I cannot easily express my inner joy and gratitude for standing by me, especially during the development of this book. I love you both.

Finally, innovation is mostly about the future. My wife and I look at our future together through the lives of our three children: Shreena, Shanil, and Raina. I thank them for being the best kids a parent could ask for, for taking care of me during the late nights, and for Skype conversations while I was traveling the globe. I am who I am because of your love.

INTRODUCTION

The dictionary defines dualism "as the idea or belief that everything has two opposite parts or principles." It is said that most of the primary progress that humans have made is because of a belief in dualism. Ever since the dawn of Adam and Eve, humans see the world as a colorful tapestry of contradictions. We spend our entire life in a system of right and wrong, good and bad, left and right, control and consensus, I and He, tall and short, good and evil, love and violence.

Dualism is not bad. It makes our world go around. In fact, it is the very source of human creativity as well as misery. Dualism gives us distinctions. It allows us to see what is and what can be. It allows us a vision to move from, toward what can be. It gives us motivation for progress in society. If we didn't practice dualism, we would still be hunting for food instead of going to grocery stores. Dualism powers evolutionary progress.

Today more than ever, organizations must generate short-term profits as well as invest for the future to create sustainable growth. Unfortunately, the financial systems, organizational boundaries, and reward systems are primarily aligned for short-term results only. Today's managers and leaders are seldom encouraged or offered incentives to pursue and ensure profits from the next generation of offerings. Unfortunately, the focus tends to be only on today's products and services.

In an ideal world of commerce, everyone would agree to achieve strategic objectives by adopting the mind-set of dualism. But that is not the case. Most managers operate in silos and lack the fast, necessary agreements for utilizing their scarce resources and skills for today's *and* tomorrow's outcomes.

The New Duality: Performance Engine and Innovation Engine

The critical call for C-level leaders is to develop a growth engine that includes a short-term *performance engine* as well as an *innovation engine* that creates long-term growth.

Innovation is often sought and is in high demand today. At the same time, it is little understood and often lacks committed sponsorship. Sometimes it even creates fear and generates wrong behaviors. Why?

Over the last three decades, most executives primarily needed to know how to excel at installing, running, and optimizing a performance engine for quarterly results (short-term only). Many were not given mandates to create a long-term sustainable corporate culture fueled by an innovation engine. In fact, most organizations lack an innovation engine completely. Therefore, today most teams at the top are ill equipped to sponsor and run their organizations using both engines. This fact inhibits forward movement in a highly global interconnected business climate where dualism is the new norm.

The primary aim of this book is to help organizations complement the *operational performance* mind-set with the *innovation execution* mind-set.

Foresight

How would you have liked to have known about the emerging virtual bookstore opportunity in 1990? In 1994, Jeff Bezos launched a company called Cadabra.com; later it was renamed Amazon, and founder Bezos was named "Person of the Year" by *Time* magazine in 1999. Why didn't the mega-publishers like Simon & Schuster or retailers like B. Dalton or Borders see this coming?

In 1996, we were introduced to the first smartphones. Using one of many foresight patterns, ability to predict demand and introductions of new products and services, available to innovators, years ago we could have predicted that the web browser would move from desktop, to laptop, to smartphones.

The social networking revolution has been coming at us like a freight train. Such services were introduced over a decade ago, with Napster (music sharing) and MySpace. In 2008, Daniel Burrus helped define the market potential for social networking.[1] There is still a huge opportunity to enter the market and organizations to innovate and leverage it as a strategic opportunity. Facebook, Twitter, Instagram, and LinkedIn are examples of social networking start-ups changing the very nature of how we communicate, share information, create knowledge, transact, and build relationships. This new technology platform will change our world at a dizzying pace, faster than any other technology we have seen in the last 2,000 years. Knowing this, why do most companies still lack a "social" business strategy?

The primary reason for such organizational behavior is because most of today's management mind-set does not embrace the dualism mind-set—the organizational ability to deliver near term and also prepare for perpetual results year after year.

Each chapter of *Innovation Engine* is packed with actionable ideas, references, and resources so the reader can explore the concepts and ideas immediately.

This book has emerged out of conversations with many executives who have freely shared their experiences and knowledge, including those from Microsoft, Yahoo, ACE Group, Bristol-Myers, The Hartford, Prudential, Merck, Macy's, AT&T, and Google in the United States and from Tata, Cognizant, Axis Bank, Coromandel International, Infotech, Larsen & Toubro in India, plus many others. Through other research, it includes stories from AMD, Apple, Facebook, Nike, Twitter, Wal-Mart, Whirlpool, and many other leading brand names.

Specifically, *Innovation Engine* will help leaders and managers who are trying to:

- Create a business case for innovation and supporting *innovation strategy* linked to business vision and goals.
- Accelerate innovation outcomes by reducing time to market.
- Expand the idea landscape with solid insights about the future.
- Build a pipeline of corporate innovators—the key talent for future growth (intrapreneurs).
- Balance profit, performance, and market differentiation.
- Help create a world-class, engaged workforce.

Getting Started

Creating a roadmap for sustainable value creation requires that an organization truly masters all aspects of innovation. Organizations looking for a competitive edge frequently focus on product innovation. However, most have little sustainable competitive advantage. Many new products never generate a profit, and those that do are often quickly copied by the competition, negating any long-term advantage. The result often involves a significant investment in product development without a commensurate return on investment.

While revenue growth is often the primary driver of shareholder value and the number one challenge for every business sector around the world, growth objectives for most industries are tempered by a continuing focus on cost containment.

To achieve sustainable growth, companies must better integrate product innovation with process and service innovations. They need to find new ways to improve efficiency and customer service. This is exactly the kind of innovation customers demand, and it's the kind of innovation competitors will find difficult to replicate.

Yet some organizations have focused on product innovation for so long they don't know how to innovate in any other areas. For example, Microsoft, one of the world's best product innovators for the last two decades, launched a social phone called Kin 2010. The product was a complete disaster. Within six weeks after the launch, the entire product group was shut down. According to the company's earnings reports, Microsoft took at least a $240 million write-off. How could such a great product innovator strike out so fast? In today's climate, it happens to the best of them.

Transforming a company into an innovative enterprise is a major challenge and generally requires new strategies, processes, tools, and behaviors. It also requires a dedicated process for nurturing and commercializing valuable ideas. This type of deep and demonstrated commitment to innovation is the surest way to achieve meaningful and lasting differentiation.

Institutions with broad-based innovation capabilities enjoy higher customer satisfaction, greater loyalty, faster revenue growth, stronger earnings, and ultimately dramatic lifts in investor returns.

Barriers and Risks

Based on our firm's fieldwork and extensive observation of innovation successes and failures, we have identified five barriers to achieving the dualism mind-set for organizations. When these barriers are acknowledged and addressed, the risk of failure associated with value creation and sustainability can be mitigated and the potential results of innovation investments can be maximized. The five barriers are:

1. Absence of a required mind-set to harvest and manage new and novel ideas.
2. Lack of recognition and misalignment of resources available in organizations for investment in innovations.
3. The sheer size of human capital assets that are underutilized and disengaged from an organization's creative capacity.
4. The broad product and delivery capabilities that large-scale organizations possess, which dilutes focus on new emerging and disruptive opportunities.
5. Organizational orthodoxies and dominant logic[2] that hold on to the past and discourage risk taking.

Over a period of time, it is these barriers that create internal conditions for large companies, which are better equipped to create new innovations compared to small start-ups, to become subservient to new entrants.

The Game of Innovation

Nurturing innovation takes resources, players, and appropriate conditions. Innovation is elusive. It cannot be produced on demand, nor can it be corraled or scheduled. Real innovation that matters and has a major impact in practice is extremely difficult to achieve. At best, the organization can create an environment in which innovation as a skill can be taught, nurtured, and supported to create winning outcomes faster than others in the market.

Like a game of basketball or American football, innovation is arduous, difficult, and tricky. Be prepared to score a game-winner once or twice, but only if you are in the game of innovation first.

Are you ready to play the game of innovation? If you don't play, you don't have a chance to win. Do you have a solid business sponsor for the game of innovation in your company?

Innovation Scorecard

Once you are ready to play the game of innovation, you will need an Innovation Scorecard.

Many purists in the field of innovation say that innovation should not be measured because if you do, it will kill your innovation efforts. We disagree.

In a game, it is crucial to measure its progress and the performance of each player. The same is true for the Innovation Scorecard. You need an Innovation Scorecard to measure how well you, your team, and your organization are doing playing the game of innovation. When you begin, the scorecard you need is simpler than the one you will need three years into it or after ten years of playing the game.

What is most important is not the scorecard itself but the mind-set, method, and processes required to build the appropriate scorecard. This will depend on your current readiness for an innovation program. Scorecard statistics required in the National Basketball Association are not the same required in a high school game of basketball. Measuring the wrong things can be a waste of time, and not measuring the right things can lead to wrong investments impacting your ability to grow your program.

The Innovation Scorecard is a critical tool to help you create a robust innovation engine in harmony with the performance engine.

We explore the elements of a good Innovation Scorecard as you play the game in later chapters. The rules of baseball are different for Little League Baseball than they are for Major League Baseball. The essence of the game is the same, but the methods for preparation, motivation, communication, mentoring, and playing are drastically different. The same applies to your innovation journey.

To become a world-class innovator, you will need a scorecard to keep track of your progress. The scorecard itself will evolve as you develop maturity in playing the game just like it does from elementary, to middle school, to high school, to undergraduate, and finally to postgraduate or professional levels.

In Chapter 4, We introduce an Innovation Scorecard framework that includes examples of scorecards and how to link to your Balanced Scorecard.

Driving Innovation

Using years of experience working with companies across the globe in variety of sectors, we have developed an Innovation Execution framework that has been field tested and refined. If you and your organization are seriously ready to play the game of innovation, you need to consider the next ten steps to derive maximum benefit from your innovation investments. Each step is discussed in a different chapter. The book is designed to allow you to jump around. Feel free to go directly to the chapter that is most relevant to you at this point in your journey.

Innovation Engine is divided into three parts. Part I will help you build a business case for innovation and help create a clear innovation strategy designed to support the business strategy. Part II is about building your own playbook for innovation, and Part III provides guidelines, tools, and techniques to begin implementation of your innovation program. Here is a quick overview of each chapter to help you get the most out of the book:

Part I: Link Innovation to Business Strategy

1. "Develop a Clear Innovation Intent." In today's dynamic business environment, your strategies are constantly adapting and evolving. For innovation to

be successful, it must be linked to your current strategic intent—a unique direction for the company that will generate specific value targets (top line, mid line, bottom line).

2. "Assess Innovation Readiness." Many organizations skip this important step. How ready is your organization's propensity to innovate? By evaluating 45 components of innovation and reviewing your organizational structural, you can develop a highly customized roadmap for innovation. (Note: To learn more about an online system to help you conduct an innovation audit, please visit www.desai.com and learn more about the Innovation Readiness Assessment, which provides a measure of 15 factors and 45 components of innovation.)

3. "Creating an Innovation Strategy." First, develop a unique value creation target. Then create a vertical and horizontal organizational alignment where everyone can see themselves in the strategic vision and mission. This is essential for future financial and nonfinancial returns.

Part II: Develop an Innovation Playbook

4. "Creating a Roadmap." The final step before you commit to a long-term innovation initiative is to develop a detailed charter, a program implementation plan, and an Innovation Scorecard that will keep you on track. There are many ways to begin to create space, build strength, or accelerate growth for innovation. Each organization must evaluate where it falls on this continuum. In addition, organizational readiness, sponsorship, leader alignment, and urgency to innovate are necessary components to constructing your innovation roadmap.

5. "Building Momentum." Once you have linked innovation to your organization's specific business strategy and the intended value targets, you will need to educate employees at all levels on how the organization generates profit. After you create transparency, all employees will have a better idea of how to generate ideas that can be successfully ventured.

Part III: Playing the Game

6. "Structuring for Innovation." One of the first high-priority tasks necessary for innovation to become an integral part of the organization is to create a vertical and horizontal organizational alignment structure. This structure outlines how each employee can clearly see him- or herself and how all can contribute to the vision and mission for innovation. This plan includes effective change management and control systems to make timely decisions.

7. "Innovation Management Process." You will need to implement a formal process for managing innovation within your firm. The innovation process is the formal series of identifiable inputs, actions, and outputs that will be used to understand the relevance, risks, and value of an idea. If designed well, it should be flexible and scalable to enable rapid evaluation and the inclusion of all stakeholders in achieving success. The objective of the process is not only to identify new innovative opportunities but also to quickly discard ideas that do not have sustainable value.

8. "Building Intrapreneurs." Innovation can occur by having people who can generate real wealth, not just great ideas. Leaders who overutilize resources and underdeliver value cannot be called real innovators. Innovation requires diversity in ability and competence of your people. Pair ability and competence together as often as you can, and they will drive growth and performance.

9. "Sourcing Radical Ideas." At some point you will have exhausted all good ideas from within your company. For sustainable growth access, you will also need access to radical fresh ideas that can catapult you to the next business models. Doing this requires deliberate reimagination. By looking at trends and convergences, you can develop new ideas to put in your innovation pipeline. This chapter provides examples of important macro trends that might impact your business within next five years.

10. "The *One* Secret about Innovation." Everyone can innovate or contribute to innovation efforts. But can they do it year after year? Organizations can identify and launch an unending pipeline of great innovations if they embrace this one secret that can continually produce streams of innovation success. What is that one secret?

Jump in and explore how to build your very own Innovation Engine using these ten steps.

Notes

1. Daniel Burrus, *Flash Foresight: How to See the Invisible and Do the Impossible* (New York: Harper Business, 2011).
2. In the field of strategic management, C. K. Prahalad and Richard A. Bettis first introduced the concept of dominant logic in 1986.

PART I

Link Innovation to Business Strategy

Develop a Clear Innovation Intent

In today's dynamic business environment, your business strategies are constantly adapting and evolving. For innovation to be successful, it must be linked to your current strategic intent: a unique direction for the company that will generate specific short-term and long-term value targets (top-line, mid-line, and bottom-line targets).

Here is a challenge for you. For your organization, small or large, for profit or nonprofit, pick up your organization's strategic report, or an executive speech, or an annual report, and look for the word "innovation." You will find it described as the *way to the future*.

Then go back and look at similar material from five or ten years ago. You will find the word "innovation" used by the previous leaders of your company. Most organizational leaders always claim that innovation is the path forward. It is the most natural thing to say to employees, customers, and stakeholders.

Then look around for evidence of innovations and supporting capabilities. You may find pockets of innovation, or none at all. Why does this happen? Why is it that organizational leaders cannot embed innovation as a core capability even when they commit to do so in public?

The Vision

In Eastern philosophy, the human body is considered to be the vehicle by which you live in this world and achieve peace, liberation, enlightenment, realization of God, and so on. This philosophy says the human body is the primary means by which one can discover and experience Universal Truth. The mind and the senses are the primary tools to help along the path to inner knowing and inner being. Mind is believed to be the key that either opens the door to a higher understanding or, if turned in the opposite direction, locks the person into the unending movement of the pendulum swinging between joy and misery. The mind is given a very high premium (mind is the key that if turned one way, it opens the doors to new possibilities and forward progress; alternatively, if turned the other way, it can close doors to new opportunities and happiness in one's life) toward the path of higher consciousness. Eastern wisdom concludes that the body, mind, and five senses, which interact with the physical world, control one's destiny.

Permanent happiness is the primary motivation for most human beings. Many look outside but then, one day, they discover that real joy and happiness have always resided within them and are the most prized possession. Most human beings don't realize that happiness arises from inside. Very often they allow it to be stolen away by others. Why do we do that? It is a mystery we call life.

In the game of life, eventually we collect enough experiences to realize that the quality of our body, mind, and senses are directly linked to our ability to achieve balanced life, meaning, and deep inner joy. This awareness may take a few years, a few decades, or a few lifetimes. Often our path to this discovery accelerates due to personal calamity and tragic events.

Once we awaken to the understanding that deep inner happiness is within and not outside, we start correcting behavior and make more informed daily choices, creating an alignment between the heart's yearning to achieve inner peace and the mind's desire to be successful in the materialistic world. Making such choices requires self-awareness, courage, and conviction. For many, this process is not easy and requires tremendous personal sacrifices.

Ultimately, one day we wake up and realize the universal truth: Permanent peace and joy in life cannot occur along with increased desires to accumulate external possessions. The two missions are on the opposite end of a fragmented reality.

Truly committed people will begin to simplify their lives and create links between both motivations. They become energized to redesign their lives. They become healthier, smile more, and begin to experience the balance they always dreamed of. Looking back, they realize that the change started when they asked questions they had never asked before about themselves and their surroundings: Who am I? Why am I here? What is the purpose of life? What do my relationships mean to me? Why is there so much suffering in the world? Who is God? What is the difference between religion and spirituality?

If we correlate Eastern thinking to the business world, the same applies. Organizations are like human bodies. The leadership mind-set is the mind that controls the senses, and the senses are our employees who interact with all stakeholders, mainly external customers. External customers are like the external world is to a human being. We do everything to serve and seek happiness from the world outside. The organizational mind-set is designed to seek permanent joy—to grow year after year, deliver increased value to all stakeholders, uplift societies, and protect natural resources. Inherently, leaders at the top know this can occur only through strategic alignment of people–profit–planet strategies.

Unfortunately, just like human beings, the organizational "being" is mostly unhappy. The culture is not creative, lacks meaning, contains unfair practices and politics, and is profit focused only, with unclear vision.

Why?

Humans are unhappy because they lack spiritual integrity of thoughts–words–action. Organizations are unhappy because they lack strategic alignment among people, profit, and planet. By only seeing rewards based on satisfying external customers and Wall Street analysts, leaders overemphasize decisions that will mostly satisfy external stakeholders and forget to seek long-term happiness and growth by satisfying internal stakeholders as well: the employees. In other words, we have created a business model that is designed for short-term joy instead of long-term happiness.

When we forget to engage our employees, it is like forgetting to engage our passion and the human spirit within us. Employees are the very source of ideas that can help us create and innovate. When employees become disheartened, how is it possible to grow year after year, decade after decade?

Joy, fear, and sorrow are mostly stimulated from outside—the quality of relationships, customer satisfaction, market analysts, suppliers, and so on. Joy doesn't last. Expectations from external constituents are constantly changing, especially in today's unforgiving markets. Happiness, however, comes from within based on how we see the world and what we value. The universal human values within all of us are compassion, helping others, acting with integrity, peace, and love. When people say life lacks meaning, it means their universal human values are dormant and they are not able to bring out these values in work, life, and play.

Happiness for organizations also comes from within by focusing the entire organization on a vision that is significantly bigger than any one person and engaging each employee to their maximum potential toward that mission. Every organization has vast amounts of unharnessed potential. In other words, every person has ideas that can help improve organizational performance, but there is no clear process and system to unleash such potential. Due to the organization's gravitational pull, most employees learn to shut up and lie low.

Examples of such disconnected cultures were visible at Enron when it filed for bankruptcy in 2001, at Satyam Computers in India in 2009 with its accounting fraud, and at WorldCom in 2002 when its accounting scandal broke. Hundreds of low-integrity scandals occur in every part of the world today; unfortunately, they will continue for a long time into the future.

The best leader innovators in the world have figured out how to achieve joy *and* happiness. These people lead organizations to great heights because they are extremely focused first on being internally happy in their own lives. They have created a bridge between their innermost passions and the organizational vision. They see themselves in a very grand mission at large. They feel they are co-creators of a better future for citizens of this planet.

These innovators know that focusing on running a business that generates new profits from products and services alone is only a third of their job. The satisfaction of their employees (people) and changing the world for the better (planet) are the other main reasons they get up every day. They know that short-term profits are essential and that, without them, they are not performing their duties as leaders. But they also know how to organize for long-term success.

Innovation Engine requires leader innovators who have an exciting, grand vision for the company, a point of view about the future, and who can engage everyone in the company toward making their vision become reality.

I offer this viewpoint in the spirit that you and your organization want to survive and create a joyful future ahead. Embrace such a vision by using innovation as the core competency and by developing a pipeline of innovative leaders from within.

The Seismic Shift

America has finally awakened from what Tyler Cowen calls the *Great Stagnation*. In one of the most influential books of 2011, the *Great Stagnation,* Cowen says that for the past 300 years, America has been eating all the low-hanging fruit (such as abundance of land, technological advances, and basic education for the masses) and now it is all exhausted.[1] He argues that the dominant economic powerhouse is our self-deception in thinking that the fruit would never run out. It did. Even then, America kept pushing ahead as if nothing was wrong for last two decades, until the recent financial crisis. Cowen claims that the leadership mind-set that ran us in the ground was this: "We thought we were richer than we were."

In the 1950s, all business communication was based on analog technologies such as telephone and telegraph. In the 1970s, communication most often was dictatorial (top down and command driven) using fax machines, word-processing and audio conferencing technologies. Recently we have shifted to a conversational style of communication, driven by social networking technologies. Business communication is no longer inside out but is now outside in. Organizations have less control over their brands and markets as customers have more access to insights about brands and offerings from other consumers and bloggers.

Sixty years ago, the main challenge was human survival. In the 1970s, it was the challenge of computing, and now we are being called to address societal challenges. Most educational systems are broken in every country, along with healthcare, retirement funding, and politics. All of this is causing massive gaps between the haves and the have-nots.

During the Industrial Revolution, the world speed was governed by a handful of people in power positions. For the last 30 years, it has been controlled by the just-in-time rules, and now we are in a world where the speed of life is in real-time mode. Everything is starting to be connected to everything, and we are starting to see what IBM calls a Smarter Planet: intelligent infrastructure for every industry where leaders can anticipate, rather than merely react, to business events. A world where business leaders can seize competitive advantage through re-framing the issues—in unexpected, often counterintuitive ways, proactively instead of reactively.

Our experiences are also changing. Fifty years ago, all rich relationships and interactions required physical presence. Now, through video and mobile computing platforms such as Skype and iPhone with FaceTime, we can push a button and *see* anyone, anywhere in the world, instantaneously.

We are now in the era where loose knowledge communities, meaning, intentions, and deep understanding will be in high demand. Technology will become a dominant enabler for values-driven engagements. Intentions, agility, personalization, loyalty, and self-awareness (people and systems) will become the primary levers for human and economic success.

Current and next-generation C-suite leaders need to prepare for values-driven engagement and innovate for the next era of experiential systems (systems that allow real-time interaction with others anywhere, anytime, all the time with both animate and inanimate objects). These shifts will have massive impacts on societal, technological, economic, environmental, and political landscapes.

For real innovators, we have arrived at Nirvana (heaven). Why? Because it is the first time in human history, that abundant new white space is being created at an accelerated speed. These new opportunities are opening up fast and closing just as fast. The emergence of Google, Facebook, and Twitter as powerhouses is just the beginning of what we are about to experience in the near future. These and many new innovators are completely transforming the very nature of communication, connection, commerce, and competence.

Mechanical Engine versus Innovation Engine

In the past quarter century, most organizations have been focused exclusively on financial performance with the mantra of "whatever it takes." To survive in a free market economy, they have learned to adjust, adapt, or redefine themselves. However, the rate at which the companies must transform is accelerating. They have tried every management technique possible—right-sizing, unbundling, reengineering, retrenching, divesting, decentralizing, outsourcing, flattening, self-directed work teams, and forming strategic alliances.

Major companies have done all of this while eliminating thousands of jobs, closing plants, moving operations to low-cost countries, and attempting to become lean and mean. Still, they are struggling. I call such companies *mechanical organizations*.

Mechanical organizations are machinelike and effective when the environmental factors are predictable. But in today's world, it is impossible for such companies to manage the type of change occurring around them. As an example, here are eight types of environmental factors creating friction at all levels:

1. **Technological factors.** Fast new technologies causing rapid product obsolescence
2. **Economic factors.** Unpredictable prices, costs, currency rates, interest rates, taxes
3. **Competitive factors.** Aggressive, global, highly innovative, threats from niche players, competitors who are also customers and partners
4. **Labor factors.** Increased scarcity of skilled professionals, mobile workforce, increased employee benefits expenses, more reliance on contract labor

5. **Resource factors.** Scarcity, increasing specialization, unknown sources of supply, rapid obsolescence
6. **Customer factors.** More demanding, complex, market fragmentation, narrow market segments, increased acquisitions costs
7. **Legal and regulatory factors.** More aggressive, increased costs, unlimited product liability, growing compliance on free and fair trade
8. **Global factors.** Real-time communications, production, distribution, logistics, sophistication of supply chain partners, customers and competitors located anywhere in the world, outsourcing pressures, international strategic alliances

These and many other issues are generating additional pressures for today's employees and managers in an already mechanistic and heartless environment within organizations. Due to these pressures, leaders have focused primarily on survival, with little focus on achieving sustained growth.

Is there a way out? Yes.

The primary way out is to evolve today's strategic operating model based on mechanistic, bureaucratic, and hierarchical practices (*machinelike*) toward an *innovation-driven* execution model.

Machinelike companies focus on bottom-line performance as the primary measurement for most management decisions, at any cost. Focus is on the short-term. These firms are weak because they are inefficient at managing their future.

Experience shows that the companies that build an innovation engine are more adaptable, flexible, fast, aggressive, innovative, and able to adjust to dynamic, threatening, and a complex external environment. These firms do not take the external environment as a given. Instead, they embrace it as a challenge and act as an agent of change, leading customers, creating new markets, and rewriting the rules of the industry they serve.

To better understand the two machines, I'd like to use the metaphor of a bicycle (see Figure 1.1). The bicycle represents an engine. The fuel comes from a human being riding it, instead of gasoline/petrol we use in other machines.

The Tour de France is the most prestigious race in the world for biking experts. It is the World Cup of bike racing. The race covers 2,200 miles (3,600 kilometers) over a three-week period broken into daylong segments, called stages. Each stage has its own unique environmental and physical challenges, which often leads to unique stage winners. The one who wins the last stage of the day wears a yellow jersey the next day. The rider with the lowest aggregate time for all stages is the winner. The course changes every year but always finishes in Paris, France.Similarly, most publicly traded organizations are also in a race—to return the highest value to all stakeholders and dominate the industry in every way possible. Each organization's strategic intent and business strategies define the course. The environmental factors for the athlete are the road conditions, terrain, weather, and other bikers. In today's business race, the environment is volatile. It changes every day, just like the

Innovation Engine

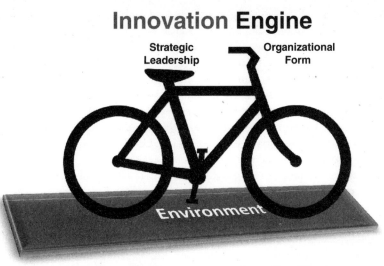

Performance Wheel
Effectiveness, efficiencies, stakeholder management

Power, resources, execution optimization

Innovation Wheel
Intrapreneurship, strategic renewal

Navigation and direction, empowerment, agility, future looking

FIGURE 1.1   Linking Performance and Innovation: A Model to Build Your Innovation Engine

stages of the Tour de France. On some days, the roads are straight; other days they are through mountains and valleys or sections with dirt road or gravel. Increasingly, unexpected rain arrives, just as regulatory changes do in business, altering investment and growth strategy.

The athlete riding is similar to the leadership team members who models the values, beliefs, skills, and behavior of the organization. The bike frame represents the organizational form—firm strategy, structure, processes, and culture.

The performance wheel is the back wheel, which represents practices for achieving organizational effectiveness, efficiencies, and stakeholder management and includes customers, suppliers, shareholders, and partners. This wheel is the source of power and acceleration for individuals, teams, and the organization.

The innovation wheel, the front wheel, represents direction and clarity about the future. It is the organization's capacity for two very important competencies: corporate entrepreneuring (intrapreneurship) and strategic renewal. The front wheel is the first to sense new opportunities to maneuver based on the eight (internal and external) environmental factors listed previously. The innovation wheel provides the first *experience* of the environmental factors, the road ahead, and the ability to conduct quick experiments in the turbulent race.

Unfortunately, today's organizations primarily focus on the back wheel to achieve bottom-line optimization, which is why it is called the performance wheel. The values of this wheel calls for power and acceleration, but if the motives of the organizational athletes (leaders at the top) are flawed, results can lead to disaster—we have seen plenty of examples. The company may move in wrong directions, lose focus on what is ahead, not make fast enough decisions to alter the path, not be sensitive to environmental conditions, and watch others pass by.

Without the front wheel of innovation, the organization has little to no strategic lens for what is possible ahead and what directional decisions to make because the front wheel is missing or ill functioning, most teams at the top make the same decisions as their competitors. The goal of this wheel is to turn the highly mechanistic athlete into an innovative competitor who can easily gather new knowledge, experiment fast, and adapt quickly to outmaneuver other competitors in the race.

Most organizations are pretty good at operating the back wheel; they just need to improve management practices and associated discipline. For managers, as practitioners, the back wheel is a safe zone because the artifacts used are metrics, scorecards, and quantitative analysis—hard stuff. For the front wheel, though, the primary values are qualitative, abstractions, and the intuition to make midcourse corrections. Due to emphasis on performance, managers lack experience operating the front wheel—the innovation wheel.

In economics, accounting, and other business-related fields, there is a concept of stocks and flows—two types of measurements. Stock is the hard tangible value measured at a specific point in time. Flow variables are measured over a period of time—the rate of change. For example, the current balance in your bank account is the stock, while the interest rate (x% per year) is the flow that increases the money in your bank account. Population size is stock, while birth rate is flow. Total number of employees in a company is a stock measurement, while rate of attrition is the flow. For a salesperson, total new revenue booking is the stock, while the close ratio (number of proposals written to number of proposals won) is the flow. Every stock measurement has related flow measurement.

Similarly, I'd like to suggest that the performance wheel is the stock and the innovation wheel is the flow for your business. Both are required to create your *Innovation Engine* to survive and for sustainable competitive advantage.

Strategic Alignment for Innovation

Innovation without clear objectives quickly loses organizational momentum and, in many cases, will never take off in the first place. Innovation should not be practiced just occasionally; it should be a repeating process of value creation and organizational adaptation. If you are serious about innovation, your first step is to create a strong strategic alignment.

Here are five critical success factors you must design to begin your innovation journey with the right foundation:

1. **Innovation intent development.** Does everyone know we need to innovate? Is your organization generating what Umair Haque calls "thick value," or is your

organization "extractive"?[2] In other words, does the organization generate more real value (not just profits and return on investment [ROI], but brand loyalty, employee engagement, and many of the facets of a meaningful prosperity: security, fulfillment, connection, humanity, purpose, etc.), or does it consume resources like the ocean-engulfing *Titanic* as it was going down? Our experience shows that world-class innovators have mandates for innovation, sometimes unspoken but clearly understood. Their innovation intent is clear and supports the organization's business strategy. For innovation to stick, this mandate from the top must be localized for each division, department, team, and individual.

2. **Innovation readiness.** How ready is your organization for innovation? Chapter 2 introduces 15 factors that are directly correlated to your organization's propensity to innovate. Assess yourself to gain learn your strengths and weaknesses and benchmark your readiness for innovation. By knowing where you stand across all the factors, you can customize a roadmap for implementation. The goal is to make sure you don't put the cart before the horse. Many organizations have made mistakes by jumping into innovation efforts without measuring leadership, cultural, and systems drivers that might hinder efforts and waste time and resources. Don't make that same mistake for your organization. Assess readiness and then develop a custom roadmap.

3. **Executive leadership program.** Do all of your leaders understand what innovation is and how to sponsor and support it for their business units? I haven't met a C-level executive who does not want her organization to be more innovative. Most often, the problem is that she may not fully understand how to build an innovation engine and enroll other leaders into the process. What the team at the top most often lacks is the knowledge and framework to make informed choices about designing an innovation program that will work for them. Someone has to help them achieve an innovation roadmap. Make sure the executives at the top are educated, ready, and willing to be the top sponsors for their respective areas. For a corporate-wide initiative, the chief executive alone cannot be the sponsor. The CEO's direct reports also must be sponsors for their respective organizations. You can't drive innovation from sideways or bottom up; it has to happen top down. An education program should provide simple frameworks for understanding innovation principles—how to support it, how to build a climate to increase strategic innovation capabilities, and how to cascade it throughout their respective organizations. This topic also is covered in Chapter 2.

4. **Develop an innovation strategy.** An innovation strategy is a strategic statement that describes innovation in the context of your business (or area), the value it promises to generate for growth, and a disciplined execution process by which to get there. It is also used to communicate to all employees answers to these questions:
   - Why innovation?
   - Who is involved, and who will be the beneficiary of our innovations?
   - What will your firm innovate that is difficult to replicate?

- How different is this from everything else you do?
- When will you know existence of the preceding four items?
- How will you know you are moving in the right direction?

These answers should fully support the business strategy or should be debated further until both are linked, as discussed in Chapter 3.

5. **Selecting and developing talent for innovation.** Where are the innovators in your company? Innovation requires innovators. The very best corporate innovators are called *intrapreneurs*, a term coined by Gifford Pinchot III. Every organization has many intrapreneurs, but they are most likely hiding. Some are easy to spot, but most are never given an opportunity to bring their best game to work every day. They used to be ready, but the organization's mechanical culture has beaten them down. How do we identify, engage, and support them? Everyone in your organization has ideas worth considering, but intrapreneurs have the DNA to build new service lines, new products, and new offerings. Innovation success is directly correlated to your organization's ability to build intrapreneurs and entrepreneurial spirit in the culture. At the end of the day, it's all about people. These great innovators have both visible and invisible traits that need to be nurtured and supported. Find them, challenge them, motivate them, and get the organization out of their way. Then watch what happens. (Chapter 8 focuses on building intrapreneurs.)

Why Innovation?

One of the most important questions that must be asked is: *Why focus on innovation now?* Or: *What is the compelling driver to change the status quo?*

For most organizations the answer will depend on a combination of these four reasons: profit, people, prosperity, and planet:

1. **Profit.** New value creation—how important is it to continuously generate differentiated new value and growth?
2. **People.** Climate and culture—how critical is it to build a culture with maximum employee engagement that allows every employee to contribute to new organizational innovations?
3. **Prosperity.** Clarity and strategy—how much are you willing to invest to improve clarity about the future and reduce uncertainty of market fluctuations?
4. **Planet.** Citizenship—how committed is the organization to help uplift society and build a corporate legacy based on ethical business practices?

New Value Creation: Innovate to Generate Differentiated New Value and Profit

The first reason executives may want innovation is to generate differentiated new value and profits. Notice the term "differentiated." Between 2008 and 2010, we interviewed many senior executives. They told us that many elements of their business strategies were not working as well as they hoped. We also discussed the desire to achieve continuous competitive advantage through innovation. "Different" implies a need to switch the business mind-set from old to the new. "New" means that managers must shift the mind-set from the current game of beating the competition to making them irrelevant and challenging industry assumptions. This mind shift implies they don't need to react to the moves of the rivals and instead learn to free up resources to identify and deliver completely new sources of value. By challenging sector boundaries, managers can look at substitute industries for new white space, just as Apple (computer manufacturer) did to Sony (consumer electronics).

DIFFERENTIATION   Differentiation in products and services means providing unique or superior functionality that generates a premium price and profit and may significantly increase market share. As shown in Figure 1.2, highly differentiated products and services have an 82% success rate compared with 18% for me-too offerings. Since most companies are incrementally competing against rivals, this may explain why so few companies are able to produce above-average shareholder returns.[3]

It is empirical fact that companies that excel at innovation generate more profit than their competition.[4] Top companies almost always lead their industries in return on equity (ROE), total returns to investors, and profit margins. There is a self-evident correlation between successful innovation programs and profitability. As shown in Figure 1.3, innovation is the best path to increase market share. Market share on an average of 40% or more is associated with pretax return in investments exceeding 20%.[5]

Since most executives sense this, why do organizations still not employ innovation as a core capability?

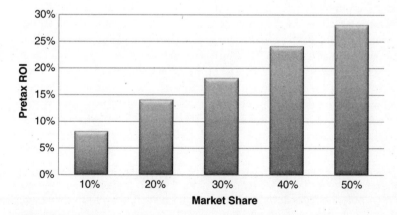

FIGURE 1.2   Strategic Choice: Impact of Differentiation

Adapted from Michael L. George, James Works, and Kimberly Watson-Hemphill, *Fast Innovation* (New York: McGraw-Hill, 2005), p. 16.

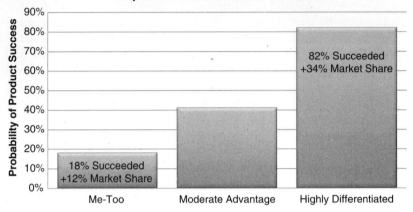

FIGURE 1.3   Market Share and Pretax Return on Investment

Adapted from Bruce Henderson's report, "Strategy Alternatives for the British Motorcycle Industry," Boston Consulting Group, 1975.

The main reason is the senior leaders at the top do not understand the fundamental contradiction that lies between a *mechanical engine* and an *innovation engine*. Mechanical engines give you scale. Innovation engines give you empowered employees.

SCALE AND INNOVATION   There are built-in trade-offs between scale and innovation and between scale and market-specific execution. As organizations get larger and achieve scale, empowerment decreases. However, innovation comes from empowered individuals and teams who break rules. To tap into their creativity, leaders must allow them to produce, market, sell, distribute, and service their innovations globally . . . often. Trying to embed innovation after scale has been achieved is much harder to do. Most large organizations are in this situation, so they don't pursue innovation. Over time as they scale, they destroy entrepreneurial spirit. Creative innovators feel lost in such environments, since scale implies following the rules, discipline, and bureaucracy. Most managers at ease with the principles of a mechanical engine. They do not have personal experience operating an innovation engine. Table 1.1 shows nine specific distinctions between the two types of engines.

To help make a case for your innovation engine, develop a dialog with the senior team or a potential sponsor(s) using Table 1.1, which shows the difference between the mechanical engine and the innovation engine management style. Are the executives in your company ready to mandate an innovation engine, or are they most comfortable with the mechanical engine alone?

TABLE 1.1 Management Style, Mechanical Engine versus. Innovation Engine

Managers	Mechanical Engine	Innovation Engine
Driven by	Seek promotion. Reward system favors conservative decision making and risk aversion. Managers seek power and upward hierarchical positions.	Highly self-motivated and seek to achieve vision, goals, and action plans with freedom and access to corporate resources. They know rewards will come.
Action	Majority of time allocated to supervise and manage downward and delegate as much as possible.	Love to roll up their sleeves, get their hands dirty, and personally dive in to get the job done.
Planning	Cyclic time management— weekly, monthly, quarterly, and yearly planning and review processes. Organize for next job.	Three- to five-year self-imposed timetables to achieve personal and corporate goals, which must include *new* ventures and projects.
Skills	Emphasis on large amounts of data for rational decision making. Pursue professional management and business school methods for analytics and people and organization management.	Would rather be entrepreneurs but realize they can achieve greater success with corporate resources to commercialize their ideas faster. Know they need help in fitting in the corporate environment, and seek it.
Failure and mistakes	Generally avoid anything that might cause failure. Avoid surprises.	Often careful at making sure the project risk being taken is controlled and does not generate political suicide. Often push the envelope for sake of learning or testing their hypothesis, knowing they might fail.
Decisions	Risky decisions are often postponed until hard facts can be gathered. Will make only those decisions the boss (or boss's boss) might want. No individual feels personally responsible.	Experimenting is more important than waiting for the numbers to line up. Very good at enrolling others into their idea at a very early stage of idea development. Often patient and willing to compromise with others if the idea can be improved and executed faster. Love to take responsibility and ownership.
Market research	Rely heavily on data from market research experts within or outside the company to help conceptualize new offerings.	Generally conduct their own market research. Rely mostly on their gut and intuition and will use formal market research surveys to validate what they feel.
Outlook	Seek approval and support from others.	Look to make a positive difference for customers and their sponsor.
Relationships with others	Hierarchy as the basis of relationship.	Intense engagement within hierarchy.

BUILDING THE NEXT S-CURVE   One clear trait of high-performance companies is how they are launch new businesses— a process of building the next S-Curve.

In 2009, Tokyo Shoko Research conducted a study of almost 2,000 of the world's oldest companies. In Japan, about 3,100 are over 200 years old. For example, the Sumitomo Group planted its roots circa 1615, when Buddhist priest Masatomo Sumitomo opened the first book and medicine shop in Kyoto. Since then, the family business has continued through the reigns of numerous shoguns and emperors as well as two major world wars. During that time it has continually grown and thrived, entering one new market after another, including electric cable manufacturing, forestry, financial services, copper smelting, sugar, trading in textiles, mining, and warehousing.

Sumitomo has achieved what most can never do: launched new discontinuous ventures while building a global brand and a sustainable fortune for shareholders year after year. Many organizations can build one brand, but the vast majority stumble badly when that business begins to mature—at the top of the bell curve. In fact, one of the main reasons so many companies—even large corporations—are here today and gone tomorrow is because they couldn't make the jump to a new, growing business from an existing, slowing one before revenues from that core market stalled.

Let's look closely at Figure 1.4.

Between T1 and T2, the mind-set required for growth is *experimentation and evangelism*. Between T2 and T3, *execution and expansion* should be the focus for

Building and Jumping the S-Curve

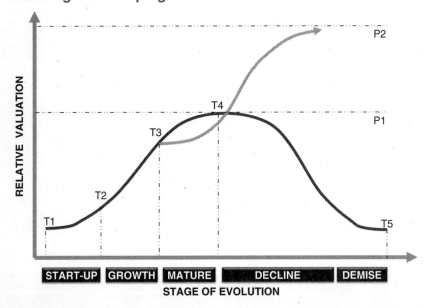

FIGURE 1.4   Building the Next S-Curve

managers, and between T3 and T4, leaders must use *evaluation and extraction* skills to protect the business. Managers who love to work in start-ups love to take risks and possibly fail, but most don't like to run or manage the business between T2 and T4. Managers who love to manage T3–T4 generally don't like the uncertainty of the start-up conditions. Most companies take their best innovators who started a new venture and turn them into managers. Soon they both realize the obvious mistake and suffer the consequences.

P1 is the physical limit every company operates in for each of its products. If you are an agriculture fertilizer company, the physical limit is the amount of land available for fertilizing crops. If you were in an electronics industry in the 1950s, you made vacuum tubes for televisions. At the time, the physical limit (P1) was maximum heat allowed inside televisions. Innovators broke through the P1 barrier by engineering transistors. Engineers soon figured out that there are only so many transistors you can put on a circuit board, which limited functionality of televisions. In order to break through that barrier, they invented integrated circuit boards (large-scale integration and very large-scale integration), which have given us innovations such as personal computers, watches, iPhones, and iPads.

If you understand the current physical limit of the raw technology in your product offerings, you can predict the next S-Curve, when to invest into building it and when to jump on it before the rivals do.

Research shows that once a company reaches the mature state (between T3 and T4), where revenues are starting to decline, margins flatten, and customers are starting to leave, chances for recovery in the current business model are anything but promising. According to one report, two-thirds of stalled companies end up being acquired, taken private, or forced into bankruptcy. Also, once the annual sales growth slows down to less than 2%, the company has less than a 10% chance of ever fully recovering.[6]

The average life span of companies on the Standard & Poor's 500 has shrunk drastically, from 75 years in the 1930s to just 15 years in the 2000s.[7]

It is important to note that the last point in time a company can build and successfully jump on to the next S-Curve is at T3. After T3, the management will not have the capital and other resources to invest into starting a new S-Curve. Remember, starting a new S-Curve requires a mind-set of experimentation. Typically, after T3, the business needs a very conservative CEO running the operation, not a risk-friendly leader who might overconsume resources.

Therefore, the best time to start building the next S-Curve is between T2 and T3, and the *last* opportunity to start a new S-Curve is at T3. This period is one of the greatest times for a company. Its performance is being strengthened for high-precision execution, expansion, and customer acquisition. Plenty of capital is being invested for the growth strategy in place. During this stage, assuming the *chasm* was crossed at T2, the business is growing very fast and everyone is happy—possibly burned out, but happy, generating personal and organizational success.[8] Paradoxically, since everyone is extremely busy executing and growing market share, leaders are ill equipped to help create extra capacity. They have no time to take on anything new, such as incubating new innovations that might pay off in a few years. Leaders become focused on putting in everything possible to manage the growth and forget to innovate. Over time, the culture and systems lose any memory of what it was like during the T1 and T2 stages, necessary for creatively building the next businesses.

An innovation engine can solidify the path of a world-class innovator (WCI) shown in Figure 1.5. The very best WCI companies are committed to maintaining their distinctive capabilities. They purposefully refuse to scale too quickly; they replicate their business in a repeatable way; and from the start they remain focused on mastering access to customer and market channels.

Innovation can help build continuous new S-Curves for your organizations.

People Express and Southwest Airlines were founded as discount airlines, but Southwest has grown its business in a decidedly different manner. It has, for example, maintained its point-to-point route system (compared to the traditional hub-and-spoke model of the legacy airlines such as American and Delta), relying more on secondary airports, such as Fort Lauderdale–Hollywood International Airport, than on primary hubs, such as Miami International Airport. And Southwest has never wavered from its high standards of hiring only those employees with certain qualities, such as a commitment to customer service and a fundamental belief that everyone should be treated with dignity and respect. People Express, however, was quickly

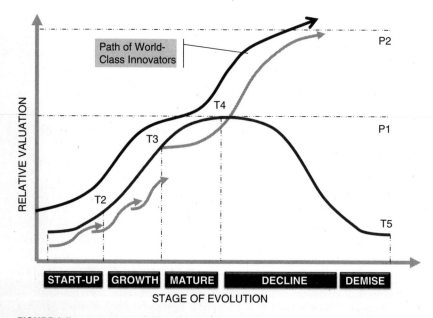

FIGURE 1.5   Path of World-Class Innovators

sold after only six years in operation as soon as it reached the top of the S-Curve at T4. It lacked an innovation engine and a clear distinctive value proposition—unlike Southwest, which had differentiated in customer service.

Climate and Culture: Improve Employee Engagement and Build a Culture of Innovation (People)

The second reason why leaders may want innovation is to build world-class employee engagement that leads to a unique corporate culture. Some organizations, such as Southwest, have figured out that by putting people first, they will retain and attract the best talent for sustainable growth.

For leaders in an environment where is a high number of disengaged employees, committing to an innovation journey is a risky proposition. Research shows that committing to innovation will increase employee engagement. Increased employee engagement drives creativity; with creativity comes ideas; and with ideas come innovation.

Without engaged employees, sustainable innovation is not possible.

Risk tolerance and employee engagement are two sides of the same coin. Intelligent failures require employees to take risks. When they do, engagement and productivity can improve. Also, it is important to remember that employee engagement arises from corporate culture. Engagement cannot be cultivated or rooted in a corporate program. It happens only when you remove barriers to work, and those barriers are unique to every work group.

According to a Gallup Group finding, when companies emphasize strengths developed through organized learning and talent management strategies, the chances are greater that a culture of innovation and creativity will exist.[9] Innovation efforts build individual strengths and bring out the very best in employees. In the 2007 report, 30% of respondents strongly agreed that their organization is committed to building the strengths of each associate. Of those, a majority (54%) strongly agreed that their current job brings out their most creative ideas. In contrast, of the nearly 50% of respondents who disagreed that their organization is committed to building the strengths of each associate, only one in ten strongly agreed that their current job brings out their most creative ideas.

When we look through the employee engagement lens, the impact of focusing on strengths and encouraging new ideas for innovation is even more evident. Sixty-five percent of all engaged employees stated that their organization is committed to building employee strengths and encouraging new ideas that defy conventional wisdom. Among actively disengaged employees, this number plummeted to a mere 2%.

It is also a well-known fact that managers play a significant role in the talent development + engagement = innovation equation. Fifty-two percent of workers who said their supervisor "focuses on my strengths or positive characteristics" also said that "my current job brings out my most creative ideas." Previous Gallup research has shown that higher levels of engagement are strongly related to higher levels of innovation.

Clarity and Uncertainty: Improve Clarity about the Future and Reduce Uncertainty (Prosperity)

The third reason why leaders should want innovation is to improve clarity and reduce the uncertainty about the future.

Most organizations have all sorts of dashboards, formulas, and metrics to monitor how the business is doing. But very few have a metric called *rate of failure*. Why is that?

FAILURE RATE   When setting a business goal and not achieving intended results, implies some level of failure. Most company cultures and systems do not tolerate even a small management failure. Although, all "failures" identify what does not work and what needs to change next time. By definition, the company has gained new knowledge regarding the original problem and process of finding the solution. In today's world, when one of the primary tool to success is access to new knowledge, shouldn't we break things that are most fragile fast? Doesn't failure increase clarity about issues and ultimately speed up outcomes?

If speed is a critical component for growth and expansion, the faster you fail, the faster you can learn what is fragile and therefore remove contradictions as you build out your solutions. The faster you remove contradictions, the faster you can implement and commercialize your ideas.

The main reason we don't use a metric such as failure rate is because it is the dark side of what we call success. Human beings don't like to fail. It hurts the self-ego.

Let me suggest that without continuous failure, there is no continuous innovation or evolution. All business growth occurs through testing an idea where most ideas don't work the first time. Just look at the beginnings of all the product and service offerings in your firm. All of them were conceived to be different from how they have been commercialized. An organization adapts quickly as it learns what is working and what is not working. The problem is that most managers spend all their time talking about what is working and only incrementally improving on the previous state.

We must challenge the organizational mind-set that primarily measures progress and growth and does not allow measuring failures. That is like saying darkness does not exist because we only have methods to measure the existence of light in lumens (we have no methods to measure degree of darkness).

Great innovators understand that increasing the failure rate actually reduces uncertainty about the future. In other words, experimentation through innovation can actually reduce uncertainty and derisk the future.

STRATEGIC CLARITY   Clarity is an important driver for strategic innovation. Strategic clarity gives access to new opportunities faster. As shown in Figure 1.6, when managers have access to clarity about opportunities more quickly than current methods of decision making, they will respond faster than by using the status quo method only.

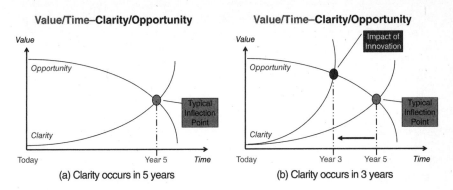

Value/Time–Clarity/Opportunity (a) Clarity occurs in 5 years

Value/Time–Clarity/Opportunity (b) Clarity occurs in 3 years

FIGURE 1.6   Opportunity/Clarity Management

In our experience, most managers are very likely to mobilize an idea if they have 80% clarity about it. No organizational system provides absolute clarity regarding what is possible. If such a discipline were available, most managers could make even faster decisions—right or wrong. There is plenty of historical data in organizations but not enough clarity regarding what is possible about future opportunities.

Clarity means deeply understanding and empathizing with what the end customers' unmet needs are today and what might be emerging as a need in the near future. It is not just about finding ideas to solve today's problems but having the insight to define new problems before others do. Do your managers do this today, consistently? Innovation can deliver this capability. Strategic clarity is about asking the right questions and finding the right answers before others do.

In Figure 1.6, our hypothesis is that every organization already has many significant opportunities. In other words, finding ideas (big and small) is not the primary obstacle. The real issue is access to the clarity about those ideas and their explicit value (before the competitors have it). No one is in charge of crystallizing and debating worthy ideas with rigor. At some point, as shown in part A—say five years from now (it could be three years, time doesn't matter)— the business will gain maximum clarity and, we hope, take an action as a response. The problem is, by that time, the size of the opportunity may be reduced by 50% or more (faster today than in previous life cycles). In the figure, the opportunity curve is controlled by external environmental factors while the clarity curve is controlled by the organizational capabilities and courage.

By embedding innovation as a core capability, companies can build a muscle that can reshape the clarity curve (part B) such that the inflection point for clarity and opportunity becomes visible much more quickly. The result, of course, is higher possible valuation of investments and faster market capture/entry.

Does your company capture the cost of being late to market? Using historical data, you can estimate the growth and margin numbers if the innovation lead times had been twice as fast. In our experience, a slow and ineffective innovation process costs companies between 20% and 50% of their potential shareholder value.

Have a conversation about failure rate, clarity, and opportunity with your management team. Do they agree that innovation actually reduces business risk? Does this create a burning platform for you and them? If so, you now have a good *innovation intent* in your hands to proceed. If not, help create urgency with the executives at the top before proceeding.

Citizenship: Uplift Society and Build a Legacy (Planet)

The fourth reason why leaders may want innovation is to demonstrate lasting impact by leaving their mark on the communities they serve. These leaders have realized that today's challenges are too great for current bureaucracy and can be met only with self-organizing systems, such as free markets, self-awareness, self-rule, and effective communities of the future. They are deeply invested in the principles that can greatly improve the intelligence, ethics, and competitive capacity of business organizations.

Free markets have provided the systems and tools to exploit our environment with extraordinary productivity and efficiency, but humans have not used wisdom to establish a balanced relationship with nature.

In the last decade, our global civilization has been experiencing nature's wrath in the form of earthquakes, tsunamis, hurricanes, snowstorms, and other natural disasters at an unprecedented rate. Mother Earth is being abused, and humans are racing toward a possible extinction by using natural resources at an unsustainable rate. Overcrowding, violence, and inhumane acts seem to be on the rise. Unfortunately, the free markets will not automatically provide the wisdom to deal with these issues, because markets love consumption growth, the very cause of these problems.

In recent years, the sustainability movement was begun by wise leaders to help respond to this urgent problem. Organizations that have mature innovation capabilities are now expanding their innovation programs to help resolve these conflicts—in effect, creating a conscious organization.

Innovation efforts to heal the planet and natural resources are not just about corporate giving but are about dealing with radical discontinuities in our way of living, playing, and working. These intelligent organizations are now merging their innovation programs with their sustainability programs. Together they are driving toward triple-bottom-line success: profit, people, and planet.

How does this actually show up in a typical business?

Businesses committing to innovation in this manner are achieving disproportionate growth increases in customer satisfaction, quality and quantity of new knowledge, new skills and capability, and improved commitment to sustainability of resources. These organizations are transforming to low-resource, high-satisfaction business models. They pay close attention to every detail to deliver exquisite customer service while staying nimble and using available inputs to produce the specific satisfaction their customers demand in products and services. To these businesses, every pound of material and each calorie of energy carries more meaning, delivers more human satisfaction, and is designed to last longer and do more.

These organizations are embedding this thinking into their culture by helping each employee understand the importance of moving away from valuing only the material success and toward valuing the quality of meaning and relationships and developing greater heart and wisdom along with technical capabilities to produce greater value per unit of resources used. Corporate Knights Research publishes some examples of such companies in its "Global 100 Most Sustainable" list each year. The 2012 report lists companies such as Novo Nordisk, Toyota, Intel, IBM, Proctor & Gamble, Hitachi, Allianz, and many others.[10]

One widely used definition of sustainability is corporate development that meets the needs of the present without compromising the ability of future generations to meet their own needs. If your organization already has an innovation program started or if innovation is a way of life, check to see if the leadership mind-set is ready for planet innovation–commitment to reaching profit goals while improving health and wellness of each citizen on Earth. If not, help create an awareness of the need to integrate the innovation efforts with the sustainability efforts—you may become a pioneer in this new movement.

Innovation Execution: Embedding Innovation

After you have clarified the role of innovation for the future of your organization, you will need a systematic process to embed it in the organization. The three broad steps of activities to imbed innovation as a core capability in your organization are shown in Figure 1.7.

1. Envision and articulate innovation intent (Chapter 1).
2. Develop an innovation strategy (Chapter 3).
3. Design your innovation program (Chapters 4–5).

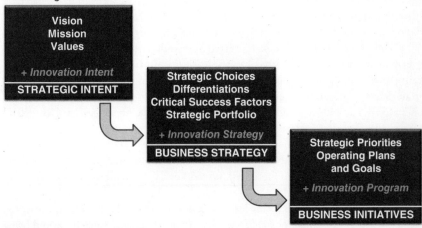

FIGURE 1.7   Embedding Innovation

There should be evidence for innovation from the top leaders. Innovation intent is articulated by the senior executive team (and sometimes the board) as part of the strategic intent. Innovation intent is top management's directional mandate on how the firm is going to win using innovation.

In our view, innovation intent is easier to identify if the senior team has already declared its strategic intent—a compelling statement about where the organization is going and defining what it wants to achieve long-term.

Yes, it is possible that, in your firm, the word "innovation" gets used a lot by the senior team and in all business reports to shareholders, but very few leaders are truly committed to actually *wanting* innovation badly enough. In other words, it is just lip service.

How do you know when there is authentic innovation intent from the top?

After working with some of the best brands over the last 25 years, we have found there are five indicators of strategic innovation intent:

1. It is being spoken about as a clear differentiator for long-term growth and success.
2. It is already part of the strategic vision and value defined, and there is a strong desire to make it part of everyone's job.
3. There is clear, authentic sponsorship from the C suite.
4. There is little evidence of resistance from top team members.
5. Senior leaders are spirited to role-model it, in spite of the guns pointed at them to stay focused on the mechanical engine.

Walt Disney, the founder of one of the most legendary brands in the world, lived his innovation intent from day 1. He launched the first theme park, Disneyland, in July 1955. Originally the project was budgeted for $4.5 million, but it ended up costing near $17 million to complete. His strategic intent was to build a theme park that would unleash the imagination and joy of children around the world. Disneyland became the most visited tourist attraction in the United States and became the foundation of one of the most enduring entertainment brands in history.

While being built, financiers exerted tremendous pressure on this massively over-budget ambition and forced Disney to shut it down. He ended up selling his Palm Springs home to finance it and sacrificed everything he had to stay true to his strategic and innovation intent. When opened, only one-third of the park was fully operational. Later Disney said, "I could never convince the financiers that Disneyland was feasible, because dreams offer too little collateral."

Walt Disney was a visionary leader. He understood the power of imagination and ideas in the face of numbers—the guns pointed at him every day. He was willing to chase a dream that had no precedent, no market data, no corporate ROI, no focus group to validate.

Disney deeply believed in his father's values of being a hardworking carpenter, farmer, railroad machinist, postal carrier, and a hotel manager. Later he would bring all of those jobs to help build Disneyland.

Disney died when he was just 66. But before then, he reflected back at the grand success of his life's accomplishments and specifically the cultural impact of Disneyland on the nation. He explained the kind of energy he brought to his new vision: "In the lexicon of youth, there is no such word as 'fail.' Certainly we have all had this confidence at one time in our lives, though most lose it as we grow older. Perhaps, because of my work, I've been lucky enough to retain a shred of this youthful quality."[11]

Very few leaders impacted society and the transcended societal cultures like Walt Disney did.

Strategic intent and innovation intent require unwavering clarity, focus, and perseverance to realize the value of installing an innovation engine in your firm. If you are lucky enough to work at an organization that already exhibits such intent, leadership, and values, you are already 60% done with the core message of this book.

Conclusion

Competition in the global market in every sector, product, service, and market segments is fierce, and that is the new status quo. In order not only to endure but to prevail, global organizations need to deliver innovative differentiated offerings that create substantial additional value, relative to what customers can already buy. Most organizations will fail unless they have an innovation engine that is looking at the future while delivering near-term value and profits.

In our experience, most executives want innovation in order to create differentiation in the marketplace, but they lack the education, knowledge, and skills regarding the innovation engine—they are stuck operating the mechanical engine. Don't minimize this issue. When a program manager is given a charter to "go innovate" by the CEO, the most important first step should be to educate the leadership team about the game of corporate innovation and engage them in a professional debate that can lead to clarity and decision on why they should implement innovation.

The innovation engine will work only when there is informed decision making and unwavering sponsorship—your first and most important step before you journey too far.

The second step is to assess the readiness of the organization for innovation (see Chapter 2 for details). The third and final step required to build a solid foundation for your innovation journey (Chapter 3) is to link innovation to the business strategy—not an easy task. If done correctly, the output should be a clear, articulated innovation strategy linked to the business strategy.

The innovation strategy communicates clear directional statement(s) from the CEO to everyone answering the question: *What will innovation give that nothing else can?* It should always be aligned to the appropriate business strategy. When it is working, it will inform the business strategy in the long run.

After the innovation strategy is in place, you are ready to build your innovation roadmap (see Chapters 4 and 5).

Key Questions about Innovation Intent

To help clarify strategic innovation intent, here are some questions worth posing to your seniormost leaders:

1. How much more cost savings can we squeeze out of our current business? Are the incremental savings worth the time spent by managers?

2. How much more top-line growth can we achieve out of our current business? Is the cost of new-customer acquisition going up?

3. To generate real wealth, how many share-increasing tactics are remaining to be tested beyond the ones already tried by the leadership team, such as buy-backs, spin-offs, and other forms of financial engineering?

4. For achieving scale, how many more mergers and acquisitions can be absorbed before altering the business model and losing strategic focus?

5. How different is our business model and the value proposition it offers in comparison to others in the marketplace?

Notes

1. Tyler Cowen, *The Great Stagnation: How America Ate All The Low-Hanging Fruit of Modern History, Got Sick, and Will (Eventually) Feel Better* (New York: Dutton, 2011).

2. Umair Haque is director of Havas Media Labs and author of *Betterness: Economics for Humans* (Boston: Harvard Business Review Press, 2011) and *The New Capitalist Manifesto: Building a Disruptively Better Business* (Boston: Harvard Business Review Press, 2011).

3. Michael L. George, James Works, and Kimberly Watson-Hemphill, *Fast Innovation* (New York: McGraw-Hill, 2005).

4. James P. Andrew, Joe Manget, David C. Michael, Andrew Taylor, and Hadi Zablit, "Innovation 2010: A Return to Prominence—and the Emergence of a New World Order," *BusinessWeek*, August 15, 2005. A report by Boston Consulting Group of 940 executives in 68 countries.

5. Bruce Henderson, "Strategy Alternatives for the British Motorcycle Industry," Boston Consulting Group, 1975.

6. Matthew S. Olson and Derek van Bever, *Stall Points: Most Companies Stop Growing—Yours Doesn't Have To* (New Haven, CT: Yale University Press, 2008).

7. Richard Foster and Sarah Kaplan, *Creative Destruction: Why Companies that Are Built to Last Underperform the Market—And How to Successfully Transform Them* (New York: Crown Business, 2001).

8. G. A. Moore, *Crossing the Chasm: Marketing and Selling Disruptive Products to Mainstream Customers* (New York: Harper Business, 2002).

9. *Gallup Business Journal,* May 10, 2007.

10. "2012 Global 100 List of Most Sustainable Corporations in the World," Research by Corporate Knights. www.global100.org/annual-lists/2012-global-100-list.html

11. J. Kevin Sheehan, *A Leader Becomes a Leader* (Belmont, MA: True Gifts Publishing, 2007).

CHAPTER 2

Assess Innovation Readiness

Assess organizational readiness for innovation: Many organizations skip this step. With a better understanding of your organization's propensity to innovate from a structural standpoint, a highly customized roadmap for innovation can be developed.

In a recent report by IBM, CEOs said they feel ill-prepared for today's more complex environment.[1] Increased connectivity has also created strong, and too often unknown, interdependencies. For this reason, often the ultimate consequence of any decision is poorly understood. With few exceptions, CEOs expect continued disruption in one form or another. The new economic environment is substantially more volatile, much more uncertain, increasingly complex, and structurally different. An industrial products CEO in the Netherlands summed up the sentiments of many when he described the last few years as a "wake-up call," adding that "it felt like looking into the dark with no light at the end of the tunnel."

Many leaders complain about the past failure rates of strategic initiatives during implementation. However, few realize the manner in which they contribute to the failure rate. A key element to the challenge of change is understanding how sponsors inhibit their own efforts to successfully execute important initiatives.

The recent economic cycle has not helped the situation and, in fact, has made it even more challenging for leaders to have clarity and better prepare their organizations for the future.

The rampant commoditization and disorder engulfing nearly all industries suggest that old methods of diagnosing growth challenges have been wrong. *Even the premise of strategy itself is under review, as many management teams thoroughly engaged in the discipline have failed to address systemic performance declines.*[2]

Reasons Why Executives Want Innovation

From 2008 to 2010, we surveyed over 300 executives all over the world and asked: "Why are you interested in innovation?" In other words, what will innovation deliver that nothing else can? The next sections describe seven themes that came up.

1. We Need to Get Off Commodity Island

Executives said their offerings (products and services) are being commoditized. For every move they make, competitors are responding fast and at lesser cost. For this reason, the organizational focus has shifted to a win-at-all-cost mentality with very complex pricing models. Everyone is doing the same to differentiate, and now everyone looks and feels the same to the customer.

2. Globalization and Automation Are Causing a Shortened Life Span for Our Products and Services

Globalization and automation are two macro trends that are fast changing the rules of business operations. Thomas Friedman, Ray Kurzweil, Daniel Pink, Tom Peters, Ram Charan, Peter Senge, Tyler Owen, Tom Kelly, and many others have written articles and books on hundreds of topics in the areas of strategy, operations, leadership, and new technologies that are changing our world at warp speed. They have tried to prepare teams at the top for their roles in shaping the future (including ethical conduct, workforce development, and the importance of the triple bottom line) in the ever-emerging, highly connected, customized, and creative world. These two disruptive trends have shifted the power from the ivory tower to the crowds outside (customers, suppliers, partners, and industry experts).

3. Our Strategic and Annual Planning Processes Are Not Working

Every company has some annual planning process. Many have a five- or ten-year strategic plan. These plans are adjusted and updated on an annual basis. The executives we interviewed espoused very little confidence in the processes they used for strategic thinking and planning; especially in today's fast moving business climate. Here are the typical major steps most mature businesses use to conduct annual planning for:

1. Gather all current operational dashboard data and their supporting material from each part of the business.
2. Collect market data: Where is the market going? How much is it growing? How does the growth compare to GDP growth? What is the expected demand in the next three to five years? What are major market trajectories in our markets and in other significant markets in the world we may want to pursue?
3. Collect competitive intelligence data: What are our numbers compared to our top five competitors? How are we doing compared to them in each major

category? Where have we been compared to them and where are we going to be compared to them? Are they competing in ways that are unique?

4. Review the current year's achievement relative to the plan: What is the delta? What does the order book look like? What is happing to our margins, cash flow, and ROI metrics? How are these numbers compared to last year's data? How are we doing against industry benchmarks across the board — people, process, quality, and so on?

5. Making choices: After all of the items are collected, organized, and synthesized, the key leaders at the top assess how much courage they want to take on for next year. Using the historical and competitive situation and mostly their gut, they come to consensus on new growth targets. Nine out of ten times, these targets are in the same neighborhood as numbers from the last years with some variations for each business unit's context. Generally the new growth numbers will be within a few percentage points of the industry GDP growth numbers.

Typically, this is the end of the annual goal planning exercise. Rarely do new strategies get debated because the exercise as a whole requires labor-intensive preparation. During this time, the executives are under heavy pressure to close the year while maintaining engagement with top customers and stakeholders. Therefore, discussing a long-term strategic change to the business model or product/service extensions is ignored or postponed to the next executive meeting. Very little time is actually spent discussing long-term changes to alter the strategic plans. This means the strategies don't change much year after year, while the environmental factors are changing at a much faster pace.

How is it possible to stay nimble in regard to market conditions if there is no fundamental process for nimbleness for the top team?

In most companies, future-related decisions are based primarily on use of recent most historical data. Hardly anyone brings explicit data about the emerging needs of current customers or defines new opportunities for evaluation that are within reach. Most strategic planning processes rely heavily on current and historical performance data only and almost completely ignore input regarding blue oceans and availability of new breakthrough technologies.

In the same manner, and in most cases, the process lacks the collective wisdom and knowledge of the entire organization at large. No pipeline process takes opportunity insights from the front line and the field systematically for the sole purpose of the strategic planning process. This might be because it is assumed that the top team, albeit most distant from the front line, has the required knowledge about the ever-changing markets, products, technologies, and issues. This is an orthodoxy that is rarely, if ever, challenged.

Innovation, if done right, should be an input to strategic planning, not an outcome.

---

4. Our Organization Lacks Nimbleness

In his seminal book *Future of Management*, Gary Hamel argues that "sometime over the next decade [every organization] will be challenged to change in a way for which it has no precedent. It will either adapt or falter, reinvent itself or struggle through a painful restructuring. Given the recent performance of industry incumbents around the world, the latter is more likely than the former." He continues to say that very "few companies are able to change ahead of the curve."

Nimbleness is the ability to quickly adapt to an environment that is ever-changing primarily due to globalization, automation, and changes to government regulations.

This is not a surprise to most businesses. But over the past few decades, every type of organization has come to think of itself as a *business*. Once upon a time, only for-profit manufacturing firms and service companies were thought of as being in business. Today, around the globe, all other types of organizations, such as government, healthcare providers, schools, colleges, nonprofits, nongovernmental organizations, and even churches/temples/synagogues, are being asked to operate in a more businesslike fashion. As a result, organizations must:

- Have a dynamic and nimble execution strategy.
- Plan for any unforeseen surprises from external environment factors.
- Explore and discover what opportunities exist for growth.
- Quickly enhance new unique capabilities in individuals, teams, business units, functions, and other stakeholders.
- Be accountable to stakeholders for continued growth.

5. Multigenerational Talent Gaps Are Widening

It is already very difficult to retain the best employees and attract those who fit in today's environment. Today as many as four generations are working in a typical multinational organization. Each generation brings its own values and motivational systems. Every motivational model shows that people are highly engaged when they feel their job requires using a wide variety of skills and abilities. All too often, professionals who work in well-defined jobs or project positions become dissatisfied and even disillusioned when narrowly structured tasks require them to use only a small portion of their overall competencies and educational training. How can we keep the existing managers and leaders highly challenged and motivated while also assimilating new talent, without seeing knowledge and skills walk out the door?

Another big driver for motivation and engagement is the ability to show results. If professionals cannot see that their work is making a difference, they have no basis for trying to improve. This is especially true for younger generations — they can pack up and go elsewhere easily in today's LinkedIn world. The best innovators are highly motivated employees with diverse perspectives who can visibly see the impact of their own work.

6. We Are Not Able to Keep Up with Breakthrough Advances in Technology and Scientific Innovations

This should be no surprise to anyone. Google is said to almost double its number of pages indexed every 18 months.[3] Wikipedia, the world's largest encyclopedia, is growing at an astronomical pace with over 3.9 million articles in English. The full

Wikipedia totals 8 billion words, in 19 million total articles, in approximately 270 languages. In June 2011 alone, 11 million edits were made in the Wikipedia system.[4] That is a lot of new knowledge being created.

The Human Genome database has been defined; it includes 25,000 genes and the 3 billion chemical pairs that make up human DNA. No doubt, this will create thousands of white space opportunities and revolutionize the healthcare industry in the coming years. Scientists are crediting these advances with helping us live longer and healthier lives in years ahead.

New technology segments, such as nanotechnology, biotechnology, bioinformatics, biopharmacology, agro-biotech, and biomemetics, are already making huge shifts in research. As a result, new innovations are created faster than ever before. These new fields will shape the twenty-first century much the same way as aviation and mass production did in the twentieth century.

Cosmeceuticals is the new industry emerging from the convergence of personal care/cosmetic and pharmaceutical industries. This industry is fueled by advances in chemistry and biotechnology that allow the use of pharmacological and cosmetic therapies in areas where previously surgical intervention was needed.

Nutraceuticals is the new industry emerging from the convergence of food and pharmaceutical industries. The new products in this industry are sometimes known as functional foods and are strategic answers to consumers' growing sensitivity to health and wellness in everyday consumption.

Nutricosmetics is an industry generated by the fusion of food and beauty products.

These convergent industries are big and are growing substantially. For example, the global nutricosmetic product market for 2010 was $2.4 billion, up from $1.9 billion in 2005.[5]

7. There Are No Safe-Haven Sectors

In the last three decades, only a handful of sectors were being transformed. Today every industry is being reshaped from the inside out. A business used to be able to dominate a single-sector strategy with a traditional business model of product design, manufacturing, distribution, fulfillment, and service for twenty to thirty years without much competition from others. Those surveyed said they now have to diversify in other industries, new segments, and new geographies more than ever before. No one sector or one market segment is stable. As an example, the financial services sector spends about $11 billion on product development annually. In the United Kingdom alone, there are more than 29,000 different financial products.[6] Studies show the average cost of bringing a new product to market has more than doubled in the past decade, with failure rates ranging from 60% to 80% and with the minority actually producing a significant profit. Worst news is that the average competitive advantage was about three months for these products. This means that an organization must develop a multidimensional approach that links product, service, and process innovations in a compelling proposition. Product innovation alone is unlikely to confer sustainable competitive advantage.

We can see successful examples all around the globe. GE offers solutions in consumer products, aviation, energy, financing, rail, healthcare, software service, and more. United Technologies Corporation's sectors include aviation, elevators, energy, and security. Tata, of India, has large operations in automobiles, chemical manufacturing, energy, hotels, telecommunications, software services, and consumer products, just to name a few. The German giant Siemens is in energy, telecommunications, automation, consumer products, financial solutions, and healthcare.

These companies realized long ago that no one sector can carry the growth year after year.

As a leader, it is imperative that you articulate the primary reasons for making investments in innovation. Do any of the reasons apply to you? If so, how would you rank them by importance?

Innovation Readiness

After defining the innovation intent for your organization in Chapter 1, you are ready to proceed to the next step, *assess organizational readiness for innovation.* The purpose of this step is to measure the current organizational propensity for innovation. The question to ask is how ready is the rest of the organization for the innovation journey?

Rolling out innovation should not be done in isolation. It should be designed with clear innovation intent, sound innovation strategy, and a realistic innovation roadmap. None of this should be done without an absolute alignment to the current organizational readiness for innovation.

Honda's core competence is the manufacturing of engines. It manufactures engines for cars, motorcycles, lawn mowers, garden tractors, marine engines, generators, all-terrain vehicles, and airplanes. All are engines, but each type of engine is designed for a different applications. You cannot use car engines for tractors or a jet engine in a boat. Each engine has a distinct design and features optimized for its exact usage. Additionally, within each category there are types and models of engines optimized for various customer segments.

For example, Honda makes car engines for city travel, large families, tourist vans, cargo, and even NASCAR professional racing models. Each car engine is designed with a specific user in mind.

Similarly, every organization is unique, based on its strategy, structure, industry, products, and capabilities, even though organizations market similar products. Therefore, each company's need for innovation execution is different, and the implementation approach must be customized to match the current readiness of the organization. In this example, an organization's innovation maturity is like the range of sophistication of various types of drivers (e.g., Honda's customers). For a simple organization that focuses on city cars, for example, all it needs is simple innovation engine features and tactics. An organization already having some innovation capability but desiring to improve its maturity to compete in a

NASCAR-like environment will need to invest differently for its organizational innovation engine.

Innovation maturity cannot be bought but must be developed over time. A student cannot learn and graduate from elementary grade and directly enter a college. Foundational courses in math, reading, and writing must be learned before algebra, calculus, and organic chemistry can be taught. Similarly, a multinational organization cannot become a world-class innovator in the first year. It must start by mastering the basic (arts and sciences) principles and processes of innovation.

In our experience, the innovation maturity of most organizations is on an elementary school level, some are at middle school level, and very few are at the high school level. Seldom do we find organizations optimized for innovation at the college or postgraduate levels.

It is crucial to measure the organization's current readiness for innovation and then design a roadmap for implementation. It is imperative to ensure that every investment in your innovation program sticks from day 1.

In this context, the term "innovation readiness" is synonymous with measuring "propensity for innovation." Innovation readiness is defined by these five readiness indicators:

1. **Business case.** What is the business case for innovation?
2. **Sustained sponsorship.** Who owns the ongoing responsibility to make innovations occur?
3. **Culture and systems.** How attuned are people, process, structure, and systems to adapt innovation principles and practices while the operational engine is running?
4. **Financial resources.** Are there appropriate budgets to launch and sustain your innovation program for at least the first three years? If so, is it enough?
5. **Program management.** Are the right people assigned to carry out your implementation plan, and do they have the right authority for change management?

Suppose you are driving a car from home to work. There are three things you must do really well. First, it is crucial you know how to drive (rules for driving); second, you must know the destination; and finally, you must have directions (navigation map) that show you how to get there. Similarly, innovation is a journey. It requires organizational skills, a strategic goal (e.g., valuation targets), and navigation (skills, competencies, processes, methods, and tools) to get there.

In order to optimize the performance of your innovation engine on the innovation highway, you must learn to maneuver correctly across three specific lanes: *alignment, insights,* and *mobilization.* When you manage your navigation through your organizational climate, you will achieve in a successful journey with exceptional outcomes.

If you decide to manage the journey in an informal way, without clear intent on your destination, an ad hoc roadmap, or disregarding the rules of navigation, the risks of failure will surely increase. If you decide to manage the journey as you go along, you may get there but just not fast enough or in the most efficient way possible, and probably with greater organizational anxiety.

Through applied research, we have discovered 15 organizational factors that define innovation readiness for every large organization. By manipulating each of the factors correctly, you can improve the performance of your innovation engine. Manipulating the wrong factors at the wrong time or using the wrong method can create negative impact. For example, installing ideation software before identifying a process to manage idea flow can create disengagement with employees and loss of investments.

Factors of the Innovation System and Culture

Let's look at the 15 factors that control innovation readiness and improve innovation propensity at your company.

Alignment

Five alignment factors are related to a business's ability to recognize, specify, clarify, and commit to the purpose of innovation and help achieve predefined business value—your target destination. There is no need to waste time and money on innovation unless it is critically linked to the business strategy. Alignment is about strategically sponsoring, engaging, monitoring, and supporting all innovation activities at every level of the business structure. If alignment is properly executed and adjusted as the organization matures, the result will be a climate and culture of innovation for long-term sustainable business growth. Table 2.1 defines each of the alignment success factors.

TABLE 2.1   Alignment Success Factors

	Definition
Innovation mandate	At the top, innovation is seen as critical to the future of our organization.
Leader readiness	Leaders are prepared to guide the organization's innovation efforts.
Employee engagement	Individuals throughout the organization are motivated to contribute to innovation.
Innovation support	Organization has effective systems and processes to support innovation.
Systematic approach	There is a clear framework, common language, along with a systematic and well-understood approach to innovation.

What are the signs of an aligned organization for innovation? When alignment is present, you will see focus and collaboration at the right levels for the purpose of achieving organizational and individual goals for both the business leaders and for individuals. True alignment will show up in the form of employees' desire to engage at work and be effective contributors to the organization, continually looking for new ways to support the overall vision, mission, and purpose of the organization as a whole. Alignment means that each business unit, department, team, and individual sees and understands its role and how it contributes to the overall innovation mandate of the organization. It gives them confidence that their work is valuable.

Insights

Insights reflect the importance of discovering new ideas—with art and science rather than as matter of luck. It begins with the recognition that information from many sources is essential to developing unique insights that will allow your business to achieve strategic targets. To develop deep insights about what is possible, you must involve people from all levels of the organization, including partners, suppliers, customers, and regulators. The larger the field of information and ideas, the more dramatic, sustainable, and unique will be your pool of insights. Here we capture a collection of ideas and knowledge, connected or not to each other, for potential exploitation. Once captured, the ideas must be organized and easily shared with others so they can be enhanced; the result becomes your *idea bank*. You need a disciplined process to keep the idea bank alive or, like anything else, the ideas will quickly die due to inertia. Table 2.2 defines each of the insights success factors.

How does a company develop this competency for deep insights? In most organizations, to gain insight into projects, market positioning, and corporate performance, they develop and study performance charts, two-by-two matrices, and Balanced Scorecards, respectively. Looking at data in such a way, we are able to develop certain forms of business insights. Similarly, innovation insight depends on finding (sometimes through visualization and highly diverse group exercises) new knowledge that leads to practical ideas for consideration. When executed well, insights enable

TABLE 2.2 Insights Success Factors

	Definition
Diverse perspectives	We incorporate a wide range of perspectives in the idea-generation process.
External orientation	We actively engage with the external environment.
Climate/Culture	Our organizational climate and culture support the generation of ideas/insights.
Idea flow	We have a strong flow of creative ideas.
Idea selection	We select the best ideas from those that are generated on a timely basis.

creation of innovation platforms (a plethora of ideas to pursue a large multiyear business opportunity) and fresh ideas. This helps managers quickly make investment decisions to accelerate new and novel discoveries.

What is required for an idea pipeline to get fatter and mightier? The most important is to establish climate of trust and openness that support the creative process. You will also need tools for individuals and teams to find incremental and breakthrough ideas.

Mobilization

The focus here is strictly on innovation execution. Our data show that most organizations are weakest in this area. Mobilization reflects the reality that even with strong alignment and a good flow of insights, innovation is only valuable when it is translated into results—that is, executed. The organization with the best idea is not always the winner. Rather, the organization with the *ability* to execute the best idea is the winner. Especially in today's competitive and fast-paced environment where maturation from unique idea to commodity is very swift, execution in the early stages of innovation is critical for success. Table 2.3 defines each of the mobilization success factors.

Mobilizing also means you must capture the maximum value of an innovation before it is duplicated, continually improving that product or service to stay ahead of the competition. Effective mobilization calls for sufficient resources; quick and effective decisions; clear thinking about the human impact of new approaches; and continuous learning about how to translate innovations into reality faster and successfully over time.

In summary, mobilization is set of processes, methods, tools, and structures that will allow employees and managers to operationalize ideas for implementation and venturing in an informed way to achieve targeted business outcomes.

Alignment, insights, and mobilization are all happening at the same time. All three play critical roles in the success of innovation and therefore, the long-term sustainability of your organization. To be successful, you must manage each of them

TABLE 2.3   Mobilization Success Factors

	Definition
Resources	The organization allocates sufficient resources to innovation.
Governance	There are effective governance structures and processes for innovation.
Portfolio	Through a structured process, the company effectively manages a portfolio of innovations selected for implementation.
Change management	Leaders create the adjustments required to ensure all innovations achieve full realization.
Execution	The company has a clear process for successfully bringing projects through the pipeline to achieve positive results.

and the trade-offs between them. An idea that has great merit but would struggle to be mobilized in your organization may not be as valuable as an idea with less merit that can quickly be tested and mobilized. A fantastic idea that would be great for your consumer but does not align with your organizational purpose will struggle to receive funding and support over the long term. A great idea for the market but without strong leadership alignment will stay dormant.

As your organization builds the innovation muscle and the innovation engine continues to grow, you will need to adjust the integration points as part of the overall business planning conversations and activities at the top.

Please visit www.desai.com to find more information and resources about how to assess these factors in your organization.

Our insight from working with global customers since 1983 is that *leadership readiness* is the most essential factor for success. Leaders may want innovation, but it is entirely possible that the midlevel managers are not ready, meaning they have no time and no resources and lack the mind-set, motivation, and skills. It is also possible that the current organizational structures are too bureaucratic to welcome innovation thinking.

Leading Innovation

The leader's primary contribution is in the recognition of good ideas, the support of those ideas, and the willingness to challenge the system to get new products, processes, services, and systems adopted. It might be more accurate, then, to say that leaders are early adopters of innovation.[7]

In 2011, DDI International conducted a global research project. The questions they asked assessed how ready current leaders are to handle tomorrow's business challenges. Where will the next generation of leaders come from? How ready is the organization to attract, retain, and grow its best talent?

One of the conclusions was that 50% of leaders don't feel they have the creativity and innovation skills required for success. The number of leaders citing innovation as a critical skill increased more than for any other skill. "Innovation has become a mantra for many organizations as they shift from a recessionary, cost-cutting mind-set to a competitive one."[8]

According to a 2010 report by the Boston Consulting Group, 72% of executives list innovation as a top priority, the highest percentage since it began conducting the annual research. The same study shows that those who focus on innovation enjoy up to a sixfold advantage on total shareholder return versus their industry peers.[9]

Role of Transformative Leadership

In the mid-1990s, Whirlpool determined that innovation was needed to create unique solutions for its customers. The company decided to embed innovation as a core competency.[10] The notion that organizations have core competencies has gained extensive credibility in last ten years. C. K. Prahalad and Gary Hamel have been credited with raising the issue about how competitive advantage can no longer be sustained solely from price and performance attributes, such as features, cost, and quality. Instead, sustainable competitive advantage must now be attained by defining, building, and leveraging unique organizational knowledge, skills, and experience (leveraging core competencies) in ways that competitors cannot imitate. Their view of strategy and strategic advantage involves orchestrating all the resources of an organization toward creating future opportunities and markets in areas where they hold the advantage.

Core competencies are derived from an organization's strategic business mandate. They can be resident or aspirational in nature. Core competencies need to exist at the organizational level and be embodied in the very lifeblood of the organization. As strategic mandate, they must be embedded across a wide range of employees within the human resource management systems, thereby becoming an enterprise-wide competency.

For such transformational change, the leaders at the top are responsible for embedding such core competencies into the organization. Many organizations have tried to become innovative, but few have succeeded. In the long run, sustaining core competencies for a business is critical to creating value. Prahalad and Hamel have outlined five key leadership tasks that are essential to embedding a core competency:

1. Leaders must identify core competencies as specific, deep, shared understandings around the critical few core advantages of the organization. They must assess if each competency meets the core competence test of running across market and product lines, customer benefits, and difficulty of imitation.
2. Leaders must establish a map of how current or new core competencies can strengthen positions in existing or new markets. This activity should include determining areas that leverage existing competencies, areas that might be obsolete, and areas that require building new competencies.
3. Leaders need to recognize that building core competencies requires sustained effort over a long time period, roughly five to ten years.
4. Leaders need to deploy core competencies across multiple business units and divisions in a manner that is aligned but flexible.
5. Leaders need to protect and defend core competencies over time. Core competencies may be lost in many ways, including lack of funding, loss of interest, fragmentation, or divestiture. Maintenance of core competencies is a critical aspect of strategy that can be easily overlooked.[11]

As seen in this section, leaders must play a very active role in embedding innovation into the culture. They must see this as *their work*. Relegating it to others is a sign that leaders are not ready for innovation as a core capability.

Innovation readiness can be improved by making sure your organization is not moving too quickly to skills training in innovation techniques or into small process modifications. This approach may work as a short-term solution, but it is usually ineffective at dispersing skills over wide groups of people. In contrast, while the process of building your innovation engine requires skills training, the emphasis is much more focused on creating systemic change in the infrastructure in order to reinforce the new skills and on leadership development to guide the execution process. Building an innovation engine is thus a broad and inclusive approach, whereas training is a narrower, more targeted approach, generally reserved for a defined set of people in your organization.

Leadership Dialog at the Top

What are the signs that leaders at the top are serious and ready about innovation?

The most important sign we have seen is the rigorous discussion about innovation among the leaders. All too often innovation gets derailed because "innovation" (the vocabulary and what it means in the context of the particular organization) is not clearly defined or agreed on—often not even discussed for agreement at the top. Rigorous discussion about what it is and what it is not needs to take place before innovation should be discussed or others in the organization or supply chain should be engaged. Top executives should discuss and rate their sentiment about how innovative the organization is and has been and come up with concrete messages that will engage the workforce before they communicate their commitment about innovation to the organization. It is critical that executives agree on the definition and how they will communicate it (with consistently used common language) so that employees align and understand the role and focus of innovation. Is senior management committed to being a market leader or a fast follower; a leader, breeder, feeder, or something else? What characterizes their preferred position?

From our experience, there are four key characteristics of innovation-based leader readiness:

1. **Bias toward opportunities over problems.** Peter Drucker once said that "problems cannot be ignored . . . but have to be taken care of." The danger for leaders is an all-too-pervasive tendency to allow problems to overwhelm the force field of a business, which provides it with its defining culture. Innovation cannot thrive in such an atmosphere and will not attain serious visibility. In short, "to be change leaders, enterprises have to *focus on opportunities.*" Even more to the point, they *"have to starve problems and feed opportunities."* In Dr. Stephen Covey's terminology, they need to be vigorously "proactive" in assuming responsibility for their chosen personal and corporate destiny in making whatever constructive changes are both plausible and maximally desirable within the context in which they are operating.[12] That is, they need to be working from and expanding their primary spheres of influence to achieve optimal impact by building on an abundance model rather than a scarcity model of personal

efficacy. Through such an empowering orientation, a leader can better guide his or her work unit toward more maximizing pursuits.

2. **Strong advocacy and sponsorship skills.** A high level of advocacy and sponsorship in mediating the innovative project up and down the organizational chain of command is indispensable, as is effective promotion to external opinion makers and markets. This includes the critical need to achieve a secure funding base from top management resources, along with the competence to continue making the case to the top when the project runs into difficult areas, which may cause delays or a need for additional funding. Effective mediation at this level has the added benefit of raising the project's visibility throughout the organization, where other priorities can easily override the protective space needed to nurture the developing offerings.

   An ability to draw in ultimate consumers and those who can influence them as the product nears market readiness is also essential. Such aptitude necessitates a subtle balance between the mastery of broad product, organizational, and market knowledge and highly persuasive interpersonal and emotional intelligence. Without strong sponsorship, innovative projects are much more likely to fail or become less than what they could have attained to. In that respect, they miss the mark in some fundamental aspect.

3. **Team building.** In most organizations, leadership is not an individual pursuit but involves maximizing the working ability of the entire team or unit. Many popular books on management agree because so much depends on motivation to authentically honor the intelligence, skills, and dignity of each member.[13] Clearly, when these "human factors" are missing or are viewed merely as add-ons, projects become easily derailed, or at least they don't become all they could be. Without the strong cohesiveness of trust, work becomes stymied in various subtle and not-so-subtle ways. The empowerment and skill enhancement of each team member, along with the shared commitment toward the common goal, is critical to optimizing project achievement.

   These soft skills, consistently applied, provide the underpinning of working with and through people in developing common or at least workable convergences, through diverse specializations where areas of interest and opportunities can easily collide. Here is where team building needs to merge with deep learning. Without consistent attention to team building, negative behaviors and attitudes arise more readily, giving shape to built-in limiting orthodoxies that are counterproductive. When these settle in, they inhabit the life path of an organizational culture and are extremely difficult to dislodge.

4. **Maintaining and keeping integrity.** Integrity is a function of vision, discipline, and credibility, which is synonymous with the merging of Covey's "private" and "public victories." Discipline has to do with the hard work of identifying your core values and aligning them with an organizational vision and values. This vital task of identifying purpose and values alignment is foundational to finding meaning at work. Ultimately, it is meaning that will inspire passionate output from every employee toward greatness and, therefore, innovation success.

As Drucker said:

> *The man who focuses on efforts and who stresses his own downward authority is a subordinate no matter how exalted his title or rank. But the man who focuses on contribution and who takes responsibility for results, no matter how junior, is in the most literal sense of the phrase, "top management." He holds himself accountable for the performance of the whole.*[14]

Are your leaders at the top creating an environment that provokes and promotes this behavior?

It is important to note that between advocacy and team building is the role of the leader of innovation initiatives. This person needs to be both able to evoke engagement, participation, and contributions from those needed at a particular point along the path and to provoke those who need to be challenged, kept on track, and influenced strongly.

For leaders, the hard work at this point is the willingness to grapple with the critical space between the imagination of possibilities that lies within every employee and the courage and influence required to execute as a leader.[15] Such personal creativity in turn defines a transformational leader:

> *When organizations face new problems and complexities that cannot be solved by unguided evolution, these leaders assume responsibilities for reshaping organizational practices to adapt to environmental changes. They direct organizational changes that build confidence and empower their employees to seek new ways of doing things. They overcome resistance to change by creating visions of the future that evoke confidence and mastery of new organizational practices.*[16]

In short, transformational leadership is essential to build your innovation engine,. Such leadership readiness can arise only at the nexus between core values (personal and corporate) and an inspiring vision that goes beyond the self to some greater social good, which in the marketplace translates ultimately to true satisfaction of customer desires.

In taking on such empowering work, what is important is not only the end product but the (innovation and other) processes unleashed inside and outside the organization as a result of the effort. To the extent these are perceived as liberating by participating stakeholders, the very process of creating desire for an innovation engine should enhance all engaged parties, the project team, and ultimately the customer alike.

Three Constraints for Innovation Success

A firm's ability firm to embrace and exploit innovation can be measured by three critical success factors:

1. Top managers' dominant logic
2. Organization's ability to acquire, learn, and share new knowledge
3. Firm's commitment and methods to access new technologies and resources to exploit ideas into innovations

DOMINANT LOGIC   The most critical factor is *dominant logic*. It either enables or hinders top management in recognizing the potential of innovation and to better allocating resources to exploit.

C. K. Prahalad and Richard A. Bettis first introduced the concept of dominant logic in 1986.[17] They said a firm's ability to exploit opportunities is directly dependent on how top managers deal with the increasing diversity of strategic decisions, which in turn depends on the cognitive orientation of those top managers. Dominant logic consists of the mental maps developed through these managers' experiences. Mental maps are how each manager brings to a management problem his or her own biases, beliefs, and assumptions about *how* to build, sell, and serve the firm's products and services. These points of view include how to attack markets, which technologies to use, how to invest, whom to serve, whom to hire, how to manage competition, how to develop and grow brands, and how to conduct the firm's business. These leadership competencies defines the window of how that leader scans the information and seeks the knowledge to solve business problems and identify opportunities to exploit.

For an organization, dominant logic arises out of how successful it has been with its organizational strategies, systems, technology, structure, and culture. If the firm has been successful, the dominant logic is easy to identify by listening to conversations that include statements such as "That is how we do things around here" or "Our best practice is to. . . ." The longer the tenure of the management team, the more likely it has been successful, and therefore, the stronger the dominant logic. Over a period of time, dominant logic turns into orthodoxies— deeply believed value systems, which are generally unwritten and invisible but are strong ingredients of the status quo at all levels within a firm.

Dominant logic and orthodoxies create the cement walls of the organizational box that often prevent finding new growth opportunities.

Dominant logic and orthodoxies also create comfort zones for the managers who use that logic to gain the support of superiors so they can stay in the center of this box—by not challenging assumptions, hiring the same type of people, and not taking personal risks.

LEARNING CULTURE   Due to globalization, automation, and changing government regulations, the environment we live in is highly complex, as most of us would agree. Complexity by its nature creates more uncertainty. In this highly connected world, we are creating tremendous amounts of new knowledge every day, about everything.

In companies, knowledge assets must grow at the speed of their markets, or they'll be outpaced as new entrants become the darling stars. We can see examples of this with Amazon, now the biggest retailer in the world—did JCPenney or Sears see that coming? Or how about Netflix taking over Blockbuster and then being challenged by Hulu? Or how about Skype carving out a dominant place in the telecommunication industry—did AT&T or British Telecomm see that one? In all of these cases, the incumbents lacked the knowledge to understand what was happening in the fast-moving marketplace and courage to move away from their dominant logic-driven business models.

To reduce uncertainty about the future, today's firms must develop new knowledge about technologies, markets, and the business.

New technological knowledge identifies insights about components, interdependencies, methods, and processes that go into making new offerings. New market knowledge can improve clarity about current customers, new and emerging customers, their current and new needs, expectations, how to get them to buy the products, how to have them socialize your brands to others, and how to deliver products that will satisfy them. Access to new business knowledge gives you insights about new business models in the industry, the economic engine, and macroeconomic influences, such as interest rates and government policies impacting the business today and in the future.

ACCESS TO TECHNOLOGIES AND RESOURCES   Having fresh technological knowledge is vital to building great innovations. Unfortunately, the greatest uncertainty in the world today is driven by technological life cycles. The good news is that technology actually evolves in a predictable pattern. So, if you understand these patterns, you can reduce uncertainty and can convert ideas into innovations faster.

One such model we already looked at briefly is the S-Curve. All technological S-Curves have a physical limit. By learning and using new knowledge, a firm can easily predict when a technology will reach its S-Curve maturity and what might emerge next for which markets. An example is how the single-processor personal computer reached its physical limit due to certain physical limitations of the physics and engineering of its microprocessor. Engineers quickly developed the multiprocessor technology used today in most personal computers.

To better prepare for innovation, it is critical to assess and acknowledge that dominant logic, lack of learning culture, and access to new technologies create constraints in every organization. Do these constraints exist within your company? Are they real? How would you address them? What do you need to do about them before embarking on the innovation journey?

Key Discussions for the Senior Leadership

To deploy innovation culture, you must assure a high level of readiness. We strongly suggest that your senior leadership team dialog and debate the next six questions. By doing so, you will address a critical success factor—sponsorship for innovation—required to make your organization more entrepreneurial.

1. What kind of innovation do you want to cultivate at your company? Why? Would this innovation represent a new direction for your company? If so, what do you hope to accomplish? What challenges are you likely to encounter?

(Continued)

Key Discussions for the Senior Leadership (*Continued*)

2. What type of innovation is most preferred by your board of directors? By your shareholders? What assurances do they need before approving innovation strategies? How will you reconcile any differences of vision?

3. What are your company's current best practices for stimulating innovation? In what ways are they similar to or divergent from your industry's best practices?

4. What role will your company's managers play in stimulating business innovation? Will you seek their involvement in the planning processes? Why or why not?

5. What are the top three essential components to providing an environment that is conducive to innovation? Why are these components important? How will they affect company policies? How will they influence management practices?

6. Do you plan to execute any mergers or acquisitions that could stimulate innovation at your company in the next 12 months? If so, how do you expect that your company will benefit?

Notes

1. IBM, "Capitalizing on Complexity: Insights from the Global Chief Executive Officer Study" (Somers, NY: IBM Global Business Services, 2010).
2. W. Kiechel, *The Lords of Strategy: The Secret Intellectual History of the New Corporate World* (Boston: Harvard Business School Publishing, 2010).
3. www.statisticbrain.com/total-number-of-pages-indexed-by-google/.
4. http://en.wikipedia.org/wiki/Wikipedia:Statistics
5. Yong-Li McFarand, "The NutriCosmetics Market: A Global Health & Wellness Megatrend" (Frost and Sullivan, June 2011).
6. Deloitte, "Glittering Prize—A Research Study" May 2005, p. 7.
7. James M. Kouzes and Barry Z. Posner, *The Leadership Challenge*, 3rd ed. (San Francisco: Jossey-Bass), p. 17.
8. Jazmine Boatman, Ph.D. and Rochard S. Wellins, Ph.D. "Global Leadership Forecast 2011 by DDI International," 2011, p. 19.
9. The full Development Dimensions International executive report and PowerPoint slides are available at: www.ddiworld.com/glf2011
10. Nancy Tennant Snyder and Deborah L. Duarte, *Strategic Innovation: Embedding Innovation as a Core Competency in Your Organization* (San Francisco: Jossey-Bass, 2003).
11. C. K. Prahalad and Gary Hamel, *Competing for the Future* (Boston: Harvard Business Review Press, 1996).

12. Stephen Covey, *The 7 Habits of Highly Effective People* (New York: Free Press, 2004), pp. 66–94.

13. Teresa M. Amabile, "How to Kill Creativity," in President and Fellows of Harvard College, *Harvard Business Review on Breakthrough Thinking* (Boston: Harvard Business Review Press, 1999), pp. 1–28.

14. Peter F. Drucker, *The Effective Executive: The Definitive Guide to Getting the Right Things Done* (New York: HarperBusiness, 2006).

15. Covey, *The 7 Habits of Highly Effective People*, pp. 103, 109.

16. Warren Bennis and Burt Nanus, *Leaders: The Strategies for Taking Charge* (New York: Harper & Row, 1985), p. 18.

17. C. K. Prahald on leadership: Leaders: (1) must have a point of view about the future and help fold that view into the current realities, (2) they must be like a sheepdog (they must stay behind, bark but don't bite, and make sure you don't lose any sheep). http://youtu.be/DXPFPhpnAvo

CHAPTER 3

Creating an Innovation Strategy

*C*reate *your innovation strategy:* Develop a unique value creation target. Then create a vertical and horizontal organizational alignment for everyone to see themselves in the strategic vision and mission that is essential for future financial and nonfinancial returns.

Innovation Strategy

A generic definition of the word "invention" is a new solution that has never been available before that creates value for the person, team, organization, market, or the planet. Inventions are created by applying design principles, technology, business processes, experimentation, and laser-focused persistence to solve a problem.

Additionally, we define "innovation" as a process that continuously creates inventions that generate sustainable competitive advantage for an organization. The advantage may come in terms of business model (incremental or breakthrough), channel, processes, product performance, branding, customer experience, and forms of delivery.

In order to begin your innovation journey, the leaders in your company must take time to develop your firm's *innovation strategy*.

We define "business strategy" as the firm's goals, timing, actions, and resource allocations in using new knowledge to offer new products or services.

Similarly, "innovation strategy" is an articulated statement that defines how the firm has chosen to build the right competencies and required assets, products and services, and the environment in which to operate in to actualize the business strategy.

As described in Chapter 1, innovation intent is a strategic statement that describes innovation in the context of your business (or area), the value it promises to generate for growth, and the disciplined execution process by which to get there.

To build your innovation strategy, we suggest you clarify the current business strategy first. Doing this will help shape the appropriate innovation strategy discussion with the top team, which then will help you formulate the emerging innovation mandate for the rest of the organization.

Six typical business strategies are presented next. Which one defines how your company operates today?

1. **Pioneer.** The pioneer is the first to introduce new offerings. This means the company invests to build the right competence to create growth before others. Wal-Mart created unique information technology systems to expand aggressively against Sears, Kmart, and others. Xerox created technologies that power 85% of appliances in today's modern-day office; these include the ethernet, graphics interface on a personal computer, computer mouse, keyboard, ink and laser printing, and others.

2. **Fast follower.** Wait for the offensive leader to introduce a product first, monitor the elements of the business model, identify shortcomings, and then introduce a better product that corrects errors made by the pioneer. IBM did this when it introduced the first PC by watching Altair, Altos, Televideo, and even Apple's mistakes before 1981. IBM was the first PC company to target the business consumer instead of the home user. Apple waited for all other MP3 player companies to fail and then came out with the first iPod, which solved many issues of finding, buying, playing, and sharing music, anywhere anytime by anyone in the world.

3. **Imitative strategy.** Firms of this type prefer to produce a clone of the pioneers' products. They have no intention being the first or to leapfrog the pioneer. These players have unique execution capabilities, such as low-cost labor, inexpensive raw materials, or low-cost manufacturing. These firms use one or all of these elements to innovate and compete. Many of the Chinese-branded items use this approach.

4. **Dependent strategy.** The firm is very happy with the status quo and will change features of its offerings only when requested by their best customers. It is happy to quickly adopt features from products of other stronger rivals. This can be easily seen within the auto industry.

5. **Low-cost strategy.** The goal of this firm is to stay focused on short-term profitability by limiting changes to offerings and striving to offer the lowest possible cost.

6. **Specialization strategy.** A firm with this strategy looks for some unique niche need of the market that is not being met. Generally, the markets are small and may have high barriers to entry. In such businesses, margins are attractive, but the business can be very difficult to scale. Also, such markets are often served by small players with deep domain expertise.

Which one of these six business strategies does your company employ? It may not be obvious. Engage in a dialog with the leadership team to help define your current business strategy. This will help define your innovation strategy. Then develop an innovation mandate that can be communicated down.

Defining Innovation Strategy

For every business, there are only *four unique types of growth strategies*. As shown in Figure 3.1, the dimensions are market focus and product focus. Companies seeking growth in current markets with current products are pursuing market penetration strategies. Companies seeking new markets with current products are pursuing market development strategies. Firms trying to grow in current markets with new products are pursuing a product development strategy. Finally, firms seeking new products in new markets are pursuing a market differentiation strategy.

Based on these growth strategies, your innovation strategy will fall into one of two types of corporate activities: venturing or intrapreneuring. Both paths can lead to outstanding results, but the overall focus is very different. Venturing is about diversification and adding new businesses on top of the current business or to existing lines. By contrast, intrapreneuring is about pursuing a competitive advantage within current and adjacent markets. Both strategies are difficult to pursue simultaneously, so you should pick one to start.

Your innovation strategy is a strategic statement that describes innovation in the context of your business or area, the value it promises to generate for growth, and the disciplined execution process by which to get there. It is used to communicate (see Figure 3.2):

- **Why** is innovation important to pursue now more than ever?
- **Who** is involved, and who will be the beneficiary of our innovations?
- **What** will we innovate that is difficult to replicate?
- **How** different is this from everything else we do?
- **When** will we do who, what, and how? And how do we know we are going in the right direction?

FIGURE 3.1 Corporate Growth Strategy Options

FIGURE 3.2   Designing Your Innovation Strategy

WHY   Successful global innovators have clarified the role of innovation for their firms. Why is innovation more critical today than ever before, and what can it provide that nothing else will? By now, you have answered this already through development of your innovation intent. If your innovation intent (Chapter 1) is not defined, make sure the sponsor has at least articulated a clear goal for innovation: top line, bottom line, or some other strategic objective.

WHO   At the center of innovation are people with ideas who desire to bring them to reality. Who are the primary targets for the innovation program? Is it about allowing employees to think more outside the box on a daily basis? Or is the innovation focus primarily within the supply chain? Or is it the current customer for the first year? If internal, will it be mostly radical or incremental or architectural for R&D, engineering, manufacturing, marketing, sales, service, or other functions? If an innovation is radical to R&D but marketing can't see its value, is that the right focus?

WHAT   Some firms are able to consistently stay ahead of their competition. Internally, they have the ability to perform certain activities that others can't. What activities? Is it the ability to identify the emerging white space or to quickly build new capabilities for quicker market response? Is it the type of people that the firm attracts—the best product champions, sponsors, analysts, research experts, project managers, and gatekeepers? What are the unique qualities and values you want to build? What drives your firm's ability to find the potential of an innovation?

HOW   It is said that strategic differentiation is directly correlated to the quantity and quality of your firm's knowledge and access to new technologies. How different is the existing knowledge inside your firm, and how new and unique should it be going forward? What will be the speed of product obsolescence in the next few years? Clarify how quickly you need to acquire and share new knowledge to drive incremental and radical innovations. Does the current resourcing model and structure align to implement your innovation strategy efficiently?

WHEN Once your sponsors have answered the questions about innovation, you are ready to begin innovation implementation. There are three types of innovations: radical, incremental, and architectural (unique method). Your innovation strategy must define how much new knowledge and technology it must deal with, depending on which type of innovations you have selected to pursue. This clarity will define your execution methodology and required innovation management capability. It is the innovation execution capability that allows you to deliver your innovations either early or late in the marketplace. Also, it is crucial to connect each phase of the idea-to-market pipeline with precision execution. For example, building new innovation skills to identify early blue oceans, without updating management processes, could result in getting new innovations out to market using legacy manufacturing and distribution processes.

Once you have addressed the five areas with senior leaders, you should have a pretty clear high-level innovation strategy defined. But having an innovation strategy alone is not sufficient. You must also engage senior leaders in order to gain their support for innovation implementation process.

HOW TO EXECUTE AND HOW TO ADAPT? What else do world-class innovators have in common? Once they answered the five important questions (Why? Who? What? How? When?), they had to answer two more questions: How to execute? and How to adapt? Execution is about operational efficiency and ensuring solutions are adaptable for each customer segments. Both allowed them to launch innovations to meet the local needs of their global customers faster than the competitors.

These seven important questions are central to help define your innovation strategy.

Examples from the Field

What do the following companies have in common?

1. Apple
2. Google
3. IBM
4. United Health Group
5. Proctor & Gamble
6. Walt Disney
7. FedEx
8. Genentech
9. Tata
10. Advanced Micro Devices (AMD)
11. Target
12. Cognizant

AMD, a microprocessor manufacturer and a chip competitor to Intel and Qualcomm, found the only way to survive and prevail is through great product and delivery innovations. P&G focuses on brand management, a core competency and one in which it has been expert for over eight decades. Nike, in contrast, drives its innovativeness through product designs. Target has mastered the skill to compete against the world dominance of Wal-Mart's low-cost business model. Each company listed has a successful innovation strategy in place.

Any company can generate creative ideas. Often companies lack innovation as a core capability to help bring those ideas as unique solutions for their markets.

Investing *only* in blockbuster ideas is a poor strategy for innovation. Why? Small ideas that could generate big profits don't get the air time, and the intrapreneur innovator (your top talent) walks out the door with that idea and competes against you in a few years. For example, at Time, Inc., the managers only wanted to keep building the next *People* magazine. The result was plummeting revenue and subscriber base. Only after smaller but creative ideas were used did they start to reverse the profit trend line.

Another poor strategy is to subject all ideas to the same performance engine criteria for incubation, evaluation, and experimentation. Not all ideas will generate the strict financial ROI targets within the time frame headquarters has set for capital expenditure policy. This typical trap leads to old ideas retrofitted in the current system, which results in only incremental changes to product and service offerings—a sure path for falling behind in the marketplace.

Remember, every product line and business unit may be at a different point on its S-Curve. The process and the investment mind-set must be aligned to where each business is on this curve in order to ensure that no small or big ideas get dropped or left for the rivals to find.

CASE STUDY: INNOVATION AT MCDONALD'S   McDonald's feeds over 50 million customers at over 30,000 restaurants around the world *every day*.[1] Getting the basics right is critical, but focusing only on the core capability is not sufficient enough. McDonald's went through a business downturn from the 1990s through the early 2000s. Revenues were slowing, competitors were growing, and people were buzzing about new, fast-casual dining options that were more upscale than McDonald's, threatening parts of its business. In response, McDonald's tried many things: buying Boston Market and Chipotle, with new kitchen systems designed to custom cook orders and different menu items. Nothing seemed to gain traction.

In 2003, a new CEO and chairman was appointed from within. The turnaround began by focusing on the five basics: People, Products, Place, Price, and Promotion. The "5 Ps" became the instrument of transformation for a few years. According to the VP of human resources (HR) at that time, Steve Russell, "It caused us to understand that the customer is key—it all has to center on the customer." This is in contrast to an earlier emphasis on operation, distribution, and cost. Today those things continue to be crucial, but only in the context of the customer experience.

Around 2005, the company started to focus more thought and discipline for growth through innovation. By listening to customers closely, a huge bank of ideas began to flow among the corporate offices, internal departments, and restaurants. An innovation strategy called "Think Big, Start Small, Scale Fast" was launched, a concept credited to Mats Lederhausen, managing director of McDonald's Ventures and leader in the company's strategy office.

Since 75% of the restaurants are owner-operated franchisees in the United States, the challenge was to bring the owner-operators into the innovation process in a disciplined way, without killing their entrepreneurial spirit.

How did McDonald's do it? It secured CEO-led sponsorship for a new Innovation Center, established an Innovation Council, and implemented a Strategic Innovation Process. The center, a giant warehouse with several model kitchens, solicits ideas from around the world and puts them into a restaurant-like "studio" setting. When a product is changed, often the kitchen equipment needs to change to support it. All testing now occurs in the center. Once the product is tested, the company partners with nearby restaurants to test the innovation. About 50 to 100 restaurants are used for fast prototyping of any new product or service offering. This enables McDonald's company to test the menu, the operating platform, and all the systems that need to align with the change.

The Innovation Council is made up of owner-operators, staff members at various levels, suppliers, and even company outsiders who are just smart people who love to think about the future. The primary job of the council is to challenge the status quo, remove the old mind-set, and prompt strong desires to study customers' unmet needs before customers themselves define it.

In the United States, 13,000 restaurants now use the innovation process to expedite near-term launches of new products, such as spicy chicken or new breakfast menu items.

McDonald's innovation strategy was designed for fast product innovations and customer centricity. Instead of focusing on internal efficiencies, the company decided to find innovations linked to their market growth strategy. It did this by carefully listening to both current and emerging needs of various customer segments across the globe. By centralizing an innovation process and resources, McDonald's was able to quickly test new innovations and bring them out to markets faster than ever before.

CASE STUDY: WHIRLPOOL   Whirlpool's innovation journey started in 1999 with its emphasis on embedding innovation as a core competency for everyone in the company.[2] Company leaders were committed to building a culture of innovation as the clear differentiator in their sector.[3]

They defined innovation as "any product or service that creates unique and compelling solutions valued by our customers, real and sustainable competitive advantages, and extraordinary value for our customers."[4]

At the center of Whirlpool's initiative were three innovation boards (I-boards) made up of senior leaders at the regional business levels of North America, Latin America, and Europe. Their primary role was to embed innovation in their respective units by setting financial goals, allocating resources, and reviewing processes and new ideas for further funding. The process included training and developing 600 I-mentors around the world, the innovation equivalent of black belts in Six Sigma initiatives. I-mentors were trained on innovation tools and were equipped with the knowledge and skills to facilitate innovation-related meetings and workshops. The I-boards funded big projects as well as many nascent ideas that might never have been supported. Its members realized that many smaller good ideas could become big successful and the risk of experimentation was relatively low.

The process of embedding innovation involved training over 22,000 employees to look for "market and in-job innovations." Employees were encouraged to find fresh new ideas in their daily jobs for things like systems changes, organizational design, customer marketing, delivery, core processes, enabling processes, partnerships, alliances, and product performance. As a result, the pipeline of ideas grew from $350 million in 2006 to over $3 billion by 2009.

For Whirlpool, unlike McDonald's, the innovation strategy was more about building intrapreneurship and making innovation a core capability with the culture. For it, innovation is a behavior and part of everyone's daily job. The company provided a process for anyone to find ideas and test them by bypassing internal vertical structures that often prevent good ideas from coming to the top.

CASE STUDY: HIMALAYA DRUG COMPANY India's Himalaya Drug Company (HDC), established in 1930, has become the global pioneer in the field of Ayurvedic medicine.[5] In 1934, HDC introduced Serpina, the world's first antihypertensive drug that could reduce blood pressure. Since then it has converted Ayurveda's herbal tradition into a complete range of proprietary herbal formulations backed by world-class scientific experts, with outstanding manufacturing plants and a state-of-the-art, world-class R&D center.

Today HDC is in over 70 countries with commanding presence in the domestic and international contemporary herbal healthcare product markets. The company also claims that over 300,000 doctors have endorsed their products to patients.

HDC's basic product line was pharmaceuticals until the 1990s. In 1999, it made a strategic decision to expand to the over-the-counter (OTC) segment in addition to the doctor-prescription path. The timing was perfect, as the global market for herbal formulations opened with double-digit growth while allopathic drugs were growing in single digits—as is the case today for most drug areas.

By positioning itself as a head-to-heal herbal healthcare brand, HDC was able to exploit the existing scope within the business. Compared to other manufacturers of herbal medicine in India, HDC could leverage several strategic assets in its quest to expand scope.

The core capability of HDC is its strong research assets. Its focus on scientific discovery distinguishes it from other players in the market. Each of its global drug brands took years of primary research in the world-class research center in Bangalore, India.

It is not uncommon for a middle-class family in India to use eight to ten HDC products. The company's popularity has spread to other areas of the world as well.

Unlike the previous two case studies, HDC is pursuing new products and new markets at the same time by pioneering new innovations to compete against much larger worldwide players.

CONCLUSION Once you have gained a high level of clarity about your innovation strategy, be sure to include a conversation about how you will implement and execute the strategy before finalizing the innovation strategy. It is possible that you may decide to postpone implementation due to other near-term priorities or until all the required executive sponsorship is obtained.

Just because senior leaders develop an exciting innovation strategy doesn't mean the rest of the organization is ready for implementation, especially middle management. Therefore, the next step is to make sure the sponsor(s) fully engage in directing *how* the organization will manage and govern the rollout of the innovation program.

Creativity, Design, Invention, Innovation

All innovations arise out of a creative idea. An idea, radically new or incremental, can lead to a breakthrough value for innovator and customers alike. Just because an idea is considered to be an incremental change to an existing offering does not mean it will have minimal impact. It could have a significant positive impact. Motorola opened up a huge new market when it started to manufacture beepers in a variety of colors instead of just black. Doing this required a small change—using a new raw material for the casing only. By making this change, the beepers appealed to students and women without much effort. In other words, the type of change, whether incremental or radical, is not directly correlated to the impact of an offering.

When new ideas go through a disciplined process of design, it can lead to an invention. If you search the U.S. Patent Office database, you will find abundant useless inventions as well as some so wacky they should belong in a different galaxy. Invention should be usable and welcomed by target users. To a company, a product could be a great invention because it has never produced it before, but to the market it might be an old idea. An offering is called an *innovation* only after it is brought to market (for internal or external customers), and the market attaches a value (small or large) to it and proclaims it innovative. If that invention creates a new behavior in the marketplace, or it creates completely new markets, and the company dominates those markets, then it is called a *breakthrough innovation*.

In other words, no one can claim a new offering as *their* innovation until the market says so. If the company continues to bring out innovative offerings and its market share continues to grow, society recognizes the company as a *world-class innovator* (see Figure 3.3).

Innovation management is the systematic process of turning ideas into a system of innovations year after year.

The ultimate goal for most companies is sustainable competitive advantage. Sustainable competitive advantage necessitates sustained new innovations.

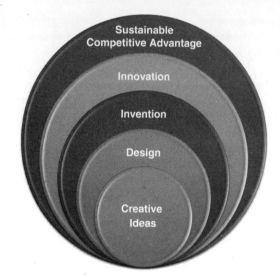

FIGURE 3.3   From Creative Ideas to Competitive Advantage

Ideas become innovations when they are quickly tested, adapted, enhanced, and implemented using the best research, design, and technologies available. Innovations generate sustained new value, competitive advantage, and therefore reduce future risk. Innovation management is the disciplined process that ensures finding, nurturing, evaluating, testing, and marketing the best ideas for success faster than competitors.

Innovation Management

In order to build a growing, profitable business, every leader and manager must possess the skill of innovation. One of the most critical skills required is the skill to manage innovation development.

Leaders need to balance unstructured and unfettered creativity while focusing on a systematic execution of those creative ideas. These two skills are imperative for successful innovation capability. The best innovative companies have achieved this balance between execution and a culture of creativity.

One of the main constraints to innovation, which senior executives and managers often believe, is that innovation happens solely in the R&D center. This implies that responsibility for innovation lies primarily with the head of R&D, and others don't need to pay attention to it. Organizations where innovation is driven primarily by R&D engineers are often bureaucratic and rarely sustain growth and profit year after year. Ideally, innovation should be a strategic process that pervades every part of the organization's value chain, as the five elements pervade our universe. Innovation should be as natural a process as breathing in and out. Innovation should drive innovative behavior throughout the organization from C suite to the mailroom.

Very often innovative products fail to deliver their intended promise because these are stuck in conventional business models that do not fit the current innovations. An example is how Kodak failed to deliver digital photographic products by using the old analog-based business model designed for the photographic film industry. Or how Sony could not exploit its dominance in the music and portable music player industries (Sony Music and Sony Electronics) because it could not get the two business leaders to work together to look at a solution to build the iPod instead of allowing Apple to do it. Without the uniqueness of iTunes and the 99-cent music download solution—a new business model offering at the time—Apple's iPod sales would have been significantly smaller. Remember, back then, Apple was just a computer company; it was not in the music industry or the consumer electronics business. Apple was successful in beating Sony (and many other music player manufacturers) because it looked outside its own conventional business model.

This is why the noun "management" is more important than the adjective "innovation" in the phrase "innovation management." Every organization has a plethora of ideas at any given point in time. The challenge is always about having access to that idea bank, creating a business case, and quickly testing the right ones that will generate growth and profit. Here are three important questions that should be taught to every idea generator:

1. **Testing validity.** I have an idea, but how can I build a business around it?
2. **Market potential.** What is the economic engine? How will I make profit?
3. **Execution.** Once I get this idea implemented, how will I sustain growth and profit?

In his book *Competitive Strategy,* Michael Porter said that "strategy formulation is 10%, and implementation is 90%."[6] Business schools quickly mandated courses on strategy. Yet it took a long time for businesses to realize that the key to successful competitive strategy was not the strategy itself but how that strategy was executed and managed. Harvard professor Robert Kaplan (of Balanced Scorecard fame) believes that companies need a VP of strategy implementation.

This same principle applies to innovation and strategy: "10% innovation and 90% innovation management." Unfortunately, the reverse is found in most companies today. Most organizations embarking on innovation efforts spend all their time on finding ideas and installing an ideation software system to evaluate ideas; they never do much to bring those ideas to life. Soon the entire innovation program gets a black eye, and it is not invited back for years to come. For such organizations, the word "innovation" becomes taboo.

Defining Innovation

Once you have developed a good strategy for innovation by answering the seven core questions mentioned earlier in this chapter, executives should next take some time to define innovation in a short, easy-to-understand sentence.

By defining innovation, you are eliminating potential confusion by other managers and staff. The definition should be a strategic public statement of what is inside and what is outside the scope of the innovation initiative at your company.

Not surprisingly, the literature on innovation contains a wide array of definitions. One useful distinction often made is the line between continuous improvement and innovation. "Continuous improvement" refers to incremental steps, while "innovation" involves discontinuous changes and breakthroughs. According to Peter Drucker, innovation is the set of tools employed to create a new business.[7] These tools can be learned and practiced. Gary Hamel redefines innovation as strategic innovation—the capacity to reconceive the existing business model in ways that create new value for customers and stakeholders and create advantages over the competition.[8]

At Harley-Davidson, innovation is ensuring that its products are newer and more leading edge than those of competitors.

At IBM, the number of new patents defines innovation.

Volkswagen defines innovation as a way of fulfillment and connection with customers by creating something novel that also pays off. The payoff may be in a new product or something as intangible as a new way to do things.

Whirlpool, in order to meet unique strategic needs, defines innovation "as any product or service that creates unique and compelling solutions valued by our customers, real and sustainable competitive advantages, and extraordinary value for our shareholders."

At CA Technologies (on the Forbes' 2011 Most Innovative Companies list), "Innovation is the conversion of knowledge and ideas into a benefit, which may be for commercial use or for the public good; the benefit may be new or improved."[9]

At one of our large pharmaceutical client companies, innovation is defined as "a creative idea that when practically applied creates new value for our customer, patient, or organization."

Cognizant Technology Solutions, an IT, consulting, and business process outsourcing Services company with over 150,000 employees worldwide, defines innovation "as additional value created for the client over and above the client requirements stated in the contract." This definition creates a clear differentiator in the highly commoditized IT outsourcing industry.

Computer Sciences Corporation (CSC) is one of the largest independent computing services firms in the world with almost 100,000 employees worldwide in more than 400 locations and revenues over $15 billion. CSC defines innovation as "the value added through applying creative ideas to a problem and implementing those ideas in the marketplace."

By defining innovation, it will become easier to communicate across the organization. At the beginning of cultural transformation work, definitions are very useful to ensure that proper change occurs. As your maturity for innovation increases, definitions will not be needed.

Defining Innovation Objectives and an Innovation Goal

Once you have defined innovation, the next is to define your *innovation goal*. To make a strategic change, it has to be measured. All too often, initiatives and programs fail because they lack measured outcomes and strong leadership sponsorship.

Defining your innovation goal will help build stakeholder alliance and commitment, especially when you link compensation plans to innovation results (we will cover this in Part II).

Air Products is a gas and chemical company with over 20,000 employees with operations in 30 countries.[10] Its senior executives recognized that growth cannot occur from organically alone. Therefore, they set a goal of 25% of future growth to come from innovation-centered efforts.[11] These senior leaders have instituted innovation as a core process.

At Coromandel, one of the largest fertilizer manufacturers in India with annual revenue of about $2 billion, senior executives have committed to enterprise innovation as a core process. Managing director Kapil Mehan and his executive team have embedded innovation as a core competency at all levels, including the HR systems' links to the Balanced Scorecard management process. Their innovation goal is to double the top line and the bottom line every five years.

Boston Scientific Corporation (BSC), founded in 1979, produces and distributes over 15,000 medical supply products in over 20 global locations and employs about 28,000 employees.[12] BSC was experiencing rapid growth (acquiring over 30 companies), complex product portfolio management issues, increased operational hurdles and costs, and growing regulatory scrutiny. Its chief technology officer imposed a solid approach and structure to minimize business risk and improve long-term planning processes using innovation as the key lever. This resulted in a broad view of innovation that includes operations, management, strategic acquisitions, and R&D. The organization decided to place greater focus on innovation from enabling technologies rather than product innovation. It emphasized two portfolios: novel and core. The novel portfolio includes both breakthrough and disruptive technologies and solutions, while core was everything else. By doing this, BSC was able to balance the entire technology portfolio with projects in new product development, core enabling technologies, core pre-product developments, novel enabling technologies, and novel product concepts.

Choosing Innovation Objectives

To help facilitate a strong leadership conversation about innovation objectives and innovation goals, here are some examples of why you might choose to enable an innovation engine for your organization:

- To differentiate your organization in the marketplace
- To build customer loyalty

- To identify savings potential
- To achieve revenue potential
- To accelerate exploitation of new business ideas worthy of pursing
- To build climate and culture of innovation as per the organization's innovation mission
- To become a leading innovation brand for products and services in the markets served and new markets you may serve
- To improve and expand current products and services
- To access new technologies
- To access new markets
- To identify market trends
- To improve product quality and associated core processes
- To improve employee attraction, engagement, and retention
- To develop new competencies

Defining the Innovation Goal

The innovation goal should be visionary and exciting. It should be something that has not seen before, measurable at least once per year (eventually more often), customer focused, and ultimately delivering value (top line, mid line and bottom line).

Following are some examples of innovation goals:

- Increase the product pipeline from x to y, to grow the top line by 5% better than your sector's GDP.
- Annually achieve 25% additional margin from new customer-driven services.
- Increase the top line every three years by 25%.
- Double the top line and bottom line every three years.
- Achieve 25% of the top line from new services created within past 24 months.
- Develop new customer-driven products from the top ten customers that will increase net margins by 5% every year.
- Build a new S-Curve: Invent a completely new business with a new category of offerings
- Improve customer acquisition ratio by 15% every year for next three years.
- Achieve a customer satisfaction index (CSAT) (or some other best practices method such as net promoter score (NPS)[13] score of 6.0 out of 7.0 (85% or better).
- Achieve 25% net profit from 3 new businesses and 25 new current product enhancements in the next five years.
- 1% profit before income tax (PBIT) above the current PBIT targets.
- Top customers rate us as most innovative in markets and categories we serve.
- 2x/3y: Grow 2x every three years, both top line and bottom line.
- 3/30/3: Within three years achieve a rate of 30% *new* revenue from products/services introduced in last three years.
- 20/20: 20% of new business (top line) should come from 20% of new customers every year.

- 10/20/30: Ten new offerings that yield 20% growth in revenue and 30% growth in profitability.
- 50% of all products should be engineered or should include technologies from outside the firm by 2020.

These are good examples of innovation goals to consider. Use the list to engage senior leaders in dialog, debate, and consensus. Then define innovation goals for your company and for each business unit.

If your innovation initiative is for the entire enterprise, one goal should be directly linked to the business strategy.

If you are rolling out innovation only in your own business unit or information technology department, the goal should be aligned to the area's business or operational strategy. Whatever you choose as your innovation goal, it should be fixed for minimum of three years. At the end of three years, you can always enhance it or pick an alternate.

Key Questions about Innovation Strategy

Once you have defined the innovation strategy, objectives, and a goal, you and your top executive team should try to answer these questions before communicating the innovation agenda to the rest of the organization:

1. How do you plan to motivate your company's employees to generate innovative ideas and products? What promotions/incentives should your company offer to employees for making substantive contributions to innovative efforts?

2. What is your goal for company innovations in the next 12 months? How will this affect your company? How do you expect innovation to benefit the company? How will you resource the incremental costs to test new innovations?

3. What percentage should your company's revenue and profit grow moving forward as a result of innovation over the next five years?

Notes

1. E. Gubman and S. Russell, "Think Big, Start Small, Scale Fast," *Journal of the Human Resource Planning Society* volume 29, Issue 3, (2006): 21–34.
2. Ibid.
3. Nancy Tennant Snyder and Bill Stopper, "Innovation at Whirlpool: Embedment and Sustainability," *Journal of the Human Resource Planning Society* 29, No. 3 (2006): 28–30.

4. Nancy Tennant Snyder and Deborah L. Duarte, *Strategic Innovation: Embedding Innovation as a Core Competency in Your Organization* (San Francisco: Jossey-Bass, 2003).

5. S. Maital and D. V. Seshadri, *Innovation Management: Strategies, Concepts and Tools for Growth and Profit* (Thousand Oaks, CA: SAGE, 2010).

6. Michael E. Porter, *Competitive Strategy: Techniques for Analyzing Industries and Competitors* (New York: Free Press, 1998).

7. Peter Drucker, *Innovation and Entrepreneurship* (New York: Harper Business, 1985).

8. Gary Hamel, *Competing for the Future* (Boston: Harvard Business Review Press, 1996).

9. http://community.ca.com/blogs/perspectives/archive/2011/08/01/how-do-you-define-innovation.aspx

10. M. Brown, G. Swift, and P. Penaloza, *Successfully Embedding Innovation* (Houston: APQC Publications, 2007).

11. APQC Report, "Successfully Embedding Innovation: Strategies and Tactics," 2007.

12. Ibid.

13. www.netpromoter.com/

PART II

Develop an Innovation Playbook

CHAPTER 4

Creating a Roadmap

The next important step before you commit to a long-term innovation initiative is to develop a detailed charter, a program implementation plan, and an innovation scorecard that will keep you on track. There are numerous implementation methods on a continuum of create space, build strength, or accelerate growth for innovation. Each organization must evaluate where it falls on this path. In addition, organizational readiness, sponsorship, leader alignment, and urgency to innovate are necessary components for constructing your innovation roadmap.

The purpose of Part I was to ensure a solid foundation for your innovation journey to maximize your investments. By now, you should have completed the following:

1. **Innovation intent.** You have defined and integrated your innovation intent into your business intent.
2. **Innovation strategy.** You have defined and linked your innovation strategy to your business strategy.
3. **Innovation goals and objectives.** You have defined expected outcomes.

Your next step is to design an optimal innovation program specific to your environment. Many choices will need to be made, including process, structure, resources, governance, and measurements of your innovation initiative.

Innovation Playbook

The *innovation playbook* is the 24- to 36-month roadmap for your innovation program rollout. It should contain specific decisions completed so far as well as the specific organizing elements required to proceed.

A suggested architecture for your innovation playbook is presented next.

1. **Innovation charter.** The charter sets out the vision, mission, strategy, goals, and objectives of innovation at your firm. It includes an inspirational message by the CEO.

2. **Innovation principles.** The principles specify the ideal cultural and operational attributes required for your organization to deliver innovation results.
3. **Innovation processes.** There are four major idea generation processes, all of which are eventually required to become a world-class innovator. However, you need to pick one or two to start with. You also need an overall program management process.
4. **Intrapreneurs.** Here you select, develop, and reward talented people and teams. Not everyone can or may want to participate.
5. **Structure and governance.** Here you decide how the entire program will be managed, including idea selection processes, funding, review, and reporting.
6. **Innovation scorecard.** The scorecard defines how you will measure, monitor, and reward for innovation success.

1. Innovation Charter

The charter defines the innovation vision, mission, strategy, and goal for your initiative.

The *innovation vision* is an aspirational statement linked to the business vision. An example is "Make a difference in our customers' standard of living by introducing great innovations for a better world."

The *innovation mission* asks and defines what innovation will do for the company. An example might be that innovation provides a "transition to a remarkable *innovation culture* that will expand the minds and hearts of our associates. We will achieve this by educating them on innovative tools and techniques that they can apply to everyday problems as well as help find disruptive solutions to outcompete in the marketplace."

The *innovation strategy* falls into one of two types of corporate activities: venturing and intrapreneuring. Both paths can lead to outstanding results, but the overall focus of activities is very different in each. Venturing is about adding new businesses on top of the current business or adding to existing lines. By contrast, intrapreneuring is for producing large-scale innovations that can be adopted to assist the company's desire to pursue a competitive advantage. At the beginning, both paths are difficult to pursue at the same time. Eventually both paths should be implemented to become a world-class innovator.

The *innovation goal* is a specific business target you expect to reach from your investment in an innovation program. The goals are hard, soft, or hybrid. Hard goals are specific measurable outcomes, such as 2x revenue growth in three years. Soft goals are harder to measure, such as cultural capability to *enable* something else to happen. One example is an improved technology platform that will help develop innovative solutions. Our recommendation is to make the goal as hard as possible. See Chapter 3 for examples.

The *innovation program* name is the brand name of the program. When starting on this journey, having a program brand will be easier for communication and to rally support. Some cultures resist a program name; others welcome it.

2. Innovation Principles

Based on the last 25 years of working with local and global firms, we have identified a few fundamental innovation principles. When embraced, these principles create a significant difference when searching for innovations or venturing for new businesses. These principles are industry agnostic. Based on your industry, company culture, and business context, some may have more importance than others. They are all crucial to a great program design. You will need to uphold these as *truths* and make sure they take deep roots from day 1.

1. Organizational Success Principles
   1.1 Seek innovation to alter or identify new business models. Due to the abundant number of convergences (as we looked at in Chapter 2), there is more white space today (in every sector) than ever before. Old business models are dying fast. Challenge your current business model, and perform acts of creative destruction. Work from the future back.
   1.2 Listen for 360-degree voices. Your customers and partners are communicating their unmet needs faster and though a variety of media. Learn to listen faster. The voice of the customer alone is no longer enough. You must empathize with customers and gain new insights for their *emerging and unmet* needs.
   1.3 Develop an *innovation charter* that defines innovation for your business. Tell everyone why it is important and what is expected of each individual at all levels as behaviors of innovation. Allow everyone to see themselves in your innovation vision.
   1.4 Focus on developing microclimates for innovation, not the culture of innovation. This means you must find ways to make teams innovative. As more teams become innovative, culture will take care of itself.
   1.5 Integrate innovation behaviors into your human resources performance management process.
   1.6 C-suite and senior leaders should role-model innovation behaviors expected of others.
   1.7 Provide basic innovation education to as many people as possible, and provide extended training to help build intrapreneurs. A good target ratio is 1% to 2% (develop 50 intrapreneurs if you have 5,000 nonfactory employees).
   1.8 Focus on fast experiments. Develop 90-day experiment plans for ideas that come from teams across the organization. Some of these ideas will surely drive powerful outcomes for your customers.
   1.9 Define stretch challenges with a vivid vision of a future that is believable. Bigger challenges bring the best innovators forward. Real intrapreneurs are those who need stretch challenges and the freedom to test their wacky

ideas—that is their currency. Liberate them to fail fast and discover new ways to serve your customers. Give them candid feedback and recognize them quickly, no matter what the outcome for an experiment or a pilot. When they produce results, reward them handsomely.

1.10   In the beginning, provide access to off-budget funds for those who can work on challenging problems and produce fresh new solutions for growth.

1.11   Manage the idea bank closely—the bigger the pipeline (quantity and quality), the better the future.

2. Individual and Team Success Principles

2.1   Promote cross-functional volunteerism. Research shows that the majority of your employees bring only a portion of themselves to work. This means there is unharvested organizational potential waiting to be leashed. Allow anyone to form cross-functional teams for their great ideas. Diversity of thought is the catalyst for ideas. What any one person sees is only a part of what needs to be seen.

2.2   Teach people how to make what is invisible visible. No one person can see the future as clearly as a team of intrapreneurs can. Humans can see only through a lens of their past experiences. This means they never see a full reality of a situation. This thought can be humbling and, at the same time, very energizing for your best talent.

2.3   Learn to ask new questions before generating new ideas. Most organizations are solving the wrong problems in today's fast-paced world.

2.4   Prototype fast—think design on day 1. Always promote action over analysis. Sitting in the corner office idealizing issues and solutions is less effective than two people role-playing the situation for new insights.

2.5   Diverge then converge. Then do it again. Then do it once more. Three cycles will improve the clarity of an idea as it moves along the innovation pipeline. The very best ideas will survive.

2.6   Greenhouse ideas. At the very early stages, ideas must be protected just like a seed has to be protected for a plant to grow. Never dismiss an idea. Put them all in a greenhouse and protect them so they don't get shot down. Keep playing with them. It might take a few weeks or months before they are ready to be shared.

3. Leadership Success Principles

3.1   Show everyone how to derisk the future. Taking no risk can lead to stagnation. Not taking enough risk can create commoditization and price wars. Taking just enough risk at the right time can lead to market differentiation; that is called derisking the future.

3.2   Create healthy discontent. Provide stretch challenges and demand breakthrough solutions—once in a while. Most work is incremental. Your best innovators get bored easily. Often they are most sought after for all incremental challenges. Manage their intellectual capital between easy and complex assignments. This will keep them engaged and at peak levels of performance.

3.3   Communicate how innovation decisions will be made. Create an environment of transparency for idea generation, evaluation protocol, funding, and experimentation.

3.4   Implement a reward and recognition policy that encourages proper behaviors for all, especially middle management.

3.5   Exhibit personal passion for innovative thinking and creativity.

3. Innovation Processes

There are many types of innovation problems. Different problems yield more readily to different approaches. Certain types of innovation challenges require tasks performed frequently, while other challenges need to be undertaken occasionally. Additionally, each innovation worker has a different role to play in the organization. Some are great at finding problems, others are good at finding solutions, while others are best at bringing out the best from others, and many others are good at connecting various parts in a cohesive entrepreneurial activity. Therefore, no single process or tool can meet the needs of everyone or all types of innovation challenges. Many organizations do not maximize on innovation investments because they use only one process.

There are four specific enterprise *innovation processes* to help find ideas. Based on the goal for innovation, business context, and current organizational environment, the correct blend of all four types of these processes should be used to help find innovations.

Great innovations happen when the insightful domain expert embraces the confluence of relevant knowledge and technology and thus can synthesize something new. Doing this requires easy-to-use innovation processes that will aid the participation of every employee in any innovation activity, based on their ability to contribute—in a small or a big way.

Additionally, information technology should be used properly to help place the innovation worker at the apex of relevant and actionable knowledge.

The four processes we recommend (see Figure 4.1) are:

1. **Bottom up.** This process allows the entire organization to participate in idea discovery activities. Generally it involves all types of ideas that can be implemented for internal cost savings as well as market commercialization. If the process is designed correctly, people at all levels can be involved and empowered to find small and radical discoveries. In our experience, this approach also helps to bypass vertical hierarchy that may impede innovative ideas from reaching the top. This is required if you want to create a climate and culture of innovation.

2. **Top down.** Here, top-down strategic *innovation platforms* (large organizational challenges) are defined by senior leaders. In our experience, there are always three to five such platforms critical to the future of the business. Each platform may contain hundreds of unique business ideas (to keep profits, to enhance profits, or to find completely new profits). The objective is to identify the platforms and best opportunities to pursue. Unlike the bottom-up approach, here team members are selected (cross-functional and sometimes from outside) for a short period of time (12 to 16 weeks) to find and build early innovative solution to a designated business challenge.

3. **Outside in.** The primary motivation for this method is "customers want to be part of the business." Using a discovery process, a funnel of ideas is created based on what customers care about the most. The output of this process can be an input to the standard product design and development process you may already have. The key is to identify *current and emerging desires* of current as well as future customers. Within this process, there are three specific activities:

   a. Ethnographic study of customers and how they interact with your current offerings

   b. Prioritized list of product portfolio based on customer outcomes with knowledge of overserved and underserved features

   c. Understanding and predicting strategic next moves by your competitors

4. **Inside in.** In this method, the goal is to improve intracompany collaboration, learning, and knowledge sharing. Most businesses are weakest in this method. The goal is to break down the internal silos through structured facilitation and cross-pollination among technical and nontechnical staff. If implemented well, the result would generate innovation opportunities by engaging forums that meet periodically (monthly, quarterly, or twice a year). Also, this method can be used in combination with the top-down method to address specific platform challenges impacting two business units, such as cross-selling of products and services.

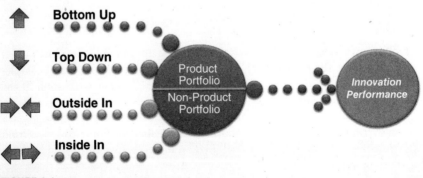

FIGURE 4.1 Four Innovation Processes

Each process is designed to achieve specific outcomes. All four innovation processes are not needed to *begin* your innovation rollout. Your *innovation strategy* will inform which process to start with and when to add on another. To be a world-class innovator, you must implement all four processes across the entire organization.

As shown in Figure 4.1, the role of these four innovation processes is to build your offerings portfolio, which sometimes is called an *idea bank* or *innovation pipeline* (Chapter 7). Our experience shows that the larger the idea bank, the higher the chances of new innovations and overall business growth. Finally, *innovation performance* is your formal output measurement. It is your report card of the innovation program activities. It must be directly linked to your business performance metrics, such as your Balanced Scorecard.

An idea is a unique object that goes through multiple states of change. While the actual states are subject to process implementation, generally an idea goes through multiple states of development. Table 4.1 shows a sample.

4. Intrapreneurs

Every time the business world turns around, some radical, free-thinking biz-kid is upsetting a Fortune 500 company by operating on anything but conventional B-school wisdom. Even more unsettling, the new or sometimes reinvented entities spawned by these unconventional CEOs appear seemingly out of nowhere, disrupting industries across the board.

No one would argue that the reason so many companies are falling victim to disruptive technology and concepts is a myopic "me-too" mentality in which their strategy is based solely on their current competition. In today's suddenly-without-warning world, however, the player most likely to steal your business will be outside your known circle and, in some cases, outside your industry.

Who are these players? They are corporate entrepreneurs. We call them *intrapreneurs* (see Chapter 8 for more). These savvy individuals are already in your

TABLE 4.1   Idea States

States	Description
New	New idea that has not yet been analyzed
Archived	Idea that is not relevant today
Scored	Preliminary scoring done
Active	Under consideration.
Investigate	Under consideration—being investigated
Pilot	Under consideration—being piloted
Reject	Under consideration and rejected
Duplicate	Duplicate idea
Approved	Approved by innovation council

organization but most likely hiding. Many of your best innovators probably left the organization because their ideas were not welcomed or they weren't invited to help create your next S-Curve (see Chapter 1). They didn't have the freedom to incubate something fresh, radical, new, or novel. They were willing to put in 80 hours a week, but the culture and systems wouldn't allow them to succeed.

An article in the *Harvard Business Review* stated that "the best innovators aren't lone geniuses. They're people who can take an idea that's obvious in one context and apply it in not-so-obvious ways to a different context. The best companies have learned to systemize that process."[1]

Intrapreneurship is a *strategic competency* sorely lacking in business today. It is a term shortened from "intracorporate entrepreneurship" and refers to entrepreneurial activities of employees within the boundaries and auspices of a larger organization. Another *Harvard Business Review* article describes intrapreneurship as "bottom-up, off-the-beaten-track business building, spearheaded by people who were working as line managers or employees."[2] A popular example of intrapreneurship is Skunk Works, the term for Lockheed Martin's advanced development program, where a group of engineers step outside the bureaucratic environment of the corporation to develop successful and innovative products. One of the major benefits of intrapreneurship is the freedom to work independently (or on a team) on tasks defined by the group but still aligned to the needs of the organization.

Intrapreneurs, some of whom we will meet in Chapter 8, are well suited to transform an organization more quickly and effectively because they are motivated, free to engage in activities, and are less restricted by bureaucratic and political inertia. Intrapreneurship allows companies to grow the business, find and retain talent, and compete with peer companies. Intrapreneurship has been the key to excite and motivate the creation of innovative products, processes, services, and partnerships for companies like Procter & Gamble, Raytheon, 3M, Nokia, Tata, and Google.

In our experience working with organizations across the globe, *intrapreneurship* is what consistently drives innovation and growth.

How does one foster intrapreneurship? In 1998, Intel established an in-house new business initiative to bootstrap new businesses by financing ones that the company's own employees start. The Xbox story is similar. Game designer Seamus Blackley had joined Microsoft in 1999 after a big project failed. At Microsoft, he was able to develop his concept in relative freedom and get credit for it. Today Xbox owns a very large market share in the gaming industry.

How do you find intrapreneurs? From our experience working with thousands of people, here is a list of attributes that world-class intrapreneurs exhibit:

1. High degree of self-knowledge
   - Clear idea of their strengths and weaknesses
   - Know how to leverage their strengths and compensate for their weaknesses
2. Knowledge of the business and culture of the organization
   - Good command of the business including the financials (how we make money)

- Understand the culture, the values of the organization and their implications for getting things done
3. Excellent communication skills
   - Able to persuade and influence others
   - Present ideas clearly, can speak coherently in front of a group
   - Good networking skills (internally and externally)
   - Clear and concise business writing skills
   - Have evangelized successful ideas in the past
4. Moderate risk taker
   - Not afraid to fail
   - Are neither timid nor overly aggressive about taking risks
   - Take personal responsibility for their actions, don't blame others or the system
5. Team building and collaboration skills
   - Know how to leverage differences to form a winning team
   - Are seen as credible and trustworthy by others
6. Are forward thinking and opportunity oriented
7. Persevere in the face of obstacles and setbacks
8. Demonstrate passion and enthusiasm for their work
9. Are open to new ideas; eager to learn

We study how to find, build, and motivate corporate intrapreneurs in Chapter 8.

5. Structure and Governance

There are numerous best practices for designing an appropriate innovation organization. The choice of an appropriate design should be based on a series of design policies controllable by management that can influence appropriate employee behavior and therefore innovation success. These policies are the tools that help shape the decisions and behaviors of your organization.

The *innovation structure* (more in Chapter 6) refers to the formal way in which innovation team members will carry out their work in an existing larger organizational structure. Most organizational structures are designed by types of markets, types of products, technologies, or some other method for optimizing operational excellence. The current structure defines the basic power relationships within the organization. It is imperative to understand how current resources (people and budgets) are allocated and coordinated for execution of the business strategy and how various profit centers are configured.

There is no such thing as one best structure for your innovation program. The best structure is the one that will help the various businesses achieve their strategic goals through innovation. After understanding what innovation culture looks like, it can be suggested that most traditional organizational structure approaches for innovation programs will not work since organizations must be subject to continual experimentation and change. Jay Galbraith, internationally recognized expert on world-class organizational structures, explains, "Organizational designs are difficult to execute and copy because they are intricate blends of many different design policies."[3] However, few basic design principles can aid the design process.

Corporate innovation and intrapreneurship flourish in organizations that have these traits:

1. Few layers or levels
2. Wider span of control
3. More horizontal and less vertical organizational structure
4. Promote decentralization and empowerment
5. Communicate clarity of vision and strategies from the top
6. Promote pushing ideas from the bottom up instead of from the top down only
7. Offer support for approaches that empower teamwork
8. Highly promoted cross-functional interactions
9. Systems allow rapid communication at all levels
10. Lean and small staff functions
11. Managers freely vary their operating styles
12. High emphasis on results rather than processes or procedures
13. Informal controls with an emphasis on a standard of cooperation

Four major types of structures that are suggested are listed next (more details in Chapter 6). A business is not limited to the use of just one of these designs. Rather, your organization can employ any of them as warranted by the diversity of your innovation strategy and entrepreneurial initiatives.

1. **Traditional two-tier structure.** In this structure, there is a central innovation group and divisional/functional innovation resources. The central group has a VP of innovation reporting to the CEO. The innovation process is less formal for decision making, but innovation principles are highly emphasized. The central group develops an innovation tool kit and a formal curriculum developed by. Divisions are encouraged to designate "innovation consultants" for their area for "certification" training on the tool kit. For the divisions, participation in the innovation initiative is optional; they have the discretion to participate or to wait. If a division decides to participate, it would assign a single point of contact for all innovation activities for its area. This person would report to the business unit/function head. A small corporate budget is given to the central group to *push* innovation. Each division would put aside annual funds for its own innovation activities. Many firms use this approach to find ideas and to quickly test for viability. An advantage of this approach is that it increases the speed of idea finding and the front end of the product development funnel.

2. **Center of excellence (COE).** In this structure, the firm dedicates core central resources for the entire organization. The innovation council, generally composed of key executives, defines the strategic direction of the COE. The COE organizes facilitating the vision, goals, discovery insights, tools expertise,

process management, and knowledge management related to all innovation activities of the firm. Small groups of innovation consultants (similar to black belts in Six Sigma) shepherd the process to help various business units. These internal core consultants provide ideation services and training in tools to various staff members such as new product development experts, advise the innovation council on new opportunities, and help build world-class innovation capabilities across the firm. The COE also manages all just-in-time and external resources as required. These relationships include functional experts, domain experts, advertising/PR agencies, industry experts, industry thought leaders, market research firms, academic resources, futurists, regulatory experts and government policy makers. Such a group is funded by each business unit and runs based on the unique innovation strategies of each business unit.

3. **Strategic horizons group.** This is a dedicated group of strategy and innovation experts looking for breakthrough and disruptive new opportunities. It is primarily focused on new and long-term business opportunities. The group should have a mandate to find new markets, new products, new services, and new technologies. It can play a pivotal role in incubating creation of new competencies and identifying talent gaps for future success. Ideally this group should be located in a separate facility away from the current organizational environment, management structures, and operational policies. IBM incubated such a group in the early 1980s when it started its PC division in Boca Raton, Florida. In 1970, Xerox also started its Palo Alto Research Center, with the same intentions, away from its New York–based headquarters. In 1996, Shell started the Game Changer group that generated more than 300 proposals; by 1999, this process was generating four out of every five of the largest business opportunities at the company. One role of the strategic horizon group might be to look at new business opportunities with the potential of new revenue, such as $50 million or more, depending on the organization's size and business priorities.

4. **Intrapreneuring and venturing group.** In this bottom-up approach, there is a central innovation group with responsibilities similar to the traditional and COE structures but with a few important differences. An innovation board acts like a group of venture capitalists and meets every 90 days to listen to *venture pitches* from innovation teams (iTeams). Each iTeam is formed around the idea owner who has an innovative solution for a product, process, delivery, or strategic growth issue. An innovation-certified facilitator helps facilitate the team's work using the central group's core tools and idea development process. Each business unit is encouraged to set up its own innovation board for ideas related to its own business issues. Using this approach, the organization can find latent incremental and breakthrough ideas from every employee in the firm. A formal idea review process is implemented using an idea management portal to expedite finding, improving, and selecting ideas. Each iTeam has an opportunity to bring its ideas to reality using a fast experimentation process, funds, and resources.

Remember, structures can disable or enable corporate entrepreneurship. A good business structure with a good innovation structure can facilitate entrepreneurship and give employees room to maneuver and innovate while also allowing them to interact with others in the organization. It can generate many new initiatives and also facilitate the speed at which such initiatives move from inception to implementation. Not all innovation initiatives are the same; this fact should be reflected in the specific attributes of the structures employed to house those initiatives. A one-size-fits-all mentality with respect to structuring for innovation won't work.

6. Innovation Scorecard

Typically, innovation metrics are used for new products and services. It is easy to monitor sales figures, which give managers an immediate indication of the return on the investment that was required to take the new product from concept to launch.

Organization's innovation momentum will slow down when the company pursues making innovation part of standard key performance indicators by trying to quantify the effect on their internal process or structural innovations. Even harder is gauging the relationship between a company's culture—whether it actively nurtures innovation among all its employees—and the bottom line.

Another risk of measuring innovation is related to the nature of innovation itself. As we know, innovation involves a venture into white space. If we try to pin these unknowns down too fast, we may make them harder to recognize and realize. If we attempt to measure the wrong things at the wrong time, we can also undermine the spirit of learning, discovery, and intelligent risk taking that the innovation process requires.

If you ask a seasoned R&D executive what ROI means, he or she will say "restraint on innovation." ROI-based decision making is a short-term view of the future. Using ROI too early in the innovation process can eliminate huge opportunities that may be worth pursuing. For example, a large technology client decided only to evaluate ideas worthy of a $50 million new top-line growth. This means if an idea is below this ROI target, it would be dismissed. The problem with this approach is how does anyone know? What was included in the research plan and what was missing? At an early stage of idea development, most great innovators are just playing at solving an existing known or unmet need. While nurturing the idea in the early stages, they are not thinking about ROI.

One school of thought about measuring innovation says that if the company is growing, market share is growing, and customer satisfaction with the product or service is high, then it is not necessary to measure internal innovation capabilities as a key performance indicator.

What is the right approach for you?

Our belief is that firms must use innovation as a forward-looking measurement. Most current business metrics give enough understanding of historical activities and their relevant performance, but innovation provides insights about the future.

Any organization can quickly and easily measure product innovation as a past output. When you are looking at organizational innovation, however, you have to use other measures that look forward. Innovation, as far as company culture is concerned, is very much about individuals and teams working together.

Measuring input and satisfaction and the results of ideas is crucial to having employees who are enthusiastic about the company's goals. If people believe they are allowed to take risks and be innovative, then they are much more likely to do so than if they are part of an organization that is risk averse.

A good innovation metric framework should include:

1. **Resources.** Input measurements related to money, time, and people along with outcome measurements related to new products, services, revenue, profits, and market valuations
2. **Process.** Measurements related to quality, quantity and speed of ideas flowing through the innovation pipeline
3. **Capability.** Metrics related to quality and quantity of innovation-related skills and competencies along with knowledge assets

By using all three types of measurements, it is easier to monitor the relationship between investment and outcomes year after year. As with any other measurement framework, choosing the right measurements at the beginning is very important. Choosing too many or the wrong ones may misfire during the annual planning process.

Table 4.2 presents some suggested metrics for consideration for each element of your innovation scorecard.

If you follow the six major steps outlined in this chapter, you should have a sound innovation playbook to move ahead. Remember that this playbook is a working document. As you begin to implement, you will want to alter components as required.

TABLE 4.2 Sample Innovation Metrics

Metric Type	Example
Resource input	**Capital:** Percentage of capital that is invested for the innovation program. Innovation activities include finding ideas, incubating them, evaluating along various phases and gates, and executing. This task includes all resources required to manage the entire pipeline: software, hardware, staff, rooms, equipment, and other related expenses. **Talent.** Number of certified intrapreneurs (champions, consultants, leaders) who have completed required training. **Talent.** Number of individuals who have previously started a business, either within the company or before joining the company **Time.** Percentage of workforce time that is currently dedicated to innovation projects. **Leadership.** Percentage of leaders and managers with training in the concepts and tools of innovation.

(Continued)

TABLE 4.2   (*Continued*)

Metric Type	Example
Resource output	**Offerings.** Number of new products, services, and businesses launched in the past year through the innovation process. **ROI.** Return based on growth projects sourced through innovative activities. **ROI.** Cost savings from process and operations innovation. **Revenue growth.** Percentage of revenue from products or services introduced in the past three years. **Profit growth.** Percentage of profit from products or services introduced in the past three years. **Valuation impact.** Change in the company's market value during the past year divided by the change in the total industry's market value during the same period compared to the change in the total industry's market value during the same period.
Process	**Depth.** Percentage of associates aware of innovation activities in the company/ innovation process. **Idea bank.** Number of ideas submitted by employees in the past 3, 6, and 12 months divided by total ideas. **Idea bank.** Number of ideas submitted by suppliers in the past 3, 6, and 12 months divided by total ideas. **Idea bank.** Number of ideas submitted by customers in the past 3, 6, and 12 months divided by total ideas. **Idea bank.** Number of ideas submitted by leaders in the past 3, 6, and 12 months divided by total ideas. **Idea bank.** Ratio of successful ideas for each stage gate to total number of ideas submitted. **Idea bank.** Number of current "experiments." **Idea bank.** Number of ideas graduated from the innovation process and moved into implementation. **Efficiency.** Conversion rate of ideas in each gate of the innovation pipeline process (percentage of ideas moved from ideation to incubation, from incubation to experimentation, or from experimentation to execution). **Efficiency.** Average total time from idea submission to commercial launch/ implementation. **Efficiency.** Percentage of ideas/projects that are funded. **Efficiency.** Percentage of ideas/projects that are killed/tabled at each step of the innovation process. **Open innovation.** Percentage of projects involving external (customer, supplier, partner) collaboration.
Capability	**Competence.** Percentage of employees for whom innovation is a key performance goal. **Competence.** Percentage of managers and leaders for whom innovation is a key performance goal. **Engagement.** Percentage of employees participating in innovation projects. **Breadth** Percentage of ideas sourced by employees and customers and suppliers. **Depth** Number of innovation tools and methodologies available to employees. **Depth** Number of new markets entered in the past year. **Engagement.** Percentage of associates who received incentive linked to innovation. **Patents.** Number of new patents filed and approved (or new strategic knowledge gained that would be called intellectual property).

CASE STUDY: COGNIZANT TECHNOLOGY SOLUTIONS Cognizant, founded in 1994, is a leading provider of information technology, consulting, and business process outsourcing services, dedicated to helping the world's leading companies build stronger businesses. Headquartered in Teaneck, New Jersey, Cognizant combines a passion for client satisfaction, technology innovation, deep industry and business process expertise, and a global, collaborative workforce that embodies the future of work. With over 50 delivery centers worldwide and more than 150,000 employees, Cognizant is a member of the NASDAQ 100, the S&P 500, the Forbes' Global 2000, and the Fortune 500 and is ranked among the top-performing and fastest-growing companies in the world.

Cognizant started its innovation program journey in 2006. In 2009, Sukumar Rajagopal, the current chief information officer and head of innovation at Cognizant, stepped in to run the company's innovation efforts. He says, "One of the most critical decisions we made was to dramatically increase our group's focus of helping enable all business unit practices to generate their own innovations, shifting away from an increased focus on generating innovations on behalf of the practices"

Once this new innovation strategy was declared, the focus was on building a climate and culture of innovation for the entire organization. "Innovation coming from every employee can deliver much higher returns than that coming from just a few within an R&D organization," says Rajagopal. In 2009, Cognizant had about 75,000 employees; that figure grew astronomically to more than 150,000 as of September 30, 2012. Cognizant bypassed its two major rivals, Wipro and Infosys, within a short period of time. "Growing an innovation program during a period of fantastic business growth can be challenging in its own way. The primary obstacle is that no one has the time for a long-term imperative such as innovation," continues Rajagopal.

Rajagopal has 24 years of experience in the IT industry with strong experience in project delivery, profit and loss management, executive relationship building, operations management, and knowledge management in consulting companies.

After Cognizant evaluated past success and failures, along with the challenges of nonlinear growth, the main question was how to develop an innovation program that attracts business executives to sponsor time and resources for innovation. Like many other high-tech firms, Cognizant has a very competitive workplace culture. Knowing this, Rajagopal and his team decided to develop an "innovation index" that would create an automatic momentum for their innovation program. He knew that you can "push" innovation on to businesses, but for it to become truly game-changing, it needed to be "pulled" by the businesses, be attractive, and be useful to meet and help exceed business goals.

Cognizant defines its innovation index as "a composite measure of the level of innovation based on activities and outcomes that enable and help sustain innovation." As of 2012, Cognizant's innovation engine is cranking at very high performance levels. Here are some quick statistics:

- Average number of ideas submitted per associate: 0.83
- Value of innovation generated in 2012: $390.5 million
- Number of innovations implemented in 2012: 17,553

- Number of unique idea owners in the 2012 idea bank: 51,997
- Size of idea bank as of 2012: 125,166

The Cognizant Innovation Index 2012 tracks 11 parameters across input, process, and output. With outcomes the focus for 2012, the index was structured with 69% weight assigned to output; the remaining 31% was distributed across input and process. By this method, the index is a more realistic measure of level of innovation effort and outcomes.

The innovation index is computed based on the weighted sum mechanism of the scores computed for each parameter. The scores for each parameter are arrived at based on the raw data measure of each parameter divided by the benchmark set for each. The benchmarks are set once a year based on the organization's innovation goals.

The 11 parameters that comprise the innovation index at Cognizant are shown in Table 4.3.

Each year, all business units, corporate functions, and over 400 client account teams are measured for their innovation maturity using the innovation index methodology. During the company's annual innovation summit, all participants, winning teams, managers, and key executives gather to celebrate the past year's success and plan for next year's growth.

The summit is designed to recognize the best of innovations and to strengthen the innovation culture within Cognizant. Over the years, the summit has proved to be a platform where the best innovations from across the organization compete for the top innovation awards, which are among the most prestigious awards at Cognizant and attract the best participation across all business unit industry practices. In 2012, the sixth time Cognizant offered innovation awards, nominations were invited from each business unit practices in three categories:

1. Market facing
2. Process
3. Technology

TABLE 4.3 Cognizant Innovation Index

Input parameters	1. Innovation strategy defined and presented to customer
	2. Number of idea champions (onsite and offshore)
	3. Number of idea champions trained
	4. Number of associates briefed on innovation
Process parameters	5. Number of ideas generated
	6. Number of associates contributing ideas
Output parameters	7. Total number of innovations implemented (internal + customer)
	8. Number of innovations implemented (customer)
	9. Total value of innovations (internal + customer)
	10. Value of innovations (customer)
	11. Value of previous innovation assets reused

A total of 1,944 submissions were received in 2012 compared to 1,381 in 2011. The top three innovations in each category won financial rewards for each team member. In 2012, one innovation reached the top five at the prestigious National Association of Software and Services Companies (country and industry level) innovation awards in India (the third time Cognizant accomplished the feat) and subsequently into CIO 100 Awards by *CIO* magazine.

The innovation index is one of the primary drivers of growth and success at Cognizant.

Notes

1. A. Hargadon and R. I. Sutton, "Building an Innovation Factory," *Harvard Business Review* (May–June 2000): 157.
2. Harvard Management Update Article, "Starting New Businesses: Inside the Organization," *Harvard Business Review* (March 3, 2009): 2.
3. J. Galbraith, *Designing Organizations: An Executive Briefing on Strategy, Structure, and Process* (San Francisco: Jossey-Bass, 1995), p. 6.

CHAPTER 5

Building Momentum

Once you have linked innovation to your organization's specific business strategy and the intended value targets, you will need to educate employees at all levels on how the organization can generate growth and profit through innovation. By creating transparency, all employees will have a better idea of how to generate ideas that can be successfully ventured.

It puzzles me that so many firms think they can get a cheap competitive advantage by purchasing something on the open market. Anything that you can purchase on the open market is also available to your competitors. So the question is: How can you distinguish yourself in a world in which your competitors can copy everything you do?

The answer is this: All that separates you from others in the market are the skills, knowledge, commitment, and abilities of the people who work for you. Companies that manage and develop people well will outcompete those that don't by 25% or more. This principle applies more than ever in today's globally connected world, and it might rise to as much as 40% in the next five years.

Most leaders immediately understand this point. What they lack is the ability to hold this principle close to the center of business growth strategies.

In retail, they say it is *location, location, location*.

When it comes to disruptive and continuous growth, it is all about engaging your *people, people, people*.

Momentum

Now that you have your own innovation roadmap, it is time to start building momentum. Doing this requires proper change management planning and execution to complete your *innovation playbook*.

Building momentum is a critical next step before a rollout can occur. How many times have you seen organizations launch an idea management portal or innovation resource site to collect ideas and after a few months no one seems to be visiting or using the tools? Or organizations begin the innovation execution work and soon higher business priorities take over so full execution never happens? We have also seen instances of innovation program implementation failures because middle management was never involved to ensure support for the frontline staff.

Building momentum means beginning the process of *organizational change* for your innovation program. It is a critically important step for your innovation journey. From our observations in the field, it is not a joy ride and most often it is overlooked.

Building momentum is lot like lifting the NASA Spacecraft at Kennedy Space Center in Florida. A space shuttle weighs about 4.5 million pounds (about 2 million kg). During liftoff, Atlantis burned 660,000 pounds of solid fuel per minute. That's nearly the same weight as 44 school buses. It also used 17,000 gallons of liquid oxygen per minute and 45,000 gallons of liquid hydrogen per minute. At the 10-second mark after liftoff, the shuttle engines generated 18 gigawatts of energy (about 24 million horsepower). That is equivalent to the full installed power output of China's Three Gorges Dam and 11.25 of the projected power output of Finland's Olkiluoto 3 fission reactor (which, upon completion, will be the most powerful nuclear reactor in the world).

Lifting off your innovation program from its current static stage will require serious investment of fuel and energy, that is, leadership sponsorship and investment—to build the momentum. Building such momentum requires a major change.

There are many different definitions, beliefs, models, and assessment tools to measure people's readiness and absorptive capacity for change. Dick Beckhard, a change management expert, proposes that the amount of change and people's appetite for it (Δ) is a function of ($= f$) three parameters:

1. Level of dissatisfaction with the status quo (D)
2. Clarity of the vision about the better future state (V)
3. Clarity of a plan for practical first steps (P)

The formula is $\Delta = f (D \times V \times P)$

In a culture that does not currently support innovation, any innovation often is perceived as a major change. In this case, for an innovation program to gain momentum, the appetite for change (Δ) must exceed the perceived cost (C) of the change.

This concept and model have been around for a long time and are widely recognized and used in the field of organizational change. The simplest meaning of the model is that if D, V, or P is essential zero, you aren't going very far in the near future. If the perceived cost of the new venture is very high, in either personal or resource costs, you aren't going to see much progress either. For example, say people's dissatisfaction with the status quo is high but their vision of a better world is limited. In this case, it would probably be more productive to put your resources into validating all the concerns about what is innovation and identifying how others have benefited from innovative cultures rather than asking executives to give speeches about the urgency of becoming an innovative company.

This simple model can also help your team to discover resistance in a different way. Typical resistance is seen as something to overcome, something subversive to fight against. Instead, the formula forces you to look at what is missing and what the people need to learn so they can see what the sponsors see regarding the value and vision of innovation. Doing this can help the change leaders and change agents, including those who may initially be against innovation, thereby creating more consensus and cooperation rather than resistance.

One final thought about the power of this equation. All people have gone through changes in the course of their personal and professional lives. Not all changes have been pleasant experiences. Poorly handled or imposed change tends to leave people bitter about the ideas and approaches used. It is crucial to build momentum for your innovation program by allowing people to work through their past experience with change rather than trying to talk them out of it.

To welcome change, organizations and individuals must first realize that something has to be different from what it is now.

Momentum Framework

Here are six components of building momentum and change to help you accelerate your innovation journey and lift off:

1. **Develop your innovation story.** Develop a compelling case for innovation, what innovation is, and why the company is pursuing the innovation journey now. Include how it will benefit everyone.
2. **Evoke change leadership.** No one likes change. During the uncertainties of a change process, people don't hang onto concepts, they hang onto *people*. Create a sense of urgency and build awareness and excitement about innovation for your key sponsors and change agents.
3. **Identify innovation leaders and best talent.** Identify the natural intrapreneurs, innovation champions, and innovation igniters along with your key innovation leaders, advisors, and mentors. This talent pool will help you build the required innovation capability (more in Chapter 8).
4. **Communicate, communicate, communicate.** Go for fast and small wins and tell everyone about it. Collect momentum data showing progress, and implement and integrate a solid public relations strategy using any and all resources at your disposal.
5. **Build awareness—educate everyone.** In many ways an innovation change initiative begins and ends with education. It is the primary method of advancing and improving organizational knowledge and acceleration for desired changes in the hearts and minds of everyone involved.
6. **Protect the momentum.** Vigilantly protect innovation principles. Many will want to go back to status quo and forget the agreements, processes, and principles in the playbook. Every small win is a huge step toward the future and part of the foundation-building process. Protect the foundation.

Let's take a look at each step in detail.

1. Develop Your Innovation Story

The business section of the newspaper is filled with stories about massive financial impacts for certain companies. Stories are the only way to make sense of a rapidly changing global economy with multiple macrotransitions under way.

For organizations, leaders are the primary storytellers. The very best storytellers are the primary change agents. Through their artistic communication skills, leaders are able to connect with their audiences as human beings. These storytellers are also great innovation leaders. They communicate a vision and a path by telling a story that inspires others.

Developing and communicating a good innovation story can help achieve multiple purposes, including igniting people into action, creating urgency for why your company must embrace innovation, and transmitting innovation behavioral values required in the culture for vitality of the company moving forward.

MANAGERS AND LEADERS   Managers usually take an agreed-on set of assumptions and goals and implement more efficient and effective ways of achieving those goals. They direct, control, and decide what to do on the basis of agreed-on hypotheses, generally proceeding deductively. Leadership, in contrast, deals with the ends more than the means. It concerns issues where there is no agreement on underlying assumptions and goals—or where there is broad agreement, but the assumptions and goals are heading for failure. In fact, the principal task of leadership is to create a new consensus about the goals to be pursued and how to achieve them. Once there is such a consensus, then managers can get on with the job of implementing those goals.

Leadership is essentially a task of persuasion—of winning people's minds and hearts. Typically it includes examples supporting a more general conclusion about the goals and assumptions you should adopt moving forward.

Storytelling is inherently suited to the task of leadership. Thus, leadership must own the responsibility of developing and communicating the need for organizational innovation.

Your innovation story is the message everyone needs to hear from you as the transformative leader of change. This message will help stimulate innovation change efforts as quickly as possible and help remove inherent barriers that might prevent the program from succeeding.

My dear friend Daryl Conner, a world-renowned change management expert, has published this story about Andy Mochan:

> *At nine-thirty on a July evening in 1988, a disastrous explosion and fire occurred on an oil-drilling platform in the North Sea off the coast of Scotland. One hundred and sixty-six crew members and two rescuers lost their lives in the worst catastrophe in the twenty-five-year history of North Sea oil exploration. One of the sixty-three crew members who survived was the superintendent on the rig, Andy Mochan.*

From his hospital bed, he told of being awakened by the explosion and alarms. He said that he ran from his quarters to the platform edge and jumped fifteen stories from the platform to the water. Because of the water's temperature, he knew that he could live a maximum of only twenty minutes if he were not rescued. Also, oil had surfaced and ignited. Yet Andy jumped 150 feet in the middle of the night into an ocean of burning oil and debris.

When asked why he took that potentially fatal leap, he did not hesitate. He said, "It was either jump or fry." He chose possible death over certain death. He jumped because he had no choice—the price of staying on the platform, of maintaining the status quo, was too high.

Organizational burning platforms exist when maintaining the status quo becomes prohibitively expensive. Major change is always costly, but when the present course of action is even more expensive, a burning-platform situation erupts.[1]

As you build your innovation story, develop a sense of urgency that includes focus on the future. Make clear to everyone that it is not only important to get off the burning platform, it is a business imperative.

Increase discomfort with status quo. At the heart of creative solutions is a healthy dissatisfaction and discontent with things as they are. Otherwise why change?

People in highly vertical organizations become complacent about the organization's ability to change, and overall performance suffers. They tend to focus most of their time and energy on fighting for internal positions and their share of the current pie instead of building a bigger pie. The best global innovators are dissatisfied with the status quo.

Dissatisfaction with financial performance alone will not be the best driver of change in your innovation story. Unfortunately, such drivers will force your middle managers to focus only on short-term profitability, and therefore often means killing innovation projects too early—sometimes before they even begin.

2. Evoke Change Leadership

There are two types of change sponsors and agents: drivers and participants. *Drivers* are individuals or organizations who manage change in a way that allows them to effectively implement all aspects of transition on time and within budget. *Participants* are individuals or organizations who bring change, but significantly late or over budget and with less competitive advantage value than originally planned.

Drivers are able to achieve the full benefit of planned change initiatives. Participants passively bring change and never achieve their intended outcomes. If they do, it's only after expending a great deal more time and money than they had anticipated.

After watching some of the best innovators in many different environments, we've learned there is only one quality that motivates the driver innovators to make and sustain the push for major innovation change effort: They are scared about the status quo. They are no longer able to live with the way things are. And announcing a need for change requires no special skill. Participants do this all the time. Drivers, however, deeply understand that when the price of maintaining the status quo is higher than the price of transition, making a change is mandatory.

There are three types of players in an organization: sponsors, change agents, and targets. *Sponsors* are those who clearly want and initiate the change. *Change agents* are those who will take the changes to the people. *Targets* are the people whose work and work lives will be changed in the process. The roles are not necessarily mutually exclusive. Sponsors and targets often act as change agents, change agents ultimately become sponsors, and everyone at some point, like it or not, becomes a target.

Our experience shows that sponsorship can come from anywhere. Change agents are often nominated or enlisted, not assigned. To achieve planned change results, people in each category must do the following really well.

Sponsors must:

- Be able to communicate the innovation vision clearly and succinctly.
- Be personally invested in the effort—willing to take personal risk.
- Set rules and boundaries for change success.
- Be an exemplar role model and demonstrate genuine interest in innovation.
- Build a community of change agents to help them.

Change agents must:

- Be passionate about innovation and entrepreneurship.
- Know the answers to these questions: What is innovation? When? Why? How?
- Be detail oriented to help manage expectations and improve clarity about the change plan.
- Walk the talk and demonstrate personal commitment for the innovation program and associated process.
- Have followers, and be credible and open to new ideas from anyone and everyone.
- Be a student of the invisible, such as political forces, emotional attachment to old products, and organizational orthodoxies.

Targets must:

- Be able to see themselves in the vision.
- Understand what innovation is, why innovation is needed, when to engage, and how to engage with the innovation process.
- Proactively participate.
- Commit to self-awareness and self-improvement.

Leadership in a change effort is about helping these groups find the value, clarity, and commitment to execute their roles well.

ROLE OF SENIOR EXECUTIVE   If we assume that you want to create a fast-moving company, an innovative organization that takes the future by storm, we assume you want a steady stream of products and service offerings. Your company can achieve these things, but not if it is a bureaucratic organization. You must find a way to release and direct a wave of entrepreneurial spirit. To accelerate your innovation journey, executive members at the top have to:

- Act as one team related to the program instead of a loose confederation of opinion leaders.
- Ensure alignment of beliefs, words, and actions among the senior executives.
- Be visible, providing mentoring and developing new learners in the process.
- Sanction the innovation process, allocating resources and ensuring ideas are turning into insights and outcomes.
- Ensure your innovation champions (leadership network for innovation change) are working well.
- Assure high-touch, high-frequency communications.

ROLE OF MIDDLE AND FRONTLINE MANAGERS FOR BUILDING MOMENTUM   It is a well-known fact that every project can get stuck in the middle and can fail to reach the front lines. Here are some suggestions for managers in the middle or on the front lines to help keep the ball rolling,:

- Be skilled in stating the business case for innovation change efforts.
- Make sure you communicate this as "your" change, and not "their" change.
- Involve senior leaders and your peers to help support the related changes.
- Become engaged enough to make good decisions even if they are not your first choice.
- Make sure you say what you believe and that what you do aligns with what you say.
- Be visible and show that you are also learning and participating to help shape the future through innovation activities.
- Sanction and support the process within your area, allocate needed resources, and make sure you have a person assigned to the innovation program changes.
- Show that you have a personal investment in the effort.
- Work actively to set the parameters of success and the boundaries for change

3. Identify Innovation Leaders and Best Talent

To build momentum, you will need change leaders across the entire organization—in business units, departments, middle management, and even frontline teams. Involving such local change leaders is crucial to the success of your innovation program. They can enable the future state within their respective area based on their local business-specific context. This is the first step in helping to move innovation programs into actualization. Large-group processes, such as innovation awareness training sessions, are particular useful at this point. Bring your innovation champions into a collaborative meeting to begin their engagement early on. This will ensure there will be space to modify, clarify, or even amend your execution plan. A common error is to view this as a deployment, informing people of the new direction and innovation-related changes. On the contrary, innovation champions should be viewed as a creative body whose work is as much to decide future of the organization as it is to enable it.

One of the hardest things for leaders to do is to help manage the creative tension between current and future states. Most typical managers fall into a trap when it comes to managing critical initiatives. They create a business case for innovation, vision for the future state with innovation capability, and then move to deploy based on this desired future.

Instead, to fully engage everyone and build momentum, every member of the organization must evaluate the changes based on his or her own perception of the current state.

Members of the innovation champions group may need to spend time in their work units gathering data to develop the local business case for innovation. This could be as easy as examining current business priorities, or absorptive capacity for taking on something new, or running a complex engagement and assessment process at each work location. Decision making must be comprehensive and relevant to the needs of that particular organization.

Your best innovation change leaders are those who are naturally discontent with the way things are. They are dissatisfied and determined to make things better. They are ready to raise the bar for the rest of the organization with courage and conviction. Pick these leaders as your first group of change agents and sponsors.

REMOVE THE BLOCKERS   Nothing creates cynicism faster than an executive member who calls for innovation and then leaves in place the system and people who are very obviously blocking it. Most barriers come in two flavors: people and systems. Here are some ideas on how to manage such barriers:

People

- Ask the best innovators what and who would provide the least support for innovation and would block an innovation program. Manage these individuals so they don't get in the way. If they persist, remove them.
- You know what to do with any area managers who come to work every day to protect their turf and normally the first word out of their mouth is no: Turn their world upside down. Remember, don't let someone else do this dirty job. As a change leader, you must do it.
- Show anyone the door who is not working on building an environment where people at all levels are turning vision into reality.
- Encourage and promote those who display 100% energy toward innovation.

Systems

- Remove all unwanted paper reports no one is reading. Award people who find useless reports. Doing this will support your sustainability efforts as well.

- If you have not done it already, remove any and all useless approvals and forms. Post these in public locations, such as conference rooms and the cafeteria—people will have lots of fun with this and it gives them hope.
- Every management review report should be stamped with "Hours Spent for Preparation = x" stamp. If management knows what it takes to pull such reports together, they will take action. This awareness will encourage leaders to ask questions carefully.

Building momentum is lot like building a garden plot when you first decide to grow your own vegetables in the backyard. You must first remove the weeds, clean the debris, put in the topsoil, construct rows, and plant seeds with proper spacing. After a few weeks, some plants will start to develop. Then every few days, you will need to remove all the unwanted weeds and water it. As the plants start to grow, you will need to give them some fertilizer and even provide support for plants so they grow straight up and do not fall down. All of this is necessary during the very early stages of building a fertile plot. Your innovation program will need the same care and attention to ensure long-term impact.

IDENTIFYING INNOVATION TALENT   We know that great leaders create deliberate conditions that elicit people's ability to produce extraordinary results. We also know that results arise from the *force field* of climate and culture. That force field is instrumental in guiding toward innovation or running away from it.

Therefore, the question is this: How does a company solicit the right leaders, managers, individuals, and facilitators for maximum momentum moving forward?

Leaders as Innovation Sponsors   Every organization already has many natural innovation leaders, managers, facilitators, and idea owners. The problem is they are mostly hiding. This occurs because most workforce cultures and systems are designed for short-term performance optimization and protection of the status quo instead of risk taking and long-term investment strategies. In such environments, the very best intrapreneurs have tried to be successful, but after hitting their heads on the organizational walls a few hundred times, they decide to leave. Others decide to stay and keep trying. You need to find these first.

As your next step, identify the natural intrapreneurs already within the organization. These are people who usually appoint themselves to their roles. They generally love to move forward and then seek approval for their work activities.

To help build the momentum, recruit your initial talent pool, do not force them into participating, especially the leaders and managers. Those who don't have passion for innovation will not be able to fake it. You can't afford to misfire by having half-engaged managers and leaders sponsoring innovation efforts.

The best innovation leaders are challenge driven. They love to climb the mountain, especially when others avoid it. Companies such as Motorola create 10x stretch goals for their leaders. GE also has a very impressive process to find *natural* innovators who can produce results.

Juan Andrade is the Chief Operating Officer for ACE's International Business and President of Global Personal and Small Commercial Insurance at one of the largest insurers in the world—the ACE Group. Here is what he told us about great business leaders:

I am looking for people who are not complacent about the status quo. That sounds trite but you need people who are going to take risks and who are naturals at that. You can identify them by their track record. You can tell pretty quickly by the way they behave, the way they talk, the way they describe their plans. You want people who again are not wedded to the status quo. If our leaders don't like the rules, they should change them. This defines an ideal attitude we want in our organization, don't be defined by the box, define the box.

I am also looking for people who have an established track record of getting things done. Otherwise you can surround yourself just with strategic thinkers who can never turn anything into an operating reality. So, the bottom line is you need people who are good leaders, good communicators, good operators, multitaskers, and who can get into the details.

Also, our best innovative leaders have a DNA that says "Look, I am going to question things, I want people who are inquisitive, I want people who are not afraid to speak their mind, to challenge." Again, I like the doer capability, the "get it done" capability, most important, I want very smart people. And I would say those are sort of fundamental things that I look for in the teams when I assess them. Last, I look for individuals who demonstrate great confidence.

Like Juan, the very best leader innovators love to work on new aspects of their roles that can create exceptional value. A unique attribute of these leaders is their ability to recruit others in the creation and crafting of a new vision. They might already have a vision, but they will not force it on others. They inherently know that getting others involved in early stages can lead to a strong path of commitment instead of dissension later on. They also know how to incorporate other people's ideas as the vision evolves.

How to Find Your Best Innovation Talent   The same attributes that define your innovation leaders holds true for your innovation consultants and change agents. The first batch of individuals who can help build momentum should be carefully chosen. Generally, these people should self-select themselves and not be pushed into getting involved.

For example, in a customer contact center (call center) environment, innovation leaders are usually the ones raising their hands offering to help or offering ideas and suggestions to do different things. In other areas, they tend to be the thought leaders. These are the people colleagues tend to go to as informal leaders. They may not necessarily be the manager or team leader, but you know they are the ones the other six in that team are going to for advice and with questions.

When it comes to new project ideas, these individuals always seem to be working on any number of new ideas. Once they find a new idea, they are exceptional at *greenhousing* (keeping them safe) until they are worthy to share. They know that any new idea is very delicate. It can be killed by a casual yawn or a snide remark, or it can be thrown in a coffin by an overzealous judgmental voice.

At the early stages of idea development, your best innovators will reach out to others to help validate elements of the idea, such as feasibility, technical strength, complexity, alternatives, and financial impact. The benefit of doing that early on in the process is it allows others to help build additional layers of information and thought process and provides different perspectives.

Because of their inquisitive nature, these individuals tend to surround themselves with very smart people. Why? Because they know that no matter how smart they think they are, the fact is, somebody can always add value, an enhanced alternative perspective, a diverse insight, or a completely new hidden dimension to their original idea.

Their preference to engage many people around them not only generates diverse perspectives but also quietly crafts momentum to help covert their small idea seed into a healthy plant.

They are very comfortable and confident in their own skin, are willing to accept that their reality is only partial truth, and recognize that by engaging smarter people around them, they can create disproportionate business and personal value from their original idea.

How do they learn? The best intrapreneurs seem to spend lot of time thinking about the future rather than the present or the past.

Juan told us, "I am not someone who has ever been complacent about anything. I don't spend a lot of time looking back or even living in the present. Instead, I am always looking forward; and frankly, from day 1, I was the kid who just wanted to get out of high school so I could go to college, so I could go to work. I've always been very focused on what's next, what's ahead, as opposed to what's now or what's behind me."

How do these intrapreneurs make decisions? It seems that most of these leaders tend to rely more on their intuition than on facts alone. One school of thought says many of the best managers in the world rely 99% on data and 1% on gut.

You would expect the majority of successful executives to rely more on data than on experience. Juan says there is a balance for him. "I tend to follow the Colin Powell method that says that as long as you have 60% of the information available to you, you are good to go. I operate probably somewhere close to him, but it depends on the business. Ultimately when you get the data, you still have to make a decision, because the data is not everything. But the data helps you at least make an informed decision. You have to have the courage and the conviction to make fact-based decisions."

Juan, along with many others whom you will meet in Chapter 8, agrees that action-oriented individuals are the best innovation top talent. They are the antithesis of complacency. They display passion in what they do, are highly motivated to want to succeed, and are winners.

Of these highly talented innovators, the best of the best have two important qualities worth noting: They are somewhat humble and selfless. They invariably think of others and society first, then themselves. As Juan summarized, "These are people who have a true winning spirit. They are team oriented, they are collaborative, and they are decisive."

4. Communicate, Communicate, Communicate

We discussed the importance of change and of teaching managers how to manage and accept change. To enhance quality of life, it is critical for executives and managers to assimilate change requirements without displaying dysfunctional behaviors. People within organizations look up to seniors because of their desire for structure and predictability in our ever-changing, chaotic world. We must help managers adopt, adapt, and accept change for themselves but, more important, for their staff. In the context of innovation as a major change initiative for your firm, the single most important ingredient is to teach your managers and help them practice *strategic organizational communication.*

A number of senior executives we interviewed stated that a lack of cultural integration is a major reason why some of their strategic programs fail to deliver the intended results. It is true that most leaders have mastered the skill to roll out a program and manage the *visible* dimensions with ease. It is the *invisible* dimension—the human side of change necessary for becoming an innovative culture— that is often overlooked. Most organizations are very good at communicating such change dimensions as vision, values, goals, objectives, brand equity, and operational processes. But when it comes to invisible factors—the need for flexibility, creativity, quality, and trust building—nothing is mentioned or proactively managed.

If your innovation program is a significantly new cultural change, you must overmanage these invisible dimensions. Therefore, a strategic communication strategy and tactics become pivotal tools to ensure you are building the best possible momentum.

BUILDING A COMMUNICATION STRATEGY A good communication strategy can promote understanding and support and build momentum and readiness for your innovation program. It can help create a solid implementation network. Such a network can provide a feedback loop for listening that can continually improve the direction, design decisions, and ultimate implementation of the program. The strategy must provide clear responsibilities and support roles for communication and facilitate planning. It should include objectives, content, media, mechanisms, and schedule of communication activities.

A good communication strategy will allow proper stewardship and promote consistent messaging, ensure ready access to sources and updated content, and promote a network of internal innovation champions taking ownership of the innovation process and related material.

FIVE IMPORTANT CHANGE QUESTIONS   In our experience, when dealing with innovation as a major change initiative, employees seek answers to these five questions:

1. What is happening with the innovation program?
2. Why are we pursuing innovation as a major change?
3. When is it going to happen?
4. How will I be impacted during the rollout and after implementation?
5. Where can I go with more questions, issues, and concerns related to the innovation program in my area?

If these questions are not answered, you are leaving it to chance for employees to create their own interpretations, leading to possible negative consequences and waste of your valuable resources.

COMMUNICATION PLAN TEMPLATE   Your high-level communication plan may include these points:

1. Develop answers to the five questions. Then make sure the questions are addressed in every innovation initiative communication document, meeting, and webcast.
2. Develop a one-minute message—your elevator pitch about the innovation program. It should describe the business case and vision of the future.
3. Demand consistent dialog at all levels, especially middle management.
4. Use multiple media to teach and tell—remove uncertainties and doubt from day 1.
5. Clearly identify the objective of each communication: awareness building, skill development, network development, employee engagement, and so on.
6. Check often for alignment of process objectives and productivity for the parties in the communication activity.
7. Be open to examine and test for what people hear.
8. Actively respond to feedback and make adjustments to the plan as required.

Finally, don't underestimate the need to repeat the messages even when you know everyone has heard them time and again. Even with your best efforts, there are always many who will not understand the importance of the innovation change initiative. There have been stories where after six months of implementation activities, senior executives have publicly asked, "Why are we doing all this innovation stuff?" Although this raised a few eyebrows, the question was taken seriously and led to rather thorough discussions of the whys that had not surfaced before.

DEVELOPING A DIALOG ABOUT THE IMPORTANCE OF INNOVATION   Communication is about more than just the exchange of data and information. It is also about relationships, a foundation on which change is built. Communication should always convey the combined thoughts, feelings, and images of all the key stakeholders. There is always conscious and unconscious content. Also remember, when using a variety of media, there is always a high probability of noise in the messages and from the environment through which they travel. Ultimately, all messages end up somewhat diluted and distorted.

We don't always understand each other. In fact, sometimes it's amazing that human beings ever get along with each other at all. Misunderstanding in communication will occur. Whatever your communication intention, include some means for checking out what the parties have heard and what it meant to them.

Since people are accustomed to existing channels of communication, leverage those processes and people when possible. You want to set conditions by which everyone has the opportunity to become engaged as communicators and potential change leaders and enroll others in communication planning and implementation. Make sure to make listening and initiating contact a universal responsibility. You want people to be proactive and stay linked and integrated with each other. Build the habit and processes that allow people to come together easily and quickly seek help and support, to establish and update plans, and to coordinate actions during all the stages of the innovation implementation process.

5. Build Awareness—Educate Everyone

To ensure that everyone in your organization understands the vision, objectives, and process for your innovation program moving forward, you need to educate everyone as quickly as possible. Here are three specific tactics to help create a cascading process for your initiative.

1. **Conduct awareness sessions.** Conduct two- to three-hour awareness workshops for the top managers and key talent. Give them an innovative experience that provides answers to these questions:
   - What is innovation? (definition)
   - Why is innovation important to our firm? (the business case)
   - What will innovation give us that nothing else will? (benefits)
   - Who is this for? Who can participate? (staff involvement)
   - How can it help me (the participant) starting tomorrow? (immediate value)
   - What are the various innovation processes? (execution)
   - How is this going to be managed, and what is the governance process? (execution)
   - How are leaders involved? (top-level support)
   - As a participant, what do I need to do after this session? (action)
   - How will I be measured against the objectives of the innovation program? (rewards)

2. **Build an intranet portal for innovation.** Create a branded site for your innovation program on the intranet, and include all strategic and operational information relevant to the program. Here are a few other items to include in your Web site:
   - Messages from the CEO and other key executives on the value of innovation and target goals.

- Timeline of program rollout
- An easy-to-understand presentation on the basics of organization creativity and innovation
- A "how to get involved section" for people to sign up for training, workshops, and awareness sessions; subscribe to monthly newsletters; and so on
- Links to videos (successful examples of inventions and innovations in the world)
- Ideation tools (easy tools for the ideation process to help generate volume of new ideas and to select the very best ideas to further pursue)
- Case studies
- Strategic articles and papers
- Resource links (Web sites, conferences, thought leaders, authors, famous bloggers, books)
- HR policies (rewards, recognition, intellectual property ownership issues, time allocation, and formal approval process, etc.)

3. **Provide special attention to midlevel staff.** Just because you have a senior sponsor and clarity regarding project goals, budgets, and resources, success is not guaranteed without full support of midlevel managers. These managers control departmental priorities and budgets. They influence whether their staff members take an executive mandate seriously. It is very hard to disengage them from their typical focus on operational performance metrics and get them to work on subjects such as innovation. For them, even an hour of investment may not pay off for months or years.

   In order to engage them, you will need to remind them that the mandate is from the top down (it is hoped that you have done so already) and show how their participation in the innovation program will improve operational performance and employee engagement of their own staff. Additionally, you must help them see how their current projects will benefit through use of innovation tools and techniques.

   Knowing the daily pressures of their jobs, midlevel managers often fear that anything new may expose their weaknesses or make them look bad to their peers and superiors. Because of this fear, you will need to start with baby steps and help build confidence that creating a climate of innovation and calculated risk taking is a good thing to do.

6. Protect the Momentum

In every mature organization, we can find numbers of formal managerial systems that have evolved over the years. These systems exist to provide stability, certainty, predictability, and coordination in an increasingly complex internal corporate environment. Unfortunately, the number of such systems creates disincentives for intrapreneurship.

In the process of building your innovation engine, you will face a number of key obstacles as you try to build momentum. Here are the top six that must be addressed as early as possible:

1. **Rewards.** We assume that your reward measurement system is designed to promote safe, conservative behaviors that produce short-term payoffs. More often

than not, they are vague, inconsistent, or perceived as inequitable. It is very likely that managers may encourage new innovative behavior X but hope for Y. They will ask for or expect innovative behavior but actually measure and reward noninnovative behaviors.

2. **Performance system.** Decision support and control systems encourage managers to micromanage budgets for every dollar and establish quantifiable performance benchmarks in as many activity areas as possible. These benchmarks become ends in themselves and also convey a lack of trust in employee discretion.

3. **Budgeting.** Typically, the budgeting process is not designed to bootstrap an unplanned idea or unofficial project yet it tends to reward the politically correct and powerful. There are no resources for experimenting on the job. Costing systems are based on arbitrary allocation schemes, where any project can be made to look untenable simply as a function of the indirect fixed costs that must be recovered.

4. **Planning.** The annual planning process can also be an obstacle by becoming formulaic. Too much emphasis is placed on superfluous analysis, on form rather than content, on the planning document instead of the planning process, and on having professional planners writing the plan (instead of relying on those charged with actually implementing it). The result is an overly rigid process that will slow down your momentum and prevent your ability to respond to new opportunities.

5. **Approval systems.** By definition, innovation is about chartering into the unknown. Intrapreneurs' efforts are often undermined by organizational policies and procedures that were established to bring order and consistency for the operational success of the firm. Two of the most damaging policies for innovators are:
   a. Complex approval cycles for new ventures.
   b. Elaborate documentation requirements.

   These two obstacles often overconsume organizational energy, kill the best ideas, and sometimes destroy the idea owner's spirit.

   Deadlines and performance standards that reflect daily operations often create a motivation to compromise on truly new and novel ideas. This often leads the corporate innovator to customize innovations to performance criteria based on past and current environmental factors rather than the competitive requirements of the future.

6. **Turf protection.** Many managers driven by a need for power and status will look at innovation from a wrong perspective. Individuals who are always protecting their turf can become a huge momentum killer. They hoard resources, especially information. They resist open communication and are suspicious of collaborative efforts. Others refuse to look beyond the current field of reference for creative solutions. Those who do find creative ideas lack the skills necessary to bend the rules, build the coalitions, and work through or around the system to achieve successful implementation.

So how does a firm nurture a culture of innovation while maintaining operational controls?

The very best method is by balancing the reporting system with an environment that promotes trust, transparency, and open communication. Senior executives must act on these two fronts simultaneously. On one side, the fight should be about offering incentives for innovation through experimentation and providing proper resources. On the other side, employees should not feel negative perceived costs associated with failure. Instead, they should be helped to become comfortable with trying out new things that may or may not work out. Finally, this approach requires special communication to protect individuals in terms of their careers when ideas being tested do not deliver intended results.

Conclusion

In this chapter, we covered the importance of building momentum before applying full throttle to your innovation engine. Program teams often skip this important step and end up wasting valuable time and resources.

In summary, follow these five steps to build momentum and prepare you for innovation execution:

1. Take your innovation vision and strategy and build a compelling story that will enlist everyone's participation.
2. Identify and develop innovation change agents—your innovation champions. These are the strategic employees who will help propagate the innovation agenda and messaging and help deliver the target outcomes. These individuals will be the arms, ears, eyes, and legs for your innovation journey.
3. Rally support through systematic communication and branding activities. Ensure key sponsors visibly and frequently support innovation story.
4. Make innovation tools and tactics accessible to all target participants—through workshops, webcasts, and intranet portals.
5. Adjust control systems to accommodate innovation change, recognizing that not all plans work perfectly. Be flexible to the changing needs of participants and target audiences as your innovation program gains momentum.

Note

1. Daryl R. Conner, *Managing at the Speed of Change* (New York: Villard Books, 1993), p. 92.

PART III

Playing the Game

CHAPTER 6

Structuring for Innovation

During the implementation phase, one of the first high-priority tasks necessary for innovation to become an integral part of the organization is to create a vertical and horizontal organizational alignment structure. This structure outlines how each employee can contribute to the organizational vision and mission through innovation. It includes effective change management and control systems to make timely decisions.

How did Microsoft lose the industry innovation edge? What happened at Blockbuster, which once dominated in-home video entertainment? How about Kodak's photography business engine? And what happened at Fiat, Zenith, and Novell? Why do many companies lose their way?

Is it the changing nature of markets? Or is it competition? Some might say it is a firm's inability to exploit and push the technology edge. Others might argue that the problem is the cost of operation or an inability to retain smart people.

You might wonder if there is one *primary* element that is responsible for such failures.

I think so.

There is plentiful evidence showing how top industry leaders can lose their way just as easily as new entrants can dominate an industry overnight.

Organizational leadership, we tend to assume, is akin to spatial navigation. Either leaders know where to take their company and how to take it there or they don't.

Kurt Eichnawald of *Vanity Fair* wrote an article in August 2012 titled "Microsoft's Lost Decade." Around the same time, Greg Sandoval wrote an article for CNET titled "Netflix's Lost Year." If we look inside companies that have lost a decade or a year, it is highly probable that leaders at these firms have lost something else—something that is arguably more fundamental to long-term organizational success than the ability to strategically navigate turbulent markets. In our experience, what they have lost in many cases is the ability to enable *organizational engagement*. That's our term for the process by which key ideas and crucial information circulate within a company.

Looking over the last three decades, I believe that lack of organizational engagement caused some of the most renowned innovation opportunities at Xerox, Lucent, and IBM to be lost.

Xerox developed the early personal computer in its Palo Alto (California) Research Center (PARC) but did not have a process to bring it to the market. The company allowed a college student, Steve Jobs, to roam around in the PARC facility, and the rest is history. Lucent invented the transistor but could not envision what Intel was able to see. IBM was the dominant computer manufacturer in the early 1980s but somehow allowed Bill Gates, a college dropout, to dominate the PC industry instead. All three companies had the people to take those ideas to market but suffered with internal orthodoxies. Because the new ideas didn't fit into the core business areas of the organization, the companies drove those great ideas out along with the innovators who wanted to work on them.

I believe that many of those engineers and intrapreneurs would have stayed if an appropriate structure existed to support employee innovation, either through the creation of skunkworks labs or venture capital units to capitalize on ideas that did not fit into the current business plans or strategy.

In this chapter, we examine various organizational designs that promote organizational engagement and innovation execution while promoting intrapreneurial behaviors. We examine alternate approaches for key variables of a good organizational design and look at examples of companies that have institutionalized radical approaches to structuring their innovation programs. First let us look at key elements that make up a good organizational design to improve organizational engagement.

Components of Organizational Structure

Fundamentally, organizational structures are designed to deal with *differentiation* and *integration*. "Differentiation" means the protocol on how decision-making authority is distributed, work groups are organized, and people are assigned to work groups. "Integration" defines how people and functions are coordinated. Therefore, the role of structure is to accommodate, or inhibit innovative behaviors.

Innovation requires creative thinking and collaboration. An employee must feel a personal sense of empowerment to maneuver without feelings of fear and reprimand. Innovation necessitates a level of flexibility in terms of resource utilization and time allocations. Quick decisions are often required during the innovative process, and the decision making should be both rational and intuitive. Sponsors and team members must be able to span boundaries within the organization.

Innovation is a communication-intensive activity. It includes both lateral and vertical communication, much of which is informal and unplanned.

Finally, innovation requires ongoing experimentation and adaptation of concepts and ideas, especially across vertical silos.

Before you can design and select an appropriate innovation structure, you must first assess how your current organizational design functions. Depending on how it works, it can:

- Build bridges or walls between individuals and groups.
- Speed or slow decision making.
- Facilitate depth or breadth of expertise.
- Generate or stifle idea generation and sharing.

If an appropriate organizational design is done well, it will accelerate your innovation execution and enable the innovation strategy. It is important to note that organizational design is not just boxes and reporting structure. Every organization is made up of hard structures (how employees are grouped together by product, function, or market to form a hierarchy of departments at each level within an organizational structure) and soft structures (how departments are organized for location of power, accountability, decision-making and responsibility at each level within the organization). In other words, hard structures are boxes and titles. Soft structures are easier to implement and offer better solutions than major adjustments to hard structures.

All organizations go through stages of evolution and revolution. Structures, as key variables, also undergo changes. There are various stages of structural changes as a program develops and matures over period of time. Your innovation structure will also go through a similar evolution through five stages.

- Stage I. The initial stage is highly informal, entrepreneurial, and often without any formal title or any kind of organizational chart.
- Stage II. A functional structure is introduced with centralized control.
- Stage III. More decentralized control and geographically organized structure develop around profit centers.
- Stage IV. Eventually there is a movement toward merged product groups or strategic business units together with centralization of administrative and staff functions at the main office.
- Stage V. The company adopts matrix structures, cross-functional team approaches, reassigns head of office staff to consultative teams, and process integration. As an example, managers operate with dual or multiple reporting relationships. They may have product responsibility in a geographic region or may work both in marketing and on a major innovation project.

The evolution of structures is not as deterministic as it sounds, and many variants are possible in a given stage of a company's evolution. Each company must continually adjust its structure to reflect both external pressures (e.g., changing competitive landscape, market movements, and technology alterations) and internal priorities (e.g., productivity gains, improve responsiveness to the market, better coordination across units and functions).

In our experience, unfortunately, entrepreneurship (creativity, innovativeness, risk taking, nimbleness, and being proactive) is not viewed as an overriding consideration in restructuring efforts and so tends to be systematically undermined as the company evolves. Every formal structure has the next nine characteristics in its design. Circle one preferred style/attribute for each of the nine elements to help you assess your current organizational design.

1. **Decision power.** Who makes the decisions? Is it at the top, with divisional executives, with product marketing teams, or with technical people?
2. **Bureaucratization.** How difficult is it to get daily work done? Are the workflow policies somewhat informal, formal with detailed policies and procedures, somewhat organic, or very bureaucratic?
3. **Specialization.** How unique are the skills and expertise of the current business groups? Is there low or high specialization, or narrow and deep expertise?
4. **Differentiation.** Looking at the various existing groups and their output, how different are they from each other? Are there minimal differences or moderate, high, or very high differentiations?
5. **Integration and coordination.** Who drives workflow across various departments and units? Is it driven by the CEO or by technocrats, is it mutually integrated, or is it driven by formal committees via plans and budgets?
6. **Technology.** Depending on your industry, do you use technology that is simple or unique and sophisticated that gives you edge in the market? Or does it vary by product family?
7. **Competition.** Within your current market segments, what type of competition do you face? Is it a highly competitive environment with tremendous margin pressures on most product lines, moderate competition, low competition due to unique offerings, or does it vary by product line?
8. **Growth.** What is the recent growth experience? Does it vary based on products and segments, very slow due to various internal and external factors, or do you experience rapid growth?
9. **Barriers to entry.** Within your business model, how difficult is it for someone enter your industry and compete against you? Is it easy because there are no barriers, is it difficult to scale a barrier because it would require heavy capital investment, is unique knowledge a barrier, or does it vary depending on the segment?

The key is to assess your current organizational design and the characteristics just listed to baseline what type of innovation structures might be the best for your organization.

Types of Organizational Structures

In his book *Innovation Management*, Allan Afuah writes extensively about various organizational structures and how they can help or hinder innovations.[1] Not to simplify or minimize too much, there are three types of organizational designs in the business world: traditional, matrix, and program based. Each has unique advantages and disadvantages.

Traditional Structures

Traditional structures are sometimes called functional structures. In this type of organization, people are grouped and perform tasks according to traditional functions, such as sales, marketing, engineering, manufacturing, and so on. As shown in Figure 6.1, the managing director (MD) or CEO has a vice president that heads each of the functional areas. Each of the vice presidents has many directors and managers reporting to her or him. These managers, in turn, have other people reporting to them. The number of levels of people that directly report to a manager is called the manager's span of control. The number of levels of management in the firm is called the depth of the hierarchy. When people with similar skills, competencies, and knowledge are grouped together, they can learn from each other and increase the firm's depth of knowledge in the particular function. For example, if an insurance underwriting group wants to quickly respond to a market opportunity due to a new regulation change by the government, it doesn't need to rely solely on the sales or marketing function.

The disadvantage of the traditional structure is when a firm needs to develop a new product or a service that requires input from many other functions. First, since the allegiance of employees is to the functional group from where their performance evaluation and compensation come, employees are not likely to devote the type of energy that is needed to offer a competitive product or service. Second, functional groups can be physically and visually isolated from each other, making communications between them difficult. Each function may be housed in a different building with very little personal interaction between employees from other functions.

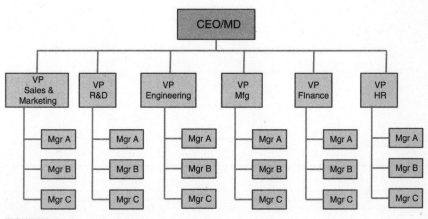

FIGURE 6.1 Traditional Structure

In traditional structures, technological and market knowledge are best transferred by some form of physical interaction. The marketing group may be starving for ideas from the engineering design group that could allow it to access huge markets faster than the competition. Another challenge with traditional structures is the orthodox mind-set that creates invisible walls. For example, the production department may view R&D as those know-it-all academics, whereas R&D perceives marketing as those laptop and latte salespeople with flashy suits.

Last, due to differences in experiences and capabilities, traditional structures may have goals that are not consistent with developing new innovations or cooperating with other functions. For example, if a VP of one function got to his current position by virtue of the existing offerings, he is very unlikely to support development of a new product that cannibalizes the existing product line and his power.

For these primary reasons, the traditional structure is conducive to product and service development that requires very little or no interaction between the different functions.

If your organization is currently designed this way, you will need to consider the right mix of innovation processes described in Chapter 4 with an appropriate innovation structure, described later in this chapter.

Matrix Structures

In the matrix structure shown in Figure 6.2, there is a VP of program management who reports to the CEO/MD. Various project managers report into this VP.

The objective of this structure is a faster response to marketplace changes in the industry. In a large global firm, the pace of change needed just to survive can be daunting. Even in a smaller company, it has become critical to deliver on operational efficiency and to keep pace with the "need changes" driven by turbulent external factors.

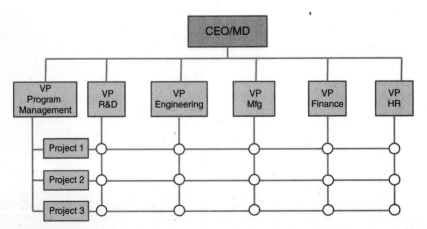

FIGURE 6.2   Matrix Structure

In such cases, the CEO and the board may sanction high-priority special programs for the sake of compliance, new regulation, technological changes, improved financial performance, product line extension, or market access. The CEO may decide that, without such focus, the organization may face high risk leading to poor performance and market loss. Examples include:

- A new enterprise resource planning system for a large manufacturing environment
- Information technology departments that must deliver better solutions while reducing unit cost annually utilizing global delivery models of onshore and offshore
- Sarbanes-Oxley regulations for U.S. firms to stay compliant with federal law and avoid financial penalties
- A new service delivery model due to the new healthcare regulations

In all of these cases, each program requires a multiyear implementation, a huge amount of change management, large-scale process changes, and a high financial burden if not implemented well. In such organizations, program managers are assigned to each major initiative. Each project manager has two bosses, one from the functional area and the other from the project management group.

Members of the same project team may or may not reside in the same physical area. This structure has three advantages.

1. Since the rate of change, quality of knowledge, and competence varies from one function to another, employees can spend time on the project commensurate with the rate of change required in their functional area.
2. Employees can keep their technical skills sharpened since they have a chance to interact with both their project teams and their functional groups.
3. Your most talented employees can be assigned to more than one project.

The biggest disadvantage to this structure is the project manager's difficulty in managing multiple bosses and building allegiance.

Program-Based Structures

Program structures, shown in Figure 6.3, are best for tasks requiring a high frequency of interaction between functions. Each group or project is under a VP, reporting to the CEO/MD, with the dedicated resources to carry out the disciplined execution requirements. Each program VP has dedicated project managers and employees with the different functional expertise, ideally appropriate for the project. These employees are assigned to the project for its duration and report to the project manager. Their performance evaluations and compensation are the responsibility of the project manager, not the functional group from which they came or to which they are assigned. For the duration of the project, their allegiance is to the project, project manager, and program manager, not to the function. Typically,

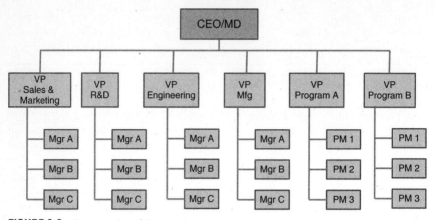

FIGURE 6.3   Program-Based Structure

members of the project are co-located in the same physical location to improve interactions and expedite sharing of knowledge and skills. This creates a clear advantage for information flow among project members. Another advantage of this structure is the protection of stakeholders' political power, neutralizing the fear of cannibalization and the emotional attachment to existing products, that can pull the blood out of implementation.

Ideally, each project team is made up of members from each critical function and, when possible, located in a separate geographic location. As an example, when IBM started its PC division, it was located in Boca Raton, Florida, away from IBM's major mainframe business unit in New York. Key members of the program team were real intrapreneurs and mavericks who desperately wanted to prove that there was a much bigger market after mainframes.

One major disadvantage of program structure is that employees can become stagnant in their functional technical knowledge due to the pace of change within their function. This is especially true when program duration is long. In other words, if the rate of change underpinning functional areas is high and the program duration is long, project members may find their functional skills outdated. Sometimes these skills are in product development or core engineering and design. The question you will need to answer is how such a loss of skills can be prevented. One answer may be in the matrix organization structure described earlier.

Planning Your Innovation Structure

Within your current organization, it may seem like all three structural designs are being used. In reality, one of the three is dominating daily operations. Once you have clarity regarding which type it is, you should be able to identify key advantages, disadvantages, and sensitivity areas you will need to manage as you begin to define an appropriate innovation structure that will work for you.

Let's say a company is beginning an innovation journey for the first time. It has been in business for over 30 years and is multilocational and global in size and footprint. The executives at the top are highly committed to innovation and the strategic objectives. Other senior leaders are also very excited about the journey of innovation. What does this company need to do to ensure proper innovation structure? Let us explore in greater detail.

First, use Table 6.1 to identify which type of organizational structure your company falls into. Then, based on your innovation intent, innovation strategies, and innovation goals, defined in earlier chapters, determine which innovation structure (see "Four Major Types of Innovation Structures" next in this chapter) will work the best for you.

Four Major Types of Innovation Structures

In Chapter 4 we introduced four types of structures that can support your innovation program:

1. Traditional two-tier structure
2. Center of excellence (COE)
3. Strategic horizons group
4. Intrapreneuring and venturing group

Let's look at organizational components of each closely.

Traditional Two-Tier Structure

In the traditional two-tier structure, there is a central innovation group and divisional/functional innovation resources. As shown in Figure 6.4, the central group has a VP of innovation reporting into CEO or COO. (It is our belief that innovation should be sponsored by your firm's highest executive who has the required passion and authority to help drive innovation.)

The innovation process is less formal than the typical rigid processes that often exists in every corner of most large organizations, but the central innovation group highly emphasizes innovation principles. The central group develops an innovation tool kit and a formal curriculum. Divisions are encouraged but not mandated to designate "innovation consultants" for their area for "certification" training on the tool kit. For the divisions, participation in the innovation initiative is optional; they have the discretion to participate or to wait. If a division decides to participate, it would assign a single point of contact for all the innovation activities for its line of business (LOB). This person would report to the business unit/function head. A small corporate budget is given to the central group to *push* innovation. Each division would put aside annual funds for its own innovation activities. Many firms use this

TABLE 6.1 Three Types of Organizational Structures

	Traditional	Matrix	Program Based
Key features	Deep technical functional expertise High efficiency levels High-quality output from each function Ideal for smaller and regional organizations Easy to cross-train others within a function Excellent team orientation within function (but not so across functions)	Nimble: Strong ability to respond quickly to market, technological, or other external changes Best for large organizations Generally organized to achieve superordinate goals Has built-in interdependencies; this can become very difficult to manage without excellent project management skills Requires use of a lot of shared resources; this can create capacity issues in each function	Focused execution to help address major business initiatives Excellent for transformative challenges Generally organized to achieve superordinate goals Allows speed and flexibility CEO sponsored, therefore can create momentum Requires excellent program and project management skills
Knowledge and learning	Excellent knowledge flow within a function but difficult across the company	Very good if there is a high support for collaboration and consensus Excellent when there are partner-style synergies within and across functions	Excellent within project teams but does not easily promote knowledge flow across business units
Decision making	Highly vertical, difficult to make big decisions	Works best when there is open line of communication and silo busting Fast when there are common performance criteria across stakeholders involved	Within program, generally, decision making is very fast and timely Each program manager needs authority and empowerment for proper execution
Resource sharing	Limited across functions since managers are not incentivized on the same performance metrics	Excellent when there is a prenegotiated focus on mutual win-win outcomes Without proper project management, can become very difficult	Excellent when there is a prenegotiated focus on mutual win-win outcomes Without proper project management, can become very difficult

New product and service development	Can be slow due to inability of functions to agree on what should come next	Excellent and fast when there is mutual understanding to win together Slow when cross-functional matrix leaders are not empowered to make fast decisions	Excellent if the focus of the program is to build new products or services. Slow if the program team does not have resources and empowerment to experiment outside of normal corporate operational focus on short-term gains and if there are ROI restrictions
Innovation challenges	Growing the top line from radical new ideas Management comfortable only with continuous and incremental improvements Middle management is too operationally focused and may not support innovation Conservative mind-set Too much short-term focus Lack of process for long-term innovation opportunities Lack of new knowledge as a fuel for growth Only a few people at the top find growth opportunities and make decisions on direction	Growing the top line from radical new ideas Too much focus on short-term profitability Too much focus on process optimization No reward system to encourage experimentation Huge focus on profit only Management comfortable only with continuous and incremental improvements Middle management is too operationally focused and may not support innovation Mostly conservative mind-set Lack of process for long-term innovation opportunities Innovations occurs accidentally	Growing the top line from radical new ideas Management generally comfortable with continuous and incremental improvements Middle management is too operationally focused and may not support innovation Generally, a conservative mind-set Too much focus on program of the month; this results in many managers' lack of engagement Lack of process for long-term innovation opportunities Knowledge sharing may not occur outside of special program teams Hard to initiate a new business opportunity without turning the idea into a program; this might take too long, and the market may have shifted by the time a decision is made on the idea

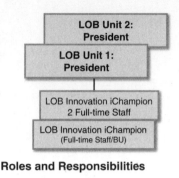

Roles and Responsibilities

- Assist in driving strategy development and ongoing application of strategy as a management tool
- Manage corporate-level leadership agenda
- Standardize on innovation tools, techniques, and methods
- Assist LOB Innovation champions
- Build more innovation consultants (ICs) and iChampions (training and project assistance)
- Revise and direct innovation processes (e.g., new product development)
- Own and drive white space/stretch opportunities that do not fit within LOB structure
- HR systems integration

Roles and Responsibilities

- Drive LOB opportunity development
- Facilitates innovation pipeline monitoring and management
- Works with IC to build more innovation *green belts* within the LOB
- Works with LOB leadership team in driving LOB strategy development and alignment
- Work with IVP of Innovation and IC in managing the ongoing leadership agenda for the LOB leadership team (e.g., innovation resourcing, platform selection, external research, marketing research, etc.)

FIGURE 6.4   Two-Tier Organizational Innovation Structure

approach to find ideas and quickly conduct worthy experiments. An advantage of this approach is that it increases the speed of idea finding and the front end of the product development funnel without requiring a big structure. It also allows various business executives autonomy to participate or wait until their other priorities are completed.

The core innovation group's primary approach is that of influence, not direct involvement, to build new clarity and opportunities for innovative ideas. Using this approach, it is possible that one business area commits to innovation activities but another does not. This approach may result in a lack of knowledge sharing across various business units and therefore slow down possible breakthrough ideas sitting between product and technical teams. Finally, since the central innovation group's role is to inspire and influence business units while relying on budgets within business units for innovation-related competency development, it may be harder to measure the direct impact of innovation efforts at the company and at the cultural level.

Center of Excellence

In the COE innovation structure, as shown in Figure 6.5, the firm dedicates core central resources for the entire organization. An innovation council, generally made up of key executives and sometimes outside members, defines the strategic direction of the COE.

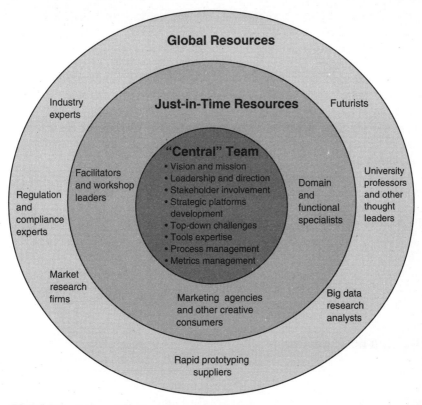

FIGURE 6.5 Center of Excellence Innovation Structure

The head of the COE is appointed and reports to a C-level executive, SVP of strategy, or SVP of R&D and innovation. The head of COE works with the innovation council, which is responsible for facilitating the vision, goals, discovery insights, tools expertise, process management, and knowledge management related to all innovation activities of the firm.

A small group of innovation consultants (similar to black belts in Six Sigma) shepherds the process to help various business units. These internal core consultants, part of COE and assigned to each LOB, provide ideation services, training in tools to various staff members such as new product development experts, advise the innovation council on new opportunities, and help build world-class innovation capabilities across the firm. The COE also manages all just-in-time and external resources as required. These relationships include functional experts, domain experts, advertising/PR agencies, industry experts, industry thought leaders, market research firms, academic resources, futurists, regulatory experts, and government policy makers. Such a group is funded by each business unit and runs based on the unique innovation strategies of each unit.

Typically, each business line will decide how much it wants to use the innovation COE services.

The COE approach is best when you are looking for mostly incremental innovations, finding adjacencies (in markets, technologies, and offerings), and overcoming organizational orthodoxies to generate medium-term success and help build intrapreneurship as a system-wide competency. The approach is the fastest way to create consistent understanding, language, and momentum for innovation within your organization.

The disadvantage of the COE approach is that some business leaders may not want to participate in the innovation journey—for their own reasons. Therefore, parts of the company may be enjoying the benefits of innovation investments but others are not. This is good news/bad news. When two lines of business need to cooperate on a big idea and one is not fully committed to innovation, it can be very difficult to move a great idea forward. This situation can create political backlash and business distractions. To prevent such occurrences, make sure the innovation council understands and deliberates on how to handle such issues to help resolve conflicts for the benefit of the overall business.

Strategic Horizons Group

The strategic horizons group is a dedicated group of strategy and innovation experts looking for breakthrough and disruptive new opportunities for growth. It is primarily focused on new and long-term business opportunities that often are disconnected from the current business model. Often the SVP of innovation is assigned and reports to C-level executive. The sole focus of this group is to look for opportunities no one else is looking for within the company.

The group should have a mandate to find new markets, new products, new services, and new technologies. It can play a pivotal role in incubating creation of new competencies and identifying talent gaps for future success. Ideally this group should be located in a separate facility away from the current organizational environment, management structures, and operational policies. IBM incubated such a group in the early 1980s when it started its PC division in Boca Raton, Florida. In 1970, Xerox also started its Palo Alto Research Center, with the same intentions, away from its New York–based headquarters. In 1996, Shell started the Game Changer group that generated more than 300 proposals; by 1999, this process was generating four out of every five of the largest business opportunities at the company. One role of the strategic horizon group might be to look at new business opportunities with the potential of new revenue, such as $50 million or more, depending on the organization's size.

This type of group is ideal when members are given the freedom to operate without very rigid current business model limitations—such as policies for financial metrics, operational constraints, technology limits, and political complexities—for ease of navigation. When leaders are allowed and empowered to take risks and operate without fear of failure while delivering performance targets, an environment for innovation can flourish.

This approach functions best when the group is located in a separate facility away from any main campus environment, with a direct funding from the top so it does not impact any of the LOB budgets, has easy access to new technologies, and has the freedom to hire the best talent as required. Generally, people in this group have multidisciplinary expertise and multi-industry backgrounds and have strong strategy development, marketing, product development, and high-tech expertise and experience with various business models.

Key operational values for this group are speed to market, disruptive business models and offerings, often pioneering ahead of competition and sometimes creating new standards for their industry, and a venture capital mind-set for experimentation and incubation.

Intrapreneuring and Venturing Group

In the intrapreneuring and venturing group, which is a bottom-up approach, there is a central innovation group with similar responsibilities to the traditional and COE structures but with a few important differences.

An innovation board acts like a group of venture capitalists and meets every 90 days to listen to venture pitches from innovation teams (iTeams). Each iTeam is formed around the idea owner who has an innovative solution for a product, process, delivery, or strategic growth issue. Each iTeam is formed by the idea owner, iConsultant (someone trained in innovation tools and methods), and a few other cross-functional colleagues who have passion for the idea as well. Idea owners use the iConsultant and other iTeam members to help nurture the idea and build an idea brief. Then the idea brief is presented to an innovation sponsor in the business area. The idea brief can be about an innovative solution for a product, business process, manufacturing process, engineering improvements, material sourcing, delivery or new strategic growth opportunities. There is no limit.

An innovation-certified facilitator helps facilitate the team's work using the central group's core tools and idea development process. Each business unit is encouraged to set up its own innovation board for ideas related to its own business issues. Using this approach, the organization can find latent incremental and breakthrough ideas from every employee in the firm. A formal idea review process is implemented using an idea management portal to expedite finding, improving, and selecting ideas as a company matures in innovation competency. Each iTeam has an opportunity to bring its ideas to reality using a fast experimentation process, funds, and resources.

The biggest advantage of this process is that it allows anyone in the company to quickly participate in the innovation journey. Any ideas can be brought up by anyone at any time for proper evaluation without too much effort. The unique advantage of this approach is that ideas cannot be killed easily. Instead, ideas can easily bypass the middle management layers that typically prevent them from reaching the top.

Remember, structures can disable or enable entrepreneurship. Therefore, company structures have to continuously evolve. A good business structure combined with a good innovation structure can facilitate entrepreneurship because it gives employees a sense that they have room to maneuver and innovate while also allowing them to interact with others in the organization. It can allow a large number of new initiatives and also facilitate the speed at which such initiatives move from inception to implementation. Finally, because not all innovation initiatives are the same, this fact should be reflected in the specific attributes of the structures employed to house those initiatives. A one-size-fits-all mentality with respect to structuring for innovation and entrepreneurship will not work.

Core Innovation Team Structure

Depending on the structure you choose for your innovation journey, this section discusses some resources you may need either full time or on an on-demand basis.

What are the skills your team must have? What are the roles of the team, and how do team members interact? Team composition varies depending on the scope, audience, and level of complexity of your innovation projects. This section focuses on the roles and responsibilities of the core team and discusses different compositions of teams based on your innovation program design.

No matter what kind of innovation solution you need to produce, there are some core (C) responsibilities and roles required. For larger and more complex organization and sites, there are extended (E) team members. Extended team members are people whose skills might not always be necessary or who might have cross-functional roles. An example of this could be a network engineer who is also a security expert. Special (S) team experts are brought in when acute skills and expertise is required that does not exist to do work that is not part of your core or extended team but may become so. For example, in a high-tech environment, there are team members who are specialists in audio engineering, security, or database architecture. Some key roles and responsibilities to consider are listed next.

- **Head of innovation program (C).** The head of the innovation program:
  - Is the primary resource for all innovation-related activities within the company.
  - Helps build entrepreneurship and innovation as core competencies.
  - Advises and/or manages internal cross-functional innovation teams to help forward their ideas.
  - Demonstrates a solid understanding of and passion for creativity and innovation.
  - Provides disciplined skills and tools that address both strategic and tactical issues for all client engagements.
  - Communicates the status of innovation activities and projects to senior leaders.
  - Provides ongoing support and counsel for internal client innovation initiatives, including planning and facilitating corporate-wide innovation processes, engagements, and programs.

- Works across multidisciplinary project teams to bring innovation expertise to the teams.
- Displays strong public speaking and facilitation skills, compelling writing ability, is comfortable discussing a broad range of business topics, and has a keen passion for creativity and innovation.
- Demonstrates intellectual curiosity and a willingness to contribute to the firm's knowledge assets while working in a team environment.
- **Account/Project manager (C).** The account/project manager, who is assigned to a business area:
  - Is responsible for scoping the work, developing the project plan, scheduling, allocating resources, budgeting, and managing the team.
  - Deals with all the political and business issues, including contracts, licensing, and other administrative issues related to innovation for that business area. (Sometimes these are two different roles (account manager and project manager) due to the number of projects being executed. In such cases, and in the absence of an account manager, the project manager or producer handles client management.)
  - Interacts with all innovation teams, external faculty, and internal resources assigned to forward innovation projects.
- **Innovation technical lead (C).** A technical lead (sometimes called a subject matter expert [SME]):
  - Oversees the project from a technical point of view.
  - Assists the project manager in ensuring that the technical content and solution strategy are sound.
  - Manages other technical staff.
  - Chooses specialized team members as required for the project.
  - Prepares technical briefs and communicates with the project manager, technical team members, and members of the client's technical team.
- **Rapid Prototype Developer (C).** These days, almost all innovation projects require some use of computers and automation technologies. A rapid prototype developer can develop quick solutions for proof-of-concept demonstrations and help define early project scope with the idea owner. These solutions could be simple PowerPoint storyboards, 3-D models, interactive simulations, smartphone apps, server-side scripts, database applications, Java applets, Adobe flash movies, or working models. This individual should be savvy enough to quickly take ideas from concept to semiworking stage, where the idea owner and iTeam members can easily create and test the hypothesis.
- **Finance and investment advisor (E).** Every serious innovation project requires resources. Business sponsors will have to be convinced through numbers that an idea is worthy of pursuing toward implementation. At an early stage of an idea development, very simple financial calculations are enough. As the idea grows, a financial proposal will need to be developed and presented. Each serious innovation proposal will require financial numbers, such as ROI, NPV, and EBIT types of justifications. If the idea is related to process improvement, typical metrics such as

cycle time improvement, waste reduction, throughput, and quality improvement benchmarks will be required and must be quantified in the financial savings proposal. A good expert with a strong corporate finance background can be a major boon to help create the business case at every stage of your innovation pipeline.

- **Intellectual property and patent expert (S).** An IP expert is someone who provides strategic inputs related to the firm's IP assets for your innovation projects. This person:
  - Is familiar with and can easily identify new IP opportunities within all your projects. IP can exist in hard technologies, methods, materials, processes, and unique business models.
  - Can help find trademark opportunities to pursue and also help conduct early global patent research to ensure no serious roadblocks exist for an early-stage innovation project.
- **Insights planner (S).** An insights planner is the person who brings unique customer/consumer insight to the team. This person generally conducts (often with help of other team members):
  - Market research
  - Ethnographic research
  - Early product testing
  - Post-product launch surveys
  - Product adaptation surveys
  - Other market-related data and insights

Conclusion

As you begin to build momentum, aligning your innovation structure to the current organizational structure will improve your chances of success immensely. Here are some hints and key questions to keep in mind as you select and finalize the design of your innovation structure:

- Within a company, all business units and functions are designed to increase their specialization and key offerings. Ask how you can help them improve their respective offerings and unique expertise while coordinating their activities to improve product development life cycle and reduce costs at the same time.
- In general, access to technology and new knowledge are two primary elements correlated to a firm's ability to innovate. How will you help each internal organization increase these two factors as quickly as possible?
- In non-product but more service-oriented sectors, unique knowledge about customers, markets, and the supply chain can create huge differentiation in the marketplace. How will you organize the innovation structure so everyone can quickly and easily share their unique knowledge with others?
- Most existing organizational structures are designed to ensure predictability, certainty, and conformity but not necessarily agility. A good innovation structure

should help organizations become more nimble, faster, and adaptive to market changes. Does your new innovation structure increase such competence or not?

If management has done its job well so far, you will begin to find ideas worthy of exploration. In the next chapter, we begin to define the innovation management process required to properly evaluate and push ideas forward in your innovation pipeline.

Note

1. Allan Afuah, *Innovation Management: Strategies, Implementation, and Profits* (New York: Oxford University Press, 2002).

CHAPTER 7

Innovation Management Process

Your innovation management process is the formal series of identifiable inputs, actions, and outputs used to understand the relevance, risks, and value of an idea. If the process is designed well, it will be flexible and scalable to enable rapid evaluation and include all stakeholders in achieving success. The objective of the process is not only to identify new innovative opportunities but also to quickly discard ideas that do not have desired value.

Creating a sustainable value creation system requires organizations to master all aspects of innovation, from idea finding to implementation. Most organizations know they must focus not only on product innovation but also on strategy, process, and delivery innovations. However, no matter which types of innovations are required in your organization, you'll need a rich basket of ideas. No ideas, no new innovations.

Then what?

Every time we work with new clients, finding ideas is not the problem. Doing something about them is the real obstacle. If there are hundreds of ideas in the funnel, which one is the best to pursue? In which order? As a knee-jerk reaction to solving this problem, many organizations will deploy an idea management software system—expecting the system to make everyone more innovative and help build new innovations. It is a good idea but often a bad strategy. For your innovation engine to perform at the maximum output level, idea management systems are required, but only after many of the tasks described in the previous chapters are completed. Implementing a software idea capture system before properly preparing to manage the idea funnel may cause negative branding for the innovation program.

Once you have a senior-level sponsor, an innovation strategy defined, goals for innovation outcomes articulated, implementation plan approved, and a proper organizational structure in place, then you will need an *innovation management process*.

Management of innovation should be part of your business strategy.

In general, innovation outcomes are based on a firm's ability to use its core competence, knowledge, and technologies in a new and unique manner, especially before competitors do. Therefore, your innovation process is heavily affected by experiences with past innovations and based on technologies the organization is already familiar with, at least to some extent.

Innovative companies often use an idea management system. Idea management is the practice of handling ideas in a structured fashion. Its aim is to select the best ideas with the most potential for further development and implementation. If ideas are the raw material for innovation, then idea management is the core of innovation management. The idea management process is not merely the generation of new ideas. It encompasses the generation, collection, development, evaluation, and selection of business ideas.

Therefore, innovation management is the key to keeping your innovation program alive and vibrant. There are three important elements of a good innovation management process:

1. Finding and generating ideas for current or emerging needs
2. Managing the innovation funnel from inception to implementation
3. Implementing or commercializing ideas quickly for a competitive advantage

Finding and Generating Ideas

Great innovations happen when insightful domain experts intersect with relevant enabling knowledge and technology and are thus able to synthesize something new. Doing this requires easy-to-use innovation processes that help every employee participate in innovation activities. Ideas are lying around everywhere in our lives—if we look hard enough.

One way to capitalize on finding the best ideas is to first understand where ideas come from.

Where did the idea of building a fuel injection engine come from? Or the electronic door opener? Or the automatic coffee machine? Or the digital quartz wristwatch? Or the automatic tire air electronic system? Or the mass manufacturing assembly line? Who thought of these great game changers, and where was that idea owner when that particular idea came to his or her consciousness?

Sources of Ideas

Lot of research has been done to prove that best ideas come from people who are highly motivated to solve a problem and are often away from their typical daily routine activities.

William C. Miller, international best-selling author, consultant and speaker on creativity and innovation, and formerly head of Innovation Management at SRI International (Stanford Research Institute) conducted comprehensive research in the late 1990s to look into where good ideas come from.[1] He compiled about a

TABLE 7.1 Sources of Great Ideas

	Internal Source	External Source
Planned: *Formal* Process	(1) Strategic plan, own market research (20%)	(2) Industry studies, consultants (5%)
Unplanned: *Informal* Process	(3) Ad hoc ideas from anyone (30%)	(4) Customers, suppliers, competitors (45%)

Miller, William C., Author of *Flash of Brilliance: Inspiring Creativity Where You Work*, 1999, Perseus Books.

dozen reports and concluded, as shown in Table 7.1, that only 20% of the best ideas (quadrant #1) come from an internal source during a formal setting, such as ideation sessions, strategic planning meetings, internal market research analysis, and formal customer surveys. The least likely source of the best ideas is to hire external specialists (quadrant #2: 5%) for your innovation ideas. Specialists might help you through the process, but it's not likely they have your next big idea.

The second best source of ideas is from quadrant #3 (30%). Often many ideas arise from unplanned and informal internal resources. An example might be when two employees run into each other in a cafeteria line. They begin to discuss individual projects and generate some innovative ideas for one or both parties. One famous example is Dr. Spencer Silver, a scientist at 3M. In 1968 he was attempting to develop a strong adhesive, but accidentally created a "low-tack," reusable, pressure-sensitive adhesive. "Dr. Spencer Silver developed a unique, repositionable adhesive, but the 3M scientist didn't know what to do with his discovery. Then, six years later, a colleague of Dr. Silver, Art Fry, remembered the light adhesive when he was daydreaming about a bookmark that would stay put in his church hymnal. That is how the Post-it® Note was invented as a solution without a problem: The rest is history."[2]

Another great example of quadrant #3 is when Upjohn scientists were testing minoxidil for efficacy in treating high blood pressure and unexpectedly discovered side effects of hair growth. The company took advantage of this occurrence and now markets minoxidil as Rogaine to treat baldness.

The best source for ideas (45%) is quadrant #4, where individuals are engaged in an informal, external setting. An example of this might be when an employee is going home on a train and sees an image of something that generates a new product marketing idea, or when a shop floor manager is at a family gathering on vacation and, while reading a book on the beach, an idea pops up in his head about a brand-new product.

One of the primary reasons quadrant #4 is a lucrative source for ideas is due to many macro issues in the world, including technological discontinuities, regulation, deregulation, globalization, changing customer expectations, macroeconomics, and social or demographics changes. Such macro issues are hard to see on a normal day-to-day basis, but they show up when people are free-thinking—away from all daily, formal settings. A company that promotes a climate that promotes innovation has mastered how to harness such impromptu conversations and fill its *organizational innovation idea bank.*

An astounding 75% of ideas (quadrant #3 and #4) come from unplanned informal occurrences. Consider again the example of the two employees running in to each other in a hallway or in a lunch line, and while sharing each other's work, a new innovation idea emerges. Informal activities are not on your calendar and are often away from your primary job role and responsibilities.

This means that the majority of the very best ideas are being generated *away* from all formal activities, such as meetings, conference rooms, and formal e-mail communications. Shocking? Not really. Your challenge is to implement an innovation management process to find ideas from all four boxes as described in Table 7.1, especially quadrants #3 and #4.

In our experience, many innovation programs often make one critical mistake— to find ideas, they focus only on quadrant #1. The very best global innovators have deliberate innovation management processes to find ideas from all four quadrants.

What if your company does not have a formal R&D or product development department? Where will you find ideas? In 2005, interviews with top-level managers of 21 small and medium-size German businesses in six industries revealed that ideas come from everywhere, not just internal R&D, product development, and marketing departments. In many organizations, most employees have ideas on how to improve their contributions by improving personal productivity or departmental efficiencies. Yes, many may be incremental in nature, but they are latent and valuable. Additionally, if a company has appropriate knowledge and an idea funnel management systems in place, it can resurface old ideas, research, and concepts that were developed in the past and can now serve as sources of innovative ideas.

For smaller organizations who lack R&D budgets, other sources and methods for collecting ideas should be explored (see Figure 7.1). According to the research, customers are the most important source for innovations. For such organizations, the study concluded that due to a lack of personnel and resources they were more likely to pursue external ideas than large companies.

Four Innovation Processes

To help maximize your idea funnel and exploit all four boxes as shown in Figure 7.2, there are four enterprise innovation processes to help find and fill your innovation funnel (this was also highlighted in Chapter 4):

1. Bottom up
2. Top down
3. Outside in
4. Inside in

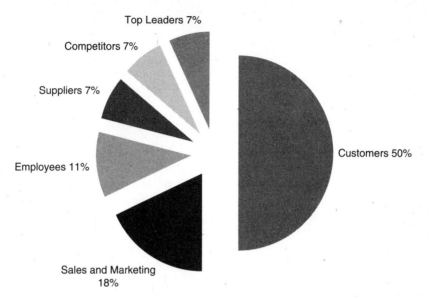

FIGURE 7.1   Where Do Ideas Come From?

Adapted from Birgit Verworn, Christian Lüthje, and Cornelius Herstatt, "Innovations management in kleinen and mittleren Unternehmen," Arbeitspapier Nr. 7, TU Hamburg-Harburg, October 2000. www.econstor.eu/bitstream/10419/55504/1/506805298.pdf.

BOTTOM-UP INNOVATION PROCESS   The bottom-up innovation process encourages the entire organization to participate in idea discovery activities. Generally it involves all types of ideas that can be implemented for internal cost savings as well as market commercialization. If the process is designed correctly, people at all levels can be involved and empowered to find small and radical discoveries.

Example: Air Products   Air Products is a multibillion-dollar, multisector company with over 20,000 employees in about 50 countries.[3] It has offerings across a wide range of industries from food and beverage, health and personal care, to energy,

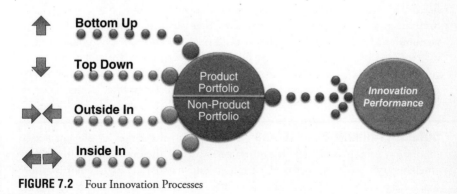

FIGURE 7.2   Four Innovation Processes

transportation, and semiconductors. It provides a unique portfolio of atmospheric gases, process and specialty gases, performance materials, equipment, and services to customers.

For its innovation process, Air Products uses an Innovation College to drive new bottom-up ideas. "Innovation College is part of the enterprise wide Air Products University. They offer roughly 20 courses, with topics ranging from creative thinking to project and intellectual asset management."

All employees are encouraged to attend a variety of courses to encourage creative thinking and to challenge orthodoxies. Air Products also provides mentoring programs for new employees and innovation awards. The company often allows employees to attend meetings and conferences that no one at Air Products attended before and that may be only tangentially related to an employee's job, as long as the employee feels that attendance would benefit Air Products. The college offers two levels of certification: one for anyone completing the basic track and advanced certification for those who are nominated by their managers for more rigorous curriculum. Courses are taught by various internal and external faculty.

TOP-DOWN INNOVATION PROCESS   Top-down strategic innovation platforms (large organizational challenges) are defined by senior leaders. In our experience, there are always three to five such platforms critical to the future of the business. Each platform may contain hundreds of unique business ideas (to keep profits, to enhance profits, or to find completely new profits). By defining these platforms, leaders channel organizational creativity to address specific challenges and opportunities.

Example: Cognizant Technology Solutions   Cognizant is a multibillion-dollar information technology, consulting, and business process outsourcing services company headquartered in the United States and listed on NASDAQ, with more than 150,000 employees worldwide. It has customers across a wide range of industries from financial services, healthcare, manufacturing, and logistics, to retail, hospitality, telecom, information, media, and entertainment.

Cognizant uses a process called Cognizant Capital to help achieve significant breakthroughs to solve a business challenge. It has established a corporate growth office at the enterprise level, headed by a senior vice president. This office is responsible for strategic business opportunities based on internally generated ideas that offer opportunities to build scalable, nonlinear businesses. Often these ideas come from an internal top-down business challenge by the C-level executive. The aim is to identify commercially viable, scalable business opportunities to grow new revenues at a faster rate. Ideas received are evaluated using the structured Cognizant Capital business plan evaluation framework.

OUTSIDE-IN INNOVATION PROCESS   The primary motivation of the outside-in innovation process is to include customers as part of the business and to discover emerging and unknown needs of customers and markets. Using a counterculture discovery process, a funnel of ideas is created based on what customers care about most. The output of this process can be an input to the standard product design and development process you may already have. The key is to identify current and emerging desires of current as well as future customers.

Example: Boston Scientific Corporation Boston Scientific Corporation (BSC), founded in 1979, produces medical supplies used in minimally invasive surgical procedures. The organization has grown through internal R&D efforts and by acquiring more than 30 companies worldwide. It is headquartered in Boston, Massachusetts, area and operates in over 22 global locations with over 28,000 employees worldwide.

With a product portfolio of over 15,000 products, the core competence is in chemical engineering and electronics. Using a variety of outside-in innovation practices and a desire to be one of the major brands for future medical technologies, the organization is pursuing mechanical, electrical, chemical, gene therapy, nanotechnology, and molecular applications. BSC spends approximately 8% to 10% of sales on R&D.

At BSC, the outside-in process is designed for investing into looking beyond the core business needs for innovations. The company calls this the noncore R&D process. By selecting third parties outside the organization to help find unmet needs of the market or other innovation opportunities, BSC can quickly acquire the competence it does not have internally. This allows each business unit manager to keep an eye on external trends and technologies. BSC spends considerable resources to manage these external relationships, which creates investment proposals for business leaders. Once a proposal is given and approved, BSC can choose to develop that opportunity internally or via outside investment. BSC uses these parameters to determine how it should proceed:

- **Cost of internal development.** What is the actual cost over time to develop the opportunity? What is the opportunity cost to existing business? How much internal resources are required to move it forward?
- **Market timing.** Is BSC first to learn about this opportunity before competitors? What is the probability of competitors catching up? Is BSC catching up with competitors?
- **Intellectual property positions.** Does BSC gain clear differentiation? Can it create new IP? Can it acquire a strategic position?
- **Net present value (NPV) analysis**

To strengthen its outside-in portfolio of opportunities, BSC has built relationships with academic institutions, including the University of Minnesota, Stanford University, the California Institute of Technology, Pennsylvania State University, the Corporate Executive Board, and Massachusetts Institute of Technology.

Example: Volvo Co-Creates an SUV with Its Customers Volvo figured out a way to tap into the collective intelligence of consumers to help it develop an SUV.

The Swedish manufacturer of cars, trucks, and buses used co-creation partners for its XC90 NPD project.

Volvo wanted to get deeper in the heads and hearts of its affluent customers. It selected women professionals in California as the co-creation partners. The company felt its traditional market research needed to be complemented with much better insights.

At the first meeting, selected women customers and company leaders explored thoughts, expectations, and opinions about SUVs in general, which would help them in the project's concept development phase. A second meeting was scheduled for about six months later and elicited more focused opinions about the manufacturer's XC90 SUV, which were fed back into its design and development process.

A number of subsequent meetings were held by the senior leaders to discuss further aspects of the project. At the final meeting, two years after the co-creation initiative kicked off, co-creators were given the opportunity to drive the vehicle. In all, the project involved 24 external participants, 16 of whom were present from start to finish.

The insights they provided gave the company a deeper understanding of its target consumer, which helped to influence its decision making and shape the final product that eventually came to the market.

Volvo is one of the first automobile brands committed to the co-creation outside-in innovation process. It is a relatively new trend that is sure to gain momentum, and soon companies will discover that it will be difficult to ignore.

INSIDE-IN INNOVATION PROCESS   In the inside-in innovation method, the goal is to improve intracompany collaboration, learning, and knowledge sharing. Most large enterprises are weakest in this method. The goal is to break down the internal silos through structured facilitation and cross-pollination among technical and nontechnical staff to lead to new innovations.

As mentioned earlier, most organizations have many ideas; one problem is executing some of them. Another problem is that those ideas are mostly incremental. Very few ideas are transformative in nature because people can only innovate based on their field of knowledge and experiences.

Many organizations lack the ability to systematically tap into the vast knowledge pool of their entire organization in a deliberate manner.

Example: India's IT Industry   For example, India's software outsourcing giants, such as Cognizant, Infosys, HCL, Tata Consulting, and Wipro have mastered the skill of how to deliver software solutions using a global delivery method—one of the best innovations in the last 20 years exported by India. The core business for these companies is software delivery or business process services leveraging the best global talent and very efficient technology platforms.

Cognizant, mentioned earlier, has instituted a venture capital model within the company under which employees are encouraged to suggest innovative business ideas. The company follows a distributed model of innovation where every employee is encouraged to innovate. The approach to innovation, which Cognizant calls managed innovation, is a two-pronged model for innovation—a centralized model with innovation clusters in every key industry practice, coupled with a distributed model of encouraging every employee to innovate for the benefit of customers.

Cognizant builds inside-in innovations by leveraging the knowledge of workers across various vertical business units. It frequently conducts "Build 24*2," its version of popular industrywide hackathon format software marathons that bring a variety of employees together for 48 hours to work on a problem. Each developer joins a team. Each team is given mentors as required. Teams compete against each other to deliver a clever and efficient software solution to a prescribed business challenge that might benefit a large set of customers in a sector.

Hackathons enable the very best talented professionals not only to showcase their skills and knowledge but also to quickly disseminate them to others. The result is an immediate increase in the quality of technical and business knowledge, achieved by each team member learning from one another. The winning team gets exciting awards. Senior officers of the company are the judges. By deploying this type of inside-in competition, the young technical geniuses can fast-track their careers as well.

Even teams that lose still win. Every team is able to bring back ideas, lessons, and best practices from other teams immediately into their respective customer areas. Therefore, ultimately, the customers win.

Size of Ideas

As you find ideas and begin to manage them, note that big bang radical innovation ideas are not always the best ones to pursue. Incremental ideas are most easily implemented and may be more profitable to pursue. The competitive advantage they provide is often not easily copied by competitors, and the implementation risks are generally low.

In their 2004 study, Robinson and Schroeder identified numerous examples of organizations worldwide that have cut costs and generated profits from seemingly small ideas.[4] Their study also established links among the number of ideas submitted per employee, the implementation rate for ideas, and the sales growth and profitability of a company. They cited numerous companies around the world with high submission rates and extraordinary profits. Those companies have average annual idea submissions per employee ranging from 25 to 110.

Another researcher, Jeffrey Baumgartner, cited Toyota as an example of a company that has mastered the skills on finding, collecting, and organizing ideas well.[5] As a part of its innovation strategy, Toyota conducts big open office meetings at least twice annually, during which time employees and managers reexamine the processes and methods of their functional areas. These meetings have produced major cost savings based on simple suggestions. Furthermore, every employee of the company is empowered and obligated by the strategy of kaizen to continually improve his or her work and the workplace. Toyota has received over one million improvement suggestions per year since the 1970s. Employees submit ideas through a formal process for evaluation; if it is feasible, it is implemented. The company has an 80% implementation rate for employee ideas. Employees who submit ideas receive recognition, such as a certificate or story in the company newsletter and small nonmonetary rewards.

Idea Finding Conclusion

Each process is designed to achieve specific outcomes. All four innovation processes are not needed to begin your innovation rollout. However, to be a world-class innovator, all four processes ultimately need to be implemented across the entire organization.

These processes will yield the best and the largest idea bank and therefore increase the probability of innovation success. Implementing one or all of these four processes will yield plenty of ideas worthy of execution. As the process matures, you will want to leverage automation, such as idea portal and idea management software solutions.

Managing the Innovation Funnel

Once you have ideas coming in, you need to put them in what we call an *idea bank*. The idea bank has to be organized to ensure optimum execution results—we call this the innovation funnel process.

The innovation funnel, as shown in Figure 7.3, is a process with a formal series of identifiable inputs, actions, and outputs that are used to understand the relevance, risks, and value of an idea as it progresses toward maturity. The idea funnel process should be flexible and scalable to enable rapid evaluation and should include appropriate stakeholders for stage gate approvals. The goal is not only to identify new innovative opportunities but also to quickly discard ideas that do not have sustainable value.

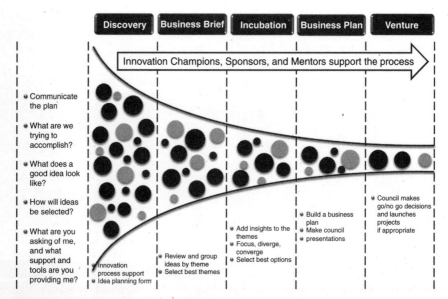

FIGURE 7.3   Example of an Innovation Funnel

TABLE 7.2 Innovation Management Terminologies

Term	Description
Idea owner	The idea initiator (an individual or a team)
Gate	Gates are go/no go decision points. Depending on the gate criteria, an idea is advanced by an individual or by a review team in a formal meeting. Typically, the first few gates are owned by innovation program champion or new business development group members, and the last few gates are managed by the business unit head or the CEO/managing director. Each idea has to face a gate at the end of every stage of the process.
Filter	Filters are the criteria on which a project is evaluated at every gate, after which the go/no go decision for the project is determined. A filter may have various parameters. For example, a financial attractiveness filter may include parameters like return on investment (ROI), net present value (NPV), internal rate of return (IRR), earnings before interest, taxes, depreciation, and amortization (EBITDA), return on capital employed (ROCE), top-line revenue, capital investment, or payback period.
Filtration process	The filtration process entails the review of the idea, concept, business case, and/or business plan generated at designated forums and meetings. This process uses the filters to determine if a project should clear the gates or not.
Categorization	Categorization involves scoring ideas, concepts, or the business case at the respective stages of the innovation funnel process and division into priority buckets: A, B, or C.
Red parameters	Red parameters are triggered when a filtration process raises potentially problematic issues that need to be studied in greater detail to determine if the project should be approved for the next stage or discontinued. By definition, a red parameter falls below the cutoff score for an individual filter during the filtration scoring at formal review meetings.

Each business unit may need its own innovation funnel besides the one at the enterprise level. Table 7.2 contains some typical terms used to manage an innovation funnel.

Organizing Ideas

An idea is a unique proposition that goes through multiple state changes. Examples of state status are shown in Table 7.3.

TABLE 7.3 Innovation Management Terminology

Idea State Status	Description
New	New idea that has not yet been analyzed
Active	Under consideration
Approved	Approved by innovation council for full implementation
Pilot	Under consideration—being piloted
Reject	Considered and rejected
Duplicate	Duplicate idea
Archived	Idea that is not relevant today

All ideas should be submitted and classified with consistent criteria. This will allow easy validation, documentation compliance, and review by the appropriate innovation governance body. Classification should be based on multiple attributes. Examples of attributes and suggested options are shown in Table 7.4.

In implementing your own innovation funnel, you'll want to expand on this template to add more fields and remove irrelevant items.

TABLE 7.4 Example of Idea Classification Template

Attributes	Options
Title	
Short description	
Detailed description	
Idea owner/submitter's name	
Business unit/department/area	
Alignment to strategy (How does this idea help our overall strategy?)	Enable growth
	Enhance reputation
	Common platforms
	Provide business intelligence
	Security and compliance
	Better workplace
	Improve financial returns
	Improve customer experience
	Customer-centric offerings
	Automation
	Supply chain

TABLE 7.4 *(Continued)*

Impact (What impact do you expect from this idea?)	Financial impact
	Operating efficiency
	External customer impact
	Other
Scalability (Who can benefit from this idea internally?)	Product
	Department
	Division
	Corporate/Home office
	Total company

Selecting Ideas to Pursue

Once ideas are submitted, a series of reviews and analyses follows. Each review is sometimes referred to as a *stage gate*: Inbound ideas are reviewed against specific predefined rules and approval criteria before they are promoted to the next gate. Typically, each gate is increasingly more challenging as it travels through the innovation funnel.

Ideas are first verified to see if they align with one or more of the organization's business strategies. If the idea does not align, it is archived. Table 7.5 is an example of a stage-gate design template with rules and review process.

TABLE 7.5 Example of a Stage-Gate Process Template

Gate Name	Rules	Reviewer
Gate 1: Discovery	Strategic alignment: All ideas are scored and queued; if rejected, the idea owners are informed about the decision and thanked for their participation in the process.	Innovation champion (certified innovation consultant), division head, or appointed innovation committee at the division level
Gate 2: Business brief	Idea opportunity and relevance: Review of financial risk, technical feasibility and risk, customer importance and satisfaction, employee engagement opportunity, and complexity factor.	Division head or appointed innovation committee at the division level
Gate 3: Incubation	Incubation: High-priority opportunity worth piloting and field testing; has potential to create significant value for customer, employees, or the supply chain	Innovation council
Gate 4: Business plan	Execution: Develop business plan that includes technical assessment, financial assessment, and overall business assessment.	Innovation team, Innovation council chair, other business unit stakeholders
Gate 5: Venture	Implementation: Move forward with solution development, deployment, and realization of expected outcomes.	Business unit head/line executive/CEO

DESIGNING GATE FILTERS   For each funnel, there is a review board. Often this review board is a cross-functional product development team, a business technology committee, or a senior innovation council of business unit heads and external members. This review board should determine specific evaluation filters that will be used for each gate to ensure consistency in the review process by all stakeholders. Each idea has to pass the filters for it to move down the funnel.

Example of Gate 1 Filters: Discovery

1.1 Alignment with company values: (Yes or No)
1.2 Attractiveness
  - Top-line potential (for next five years)
  - Growth potential
  - Access to strategic assets
1.3 Financials (Estimates from competition, industry analysis)
  - EBITDA
  - Market capitalization
1.4 Industry leadership
  - Degree of competition
  - Leadership potential by revenue or profitability

The ideas can be scored on a scale of 1 to 5 on each filter. Each idea can be categorized into four priority categories:

  - Bucket A ideas get a clear go ahead to the next stage.
  - Bucket B ideas are segregated for studying red parameters at gate 1. They are either approved as Bucket A or discontinued as Bucket C at the next board meeting, after studying the red parameters.
  - Bucket C ideas do not clear the filters at gate 1. They are documented and revisited.
  - Bucket D ideas do not clear the filters at gate 1. They are discontinued and documented.

Example of Gate 2 Filters: Business Brief

Using the innovation funnel example in Figure 7.3, the project team is ready to present a high-level business brief. A practical study should be completed that validates financial, market, and technical elements in greater detail. Here are some examples of additional filters that can be used for gate 2:

2.1 Attractiveness
  - Top-line potential (for next five years)
  - Growth potential
  - Access to strategic assets
  - Commercial assumptions (low differentiator to highly unique))

- Legal regulations
- Leverage: Synergies with core organizational competencies

2.2 Financials (estimates from competition, industry analysis)
- EBITDA
- Market capitalization
- ROCE
- Payback period

2.3 Industry leadership
- Degree of competition
- Leadership potential by revenue or profitability
- Ability to overcome barriers to entry

Example of Gate 3 Filters: Incubation   Using the innovation funnel example in Figure 7.3, the project team is ready to present a high-level business brief. A practical study should be completed that validates financial, market, and technical elements in greater detail. Here are some examples of additional filters that can be used for gate 3:

3.1 Attractiveness
- Top-line potential (for next five years)
- Growth potential
- Access to strategic assets
- Commercial assumptions (low differentiator to highly unique)
- Legal regulations
- Leverage: Synergies with core organizational competencies
- Risk analysis

3.2 Financials (estimates from competition, industry analysis)
- EBITDA
- Market capitalization
- ROCE
- Payback period
- NPV/IRR
- Capital investment

3.3 Industry leadership
- Degree of competition
- Leadership potential by revenue or profitability
- Ability to overcome barriers to entry
- Sustainability
- Competitive differentiation

ALTERNATE FILTERING APPROACH   An alternate approach can be to evaluate each idea through three detailed assessments: technical, financial, and business impact. Each gate may look at all three components using a variety of elements in each category as shown next.

Technical Assessment Technical assessment includes assessing the technical feasibility for implementing the idea. This will include analysis of one or more of the following areas:

- Assumptions and dependencies
- High-level solution description
- Functionality
- Hardware and software requirements
- Contextual requirements (government compliance, regulation compliance, etc.)
- Security
- Scalability
- Usability
- Quality
- Product(s)/service(s) impacted
- Organizational capability
- Maintenance
- Technical risks

Financial Assessment Financial assessment includes assessing the financial feasibility for implementing the idea. This can include analysis of one or more of the following areas:

- Assumptions and dependencies
- Implementation costs or investments required
- Three-year, five-year, and ten-year cost structure
- NPV and IRR of the idea (investment) based on the expected life of the idea.
- ROI
- Financial risks
- Amount of investment allowed before next review

Business Assessment Business assessment includes assessing the relevancy and importance of the idea from a business perspective. This will include analysis of one or more of the following areas:

- Assumptions and dependencies
- SWOT analysis
- Market analysis
- Focus group studies
- Marketing plan
- Business plan
- Impact on existing business
- Business risks

In some cases, the assessment team may have to collaborate with suppliers and partners. For some, additional funding may be required. Examples may include funding pilots, conducting further research, or engaging external consultants for in-depth analysis. Such funding requirements should be identified and justified to the Innovation Council.

Building a Business Brief (Gate 2)

A business brief is a mini–business plan with just enough details for senior leaders to get excited about your idea. Business briefs can build momentum—a very important requirement when the idea is somewhat new and novel.

This section presents a ten-step business brief framework you can use to sell your idea to the review board and other key decision makers. It is best to use this framework as a thinking tool and a guide to ensure you have covered all the relevant items required to make a strong impression regarding your new venture.

Do you need to answer each question in detail? The questions are guides to help you thoroughly research all aspects of your idea. Depending on the idea, its viability, the current business, the context, and the makeup of the review board, you will need to determine which questions should be answered and which ones can wait until later. Remember to anticipate the concerns that others will raise and, where applicable, try to address them ahead of time in your presentation.

Ideally, certified intrapreneurs (see Chapter 8) and mentors can be used to provide assistance.

TEN-STEP BUSINESS BRIEF FRAMEWORK

1. **Executive summary.** This short description of the product and service you are proposing includes a profile of the customer/segment. What basic problem are you solving for the customer? Be specific about why this product is in high demand. Is this a current customer problem, or is it an emerging one for them? Do customers want it solved? How do you know?
   - How will customers use this product or service?
   - What benefits will they derive from it?
   - Why will they use this solution?
   - What are the markets for your solutions: Internal? External?
   - What other insights do you have that support this idea?
   - How will your organization benefit from this?
   - Describe any elements of uniqueness, intellectual property, or patent benefits that can be derived now or in future. This can create a compelling start for your presentation.

   For best results, describe the idea, the need, and the solution in a story format.

2. **Proposed solution.** Describe the product or service and how you envision its use. To ensure clarity, test your description with several people who don't know your business or the associated idea.

   As you present it to the review board, use pictures, graphics, collages, technical diagrams, and drawings to describe it—these are worth 1,000 words. The goal is to emotionally connect the audience with your idea. Use analogies and metaphors to further clarify your point. If it makes sense, showing a working model is better than describing it.

You don't need to go into technical detail specifications in this section. Detailed design strategies and product specifications should appear as handouts or as part of the appendix. Here you should:

- Describe the basic and unique features of your solution.
- Provide basic performance specifications (including any compliance, regulatory, and legal elements).
- Give an overview of the technology and design being proposed.
- Explain how you will deliver this solution. What is the process?
- Show how your innovation will provide competitive advantage or industry positioning.
- Demonstrate how this idea can help other parts of the business, products, and services in the current portfolio.

3. **Growth path.** If your idea will take multiple years to fully commercialize, describe the growth and migration roadmap. This is especially true if you are creating a new market. Describe how to go from version 1.0 of the solution you are proposing to version 3.0.

- How far is the future?
- How will your solution evolve over time, and what parameters will influence feature changes to your solution?
- What alternative direction paths can your solution pursue?
- Which direction path is the best to pursue? Why?

4. **Market potential.** Describe the markets, geography, and demographics you will serve. Define each segment you will serve and what will happen to each segment over the next few years— is it growing, declining, merging?

- For new markets, how will you access these new markets for your solution?
- What existing market will you serve?
- How will you penetrate the targeted markets? Do you need a partner or a strategic alliance to do so? Who would that be?
- Within each market, who are the specific target customers/segments?
- How will you reach the target customer: via the current distribution method or a new one?
- How will you capture the targeted segments? How will you prevent the competition from catching up?
- How will you price the product, and why?
- How will you roll-out and launch the offering into the various segments identified?

5. **Strategic fit.** Corporate entrepreneurs must balance their ideas between helping to grow the business and minimizing potential conflicts. In this part of the presentation, you should mention all the areas of the company you will use to gain support and also any particular internal service you will provide. The more synergy you create in your business brief, the stronger the rationale will be for keeping your idea and generating momentum.

- What will define key winning formula in this space?
- Who internally benefits and how?
- How will this make us more competitive against the traditional players as well as position us for new unknown entrants (such as what Apple did to Sony's market)?
- What new competencies will our organization gain because of this idea offering? How difficult will it be for competitors to catch up?
- How will current (internal and external) competitors respond to your new offering in the market?
- What will it take to acquire the new competencies required for your new solution offering to be successful? Buy? Build? How long will it take? Do competitors already have it? How can we create a roadblock for them?
- How can we become the pioneer in this area? Is it possible to lock in the market by creating a licensing model?

6. **Brand fit.** In today's unforgiving business climate, building brand equity is crucial to long-term success. World-class innovators must ensure the new offerings support the build of the current brand and do not confuse the customers.
   - How does this new offering fit with the current brand? How does the new offering support it? How does it extend the brand value?
   - With this new offering, which brand drivers are leveraged the most:
     - Product performance?
     - Quality of service?
     - Ease of purchase and delivery experience?
     - Loyalty and relationship?
     - Communication and access?
     - Social and sharing aspects?

7. **Economic engine.** The fundamental question one must ask is: How does this venture generate profits? Most idea owners do not have the financial discipline required to put together this part of the presentation. We strongly advise you to add a finance person to your team immediately. This person should have experience with assembling budgets and financial reports for senior management. Management normally does not look at all the numbers. It relies on the finance person and controllers to report major variances between planned and actual. Being an intrapreneur, your project will surely have large variances. Without a finance person on your team, the finance department could make your life miserable. Major questions that must be addressed in this section are:
   - What are the major revenue and cost drivers? How sensitive are the venture economics to each of these drivers?
   - How does money flow in this model?
   - What investments are required to make this work? What is the time frame?
   - What does the return on these investments look like?
   - What does a detailed pro forma look like?
   - What are key drivers that can significantly alter the financial plan?

- What do the best- and worst-case projections look like?
- What are tax implications?
- Are there government rebates or low-cost loans available for this venture?
- What are ways to maximize ROI and reduce risk?

Most of the senior managers are paying attention to a few critical numbers all the time. Include some of these in your presentation to help improve your chances of success:

- Annual sales volume
- Annual sales growth
- Return on sales
- Return on capital invested
- Gross profit
- Pretax profit
- Payback
- Inventory turns
- Working capital

Find a finance person who knows which numbers matter to the review board and the decision makers, and learn how they are calculated. Often, for each metric, there are thresholds and conditions which are considered safe. For example, "Payback in 18 months" or "22% pretax return on capital invested" or "12 inventory turns per year."

8. **Risk factors.** Not all companies have a risk factor section for new entrepreneurial plans. If that is the case at your organization, you can eliminate this section. But prepare it for yourself. After all, your career is at stake.

   The main task in this section is to identify what might go wrong. Start with listing possible threats, barriers, obstacles, and then prioritize by highest negative impact—most problematic. Risks can lie in various aspects—markets, technical, people, financial, patent, partnerships, and so on.

   Describe how you plan to reduce the exposure to these risks. Can you create useful intellectual property from this venture to help create long-term value? Can you create strategic alliances to help reduce risk?

9. **Operation plan.** In this section, describe all the steps required to market the product or deliver the service. Where will you run into problems? How many person-hours will it take to complete each step? Pick two or three different volume levels to help create some forecasts.

   For each volume and proposed growth migration plan, describe the capital equipment required. Generally, for a service offering, there is very little capital requirements, unless you are in the transportation business and you need cars or trucks. Try to prove your offering with as little capital as possible.

   The operation plan should include a facilities plan showing how much space you need and how you will use it. It should also include rent and utilities, office supplies, administrative support expenses, postage, insurance, benefits, and professional services, such as legal, accounting, and bookkeeping.

Also describe if you will make internally or buy from outside. Sometimes internal sourcing and manufacturing can delay and even derail your new venture. There can be enormous pressure to use internal resource, but often internal facilities, processes, and resources are not adequately set up to support short runs and rapid delivery times. Be very clear on how you should produce the offering for success.

Related to quality and manufacturing, have clear goals you are willing to pursue. What will be your reject rate? Customer complaint rate? Rework? Customer satisfaction value? Supplier quality? Process quality? Employee satisfaction rate? Machine down time? Factory throughput rate? Plant profitability?

10. **90-day experiment plan.** This is the final and often the most important section of your presentation. The most effective innovation project teams are action oriented and focused on the goal throughout the idea's life cycle. Ninety-day plans help keep team members focused.

From the review board's point of view, a short cycle time derisks overall investment decisions, especially if the venture has a long-term time horizon.

In the 90-day experiment plan, you should definitely cover two areas:
- What do you need from the review board?
- What will you deliver in the next 90 days if the board gives you what you are asking for?

Additionally, you should address these items in your presentations:
- What will you validate in 90 days?
- What types of tests and pilots will you complete?
- What internal or external resources will you need?
- What key interdependencies will you manage to ensure you can complete the 90-day plan?
- How much investment do you need for the next 90 days?
- What could possibly go wrong? And how will you resolve it?
- What guidance and involvement do you need from the review board member(s), if any?

A business brief is a major tool used to guide the direction of your proposal; it also is the primary document in managing the idea as it moves from conceptual stage to implementation in the innovation funnel. A business brief is not just a mechanical activity of writing up sections on a checklist, outline, or a PowerPoint presentation. Ideally, your business brief is a living document of your idea. Each of the ten parts is internally consistent and connected, and the parts reinforce one another. This means that a change in one part of the document activates other changes throughout the document, resulting in many other changes, adjustments, and improvements.

Use the ten-step business brief from the start of your innovation implementation process to gather information and conduct analysis. Then continue use it to fill in the projections, numbers, forecasts, and overall decisions based on the team's progress. It provides a continuous platform for thinking and expanding your idea.

The clearer your business brief, the more powerful it becomes for continuous evaluation and access to greater support from senior executives.

Managing the Innovation Funnel Conclusion

The innovation funnel is an iterative process of documentation, analysis, and stage-gate approvals designed to solicit broad idea generation and methodically assess and advance the most worthy ideas. The stage-gate mechanism ensures that appropriate reviews are conducted at the appropriate time; the idea is not only to weed out ideas that don't align with company objectives and ROI expectations but also to purposefully advance and resource innovative ideas. Developing such a process that works for your environment is a matter of understanding the company's strategic objectives, applying a proven innovation funnel process, and ensuring review boards and management teams are trained in the art and science of incubating innovation organization wide.

Implementing or Commercializing Ideas

There can be hundreds of ideas. How does the innovation council select which ideas to move forward and which ones to postpone or terminate? Part of the answer was given in an earlier section in the discussions of filters for each gate. Another important dimension of selecting ideas is related to the overall innovation investment strategy and risk tolerance as defined by the senior leaders.

Investment Strategy

In the world of investments, financial advisors often recommend a portfolio approach to asset management by carefully allocating investments among various types of assets (stocks, bonds, foreign exchange). By diversifying, investors can reduce risk without reducing their returns.

Senior executives should use a similar approach for innovation. While small business entrepreneurs generally use one core innovative offering to establish their future, intrapreneurs and corporate innovators should use a balance of all types of innovations, from incremental to breakthrough.

Table 7.6 shows how executives within your firm can allocate a portion of innovation resources to each type of innovation (Type 1, 2, or 3) depending on the chosen innovation risk strategy.

As a senior executive in charge of innovation, as you plan for appropriate strategy, recognize that a low-risk strategy approach is highly vulnerable if your best competitor has chosen a radical innovation strategy. Paradoxically, when it comes to innovation, low-risk policies ultimately may incur the highest risk of all—as we have seen between Sony and Apple, or Blockbuster and Netflix, or Microsoft and Google.

TABLE 7.6 Innovation Portfolio Strategy

Type of Strategy	Box 1 Innovations (Keep Profits) Focus is on sustaining and protecting the current business and managing the competition	Box 2 Innovations (Enhance Profits) Focus is on incremental innovations and careful expansion into adjacencies	Box 3 Innovations (Find New Profits) Focus is on radical innovations, outthinking competition, and exploring unfamiliar business territories
Low risk	25%	65%	10%
Medium risk	20%	55%	25%
High risk	15%	35%	50%

Nature of Control

As shown in the innovation process example in Figure 7.3, some ideas will graduate from 90-day experiment plans and the business brief to the business plan and venturing stages. Special attention must be given to an idea at this stage. The review board must be very careful so the project team's hard work doesn't get stuck and the team doesn't become dejected. We often see lot of good work go to waste during this phase; ultimately senior leadership loses hope over the entire innovation management process. Typically two things happen at this stage:

1. Innovation teams are tired and afraid. These teams have been slogging extra time into the project for as much as 6 or 12 months, in addition to their day job. The exciting part of developing the idea into a tangible solution that senior leaders are willing to support is finished. For some team members, the high of working on an exciting innovative project, taking the idea and developing it, was fun. But since it was not their own idea, they are ready to work on the next thing. Some prefer to remain a team member but are not able to negotiate time for this project with their direct supervisor.

   Most important, depending on the culture of the firm, many team members do not want to work the execution phase of the project for fear of failure. In other words, they are afraid to stay with the idea, knowing it may not deliver intended objectives and, if it does not, they may not be able to return to their current job.

2. The innovation review board decided to implement the project using standard control systems moving forward.

   Control systems are the formal and informal mechanisms that ensure managers are using all obtained resources most effectively and efficiently in the execution and delivery of the firm's objectives. Controls are intended to protect against the possibility that some people may do something against the organizational norms or fail to do something they should do.

Controls are required and vital to each organization. Without controls, chaos can occur, and it would be impossible to know what is going on. Without controls, it would be difficult to deliver consistent service to customers, to be competitive, to distinguish high from low performers, or to find methods to continually improve operational success.

Unfortunately, control systems often create unintended consequences, such as lack of trust among team members, slow down decision making, and emphasis on being compliant with a control rule. Such practices often forces them to lose sight of project objectives.

In our experience, control efforts are implemented to achieve risk reduction, reduce uncertainty, deliver higher efficiencies, and promote conformity across all coworkers. Sadly, these types of desires and outcomes tend to be inconsistent with corporate innovation and intrapreneurship.

Therefore, as you design the controls for managing the innovation funnel and the decisions to take ideas forward, the review board must answer two important questions:

1. What is our concept of control in this company?
2. What control philosophy should we employ for intrapreneurial projects and project teams?

DELIBERATE DECISIONS FOR IDEA TEAMS   Review boards should carefully deliberate on this question: How will our decisions to approve or deny ideas presented by innovation teams make us become more entrepreneurial as a firm?

The answer lies in understanding characteristics of an entrepreneurial company culture and the underlying control systems that either promote or inhibit innovative behaviors among employees at all levels. In our experience, an intrapreneurial environment appears to be consistent with at least five major attributes within supportive control systems:

1. **Risk tolerance.** A greater degree of empowerment and autonomy is promoted through low organizational rigidity across various departments and less delineation about areas of responsibility.
2. **Open-minded efficiency.** There are very few formal processes and rigidity about planning for the future, budgeting mechanics are more flexible in accommodating new unplanned opportunities as they emerge, and, most important, organizational end goals are emphasized rather than the means.
3. **Less formality.** An allowance for special discretion is deliberately built into cost controls and budgeting, performance is not always measured at a fixed schedule, and success measures include both financial and nonfinancial indicators. Creating budget detours can very effectively overcome internal innovation stagnation.

4. **Harmonized goal setting.** In a climate that successfully supports innovation, often social and personal controls receive heavier weight than procedural controls designed to create goal alignment and attainment. In other words, goal achievement is important but not at the cost of personal and social relationships.

5. **Freedom for job flexibility.** In intrapreneurial cultures, employees are empowered to make decisions in their personal work with an attitude of whatever it takes to complete their projects—with proper discretion and empathy for all concerned. Control systems focus on intentions and outcomes and less on written norms and rules.

Therefore, the leadership teams, review boards, and direct supervisors who support innovation teams must be very careful to make sure proper support is given to each team once the idea is ready to graduate from the innovation funnel process and into a new business venture.

Often it is essential that innovation sponsors provide direct and appropriate involvement in the first few projects ready for implementation.

FOUR RESOURCING STRATEGIES FOR FASTER INCUBATION PERIODS A primary challenge faced by every intrapreneurial team and the supporting sponsor is the lack of resources to incubate their ideas fast enough while influencing all stakeholders during the idea development process.

Most firms are replete with countless stories of resourceful lobbying and associated politics. The best venture managers are fluid when it comes to hijacking resources, material, equipment, and extra manufacturing capacity. They are also great at concealing development activities and are flawless in daily deal making to access resources they need for their projects. What is especially very unique about these exceptional innovators is their ability to do all of that with co-optation, not competition.

In 1990, authors Jennifer A. Starr and Ian C. MacMillan identified four strategies employed by these creative corporate entrepreneurs.[6] They are:

1. **Borrowing,** or using resources that will be returned in a timely basis.
2. **Begging,** or acquiring resources by tapping into the goodwill of the resource owners. It is amazing what you can gain by simply honestly begging.
3. **Scavenging,** or securing unused or underused resources for better purposes. Sometimes the resource owner actually welcomes giving up such resources. An example of this might be obsolete inventory, idle equipment, or underutilized staff members.
4. **Amplifying,** or finding a way to achieve a far greater outcome of an asset than the original asset owner believes possible.

These four strategies allow innovation champions and idea teams to secure resources at much lower cost. These strategies provide a number of benefits:

- Underutilized company resources are used.
- Ideas get incubated faster.
- The overall cost of a start-up is reduced.
- The risk of a start-up is reduced due to lower initial investments.

Innovation Scorecard

As stated in Chapter 4, make sure you have defined your innovation scorecard by now. At this time, you will need it to ensure everything you commit to regarding innovation sticks within the organizational walls.

The innovation scorecard and relevant metrics should be published on a monthly basis. At the beginning, only a handful of people at the tip might pay attention to it. But over period of time, the executives will review it more often to help you gain momentum for your innovation program.

Conclusion

Innovation will not happen without an innovation management process from day 1. This means proper management involvement will be needed to support iTeams to find and test their ideas quickly. Here are specific questions you should answer about your innovation management process to ensure maximum clarity and design of your idea generation and innovation management processes:

1. How easy is it for anyone in the company to test their ideas without being afraid to fail?
2. How many ideas are in your idea bank and at each stage of development?
3. How rich is the idea bank—with small continuous improvement ideas, incremental profit generation ideas, or radical new profit ideas?
4. What is the percentage of employees involved in various innovation program activities?
5. How many certified intrapreneurs do you have who can help others bring their ideas forward all the way to implementation or venturing?
6. What is your firm's innovation investment strategy?
7. How easy is it for teams to find resources to get their ideas tested?

Notes

1. William C. Miller, *Flash of Brilliance: Inspiring Creativity Where You Work* (New York: HarperCollins, 1999).
2. www.post-it.com/wps/portal/3M/en_US/Post_It/Global/About/?WT .mc_id=www.3m.com/us/office/postit/pastpresent/
3. "Report: Successfully Embedding Innovation," APQC Publications, 2007.
4. Alan G. Robinson and Dean M. Schroeder, "Ideas Are Free," 2004. www.ideasarefree.com/iaf.pdf
5. Jeffrey Baumgartner, "Big and Little Innovation," Report 103, April 27, 2004. www.jpb.com/report103/archive.php?issue_no=20040427
6. Jennifer A. Starr and Ian C. MacMillan, "Resources Co-Optation via Social Contracting: Resource Acquisition Strategies for New Ventures," *Strategic Management Journal* 11 (Summer 1990): 79–92.

CHAPTER 8

Building Intrapreneurs

Innovations occur when great corporate innovators generate real wealth, not just great ideas. Leaders who overutilize resources and underdeliver value cannot be called real innovators. Innovation requires diversity in ability and competence of your people. Pair them together as often as you can, and they will drive growth and performance. Create a pool of intrapreneurs as a certified group of growth resources in every part of your business.

In this chapter, we dive deeper into the most important aspect of your innovation program—the importance of finding and building real intrapreneurs across your firm.

So far we have looked at key organizational components to build your firm's innovation engine. Systematically, we have made a case for creating a culture of innovation across your organization and proposed how to create urgency for innovation, build an innovation strategy, create an innovation roadmap, and maintain momentum to gain support from all key stakeholders in the company. I have also introduced a framework for how to manage the entire innovation program, specifically, the innovation management process—to help find ideas, evaluate them, select the best ones, and properly guide them toward successful implementation while reducing risk of failure.

In Chapter 4, we briefly touched on the topic of intrapreneurs, their importance in today's global business environment, and the strategic value of intrapreneurship as a core organizational competency. [1] We also mentioned that intrapreneurs are well suited to transform an organization more quickly and effectively because they are naturally wired differently and exhibit some critical attributes. They are highly self-motivated, free thinkers, and masters at navigating around the bureaucratic and political inertia of most large companies.

Intrapreneurship allows companies to grow business, find and retain talent, and compete with peer companies. Intrapreneurship has been the key to excite and motivate the creation of innovative products, processes, services, and partnerships for companies like Procter & Gamble, Raytheon, 3M, Nokia, Tata, and Google.

Innovations arise from great ideas and persistent problem solvers. The very best innovators are called intrapreneurs, a term coined in 1986 by Gifford Pinchot III to describe these exceptional entrepreneurs working inside the corporations. Many intrapreneurs could easily start their own businesses.

The good news is that you already have some natural intrapreneurs in your company. Some you know about, but most are hiding. An important task is to find these talented individuals and unleash their creativity with a supporting environment, as described in earlier chapters.

Intrapreneurs are not always your top talent or the rebels or mavericks. But they are unique and are certainly the opposite of organization men. When you find them, support them correctly, and magic *will* occur.

In this chapter, we address these important questions concerning building a bench of intrapreneurs—your fuel for growth:

1. What is the definition of a corporate intrapreneur?
2. How does one become a successful intrapreneur?
3. How do you find intrapreneurs within and outside your company?
4. What are methods and tactics to develop intrapreneurs and intrapreneurial teams?
5. What are the HR implications for nurturing intrapreneurs?

In our informal research, teaching executive MBA students, speaking at conferences, and working with our global clients, we have surveyed thousands of executives over the last two decades. Of all we surveyed, only six executives identified themselves as being idea poor. Ask any CEO of a public company and the same will be true. Finding ideas is not the problem. The real challenges firms face have to do with selecting the best ideas, testing them quickly, executing them flawlessly, and getting their ideas to spread. This is a crucial point.

To build your innovation engine, your firm must excel at operationalizing ideas from your energized people who are willing to do everything in their power to fight off every internal resistance without creating chaos—these are your intrapreneurs.

Intrapreneurship and Intrapreneurs

Intrapreneurship, a word shortened from the term intra-corporate entrepreneurship, refers to the entrepreneurial activities of employees within the boundaries and auspices of a larger organization. A *Harvard Management Update* article describes intrapreneurship as "bottom-up, off-the-beaten-track business building, spearheaded by people who were working as line managers or employees." A popular example of intrapreneurship is Skunk Works, the alias for Lockheed Martin's advanced development program, where a group of engineers step outside the bureaucratic environment of the corporation to develop successful and innovative products.

In many decentralized organizations, CEOs feel that they have done their part by giving strategic and operational autonomy to each line of business and then leave the rest up to them. In theory, that works if the goal of the business is to streamline, drive operational efficiencies, create certainty, reduce risk, and keep everything status quo. Most management and control systems, as we discussed in Chapter 7, are designed to dumb down decision making and restrict operational freedom.

On one hand the CEOs provide autonomy but also enforce corporate control systems (see Chapter 7) on the business units. This forces business unit barons to comply with the CEO and, in turn, block hands-on innovation efforts by their very own intrapreneurs.

For employees, one of the major benefits of intrapreneurship is the freedom to work independently (or on a team) on tasks defined by the group but still aligned to the needs of the organization.

In a firm with 5,000 employees, there are at least 200 natural innovators, and of these at least 25 are great intrapreneurs. It is these individuals who will build the next business for your firm. Don't be mistaken: The top talent your human resources group tracks are not the only members of this top 25 list.

Intrapreneurship is the process used to identify, cultivate, and make these groups successful—the 200 innovators and 25 intrapreneurs.

In the 1950s, Robert Noyce was credited with inventing technology that eventually became the microchip. After getting his Ph.D. from MIT, he worked for Shockley Semiconductor. Semiconductors was a young industry at the time, and Noyce had countless ideas. But to his frustration, the "experienced" executives did not welcome those ideas. In 1957, Noyce and seven bright engineers left to start Fairchild Semiconductor, which invented semiconductor technology. In 1968, Noyce and Gordon Moore cofounded Intel—the inventor of microprocessor technology. Today, Noyce is well regarded as the father of Silicon Valley. It was his disturbing experience at Shockley that prompted him to create a casual working environment for his young budding engineers at Fairchild and Intel. In many ways, he defined the Silicon Valley working style that has given the world innovations in every sector.

In the late 1970s, the great inventor Ed DeCastro created the extremely successful PDP-8 minicomputer for Digital Equipment. Later he was unsuccessful at convincing Digital Equipment leaders to support another new computer idea and left to start Data General, which became the fourth-largest computer manufacturer. Data General was sold to EMC Corporation in the 1990s.

Around the same time, Steve Wozniak also hit walls at Hewlett-Packard with his idea for a PC. He reluctantly left to join Steve Jobs, who had unsuccessfully pitched a similar idea at Atari, and that was the start of Apple.

When we look closely at businesses, we find that this happens all the time. Smart people leave companies to start their own ventures because their firms did not believe in intrapreneurship as a critical tool for growth.

It may surprise you that many senior leaders are actually afraid to promote out-of-the-box thinking for fear of losing their best employees to success and then to competitors; this is a sure sign of failed leadership.

Tomas Chamorro-Premuzic addresses this issue in a recent article titled "How Bad Leadership Spurs Entrepreneurship."[2] He argues that 70% of successful entrepreneurs have one thing in common: They got their business idea while working for a previous employer. These talented individuals left because the organization they worked for did not have an intrapreneurial process to pitch their ideas and their boss was unbearable. Most employee engagement research confirms this point.

This is good news and bad news. The good news is that additional new small businesses create many new jobs. Since the 1980s, America has seen 50 million jobs replaced with100 million new "skilled" jobs. Entrepreneurial ventures also attract global minds to the United States. In the same article, Chamorro-Premuzic mentions that 50% of world's skilled immigrants go to the United States for jobs. He explains: "There are at least 500 start-ups with French founders in the San Francisco Bay area, and there are over 50,000 Germans in Silicon Valley, where salaries for software engineers are much higher than in Europe (or elsewhere)."

The obvious bad news is how ill-equipped large corporations are at retaining and benefiting from such bright minds. One can argue that for large corporations, this is not bad news since most small businesses fail. So, if a large company allowed these employees to try their ideas, the corporations would experience more failure. It is true that not everyone within a company would be a successful entrepreneur outside. But if anyone can identify the best entrepreneurs, it is likely the company itself can, given its deep HR processes, expertise, and access to resources.

When there is failed leadership for innovation, it is often because managers and leaders did not create an environment for employees to master the skill of intrapreneurship. Managers must be taught to attract, develop, and retain entrepreneurial talent for strategic growth of a firm. Sheryl Sandberg understands this at Facebook, Larry Page and Serge Brin understood this when they brought in Eric Schmidt at Google. Ratan Tata understood this when he and the Tata board selected Cyrus Pallonji Mistry to be his successor, and Steve Jobs understood this when he hired Tim Cook.

Defining and Embedding Intrapreneurship

For a company, intrapreneurship is the ability to think big and small at the same time while unleashing the entrepreneurial spirit of each employee in the firm. For an individual, intrapreneurship is the method and mind-set of becoming a force of positive change and ingenuity every day.

For a long time, the business world has believed that a carefully structured product development process is the key to unplanned entrepreneurial passion. A plethora of research proves this to be false. Invariably, in large organizations, innovation never happens without an individual or small team passionately working on a unique idea. When such people start up new companies, they are called entrepreneurs. Inside large organizations, we call them intrapreneurs.

To help operationalize innovation, we recommend embedding intrapreneurship within your HR competency model.

Case Study: Medical Services Company

As an example, let's look at how a global medical services client embedded intrapreneurship competency into its organization. Table 8.1 gives a definition of "Innovation"

TABLE 8.1   Competency and Behaviors for Intrapreneurship at a Global Medical Services Company

	Strategic focus	Sponsor change	Operational excellence
Primary skills	**Strategic focus** create and share a compelling vision of the future; translate vision into strategies and priorities that generate global business growth; align people's efforts toward a common purpose.	**Sponsor change** sponsor and model innovative practices; embrace different ideas and perspectives; and demonstrate creativity, flexibility, and adaptability.	**Operational excellence** improve operational effectiveness and efficiency for flawless execution.
Executive	Creates a clear and inspiring vision and strategy based on a deep, comprehensive understanding of the industry, customers, and business. Ensures that business strategy is aligned with domestic and global policy issues and trends. Shares vision and strategy across multiple parts of the organization, generating understanding, enthusiasm, and commitment.	Actively champions major cross-divisional and/or cross-geographical change initiatives and ensures appropriate support. Promotes and models prudent risk taking across the organization. Creates and capitalizes on new ways of doing business.	Rapidly and accurately identifies and acts to eliminate overlapping responsibilities/processes, structural inconsistencies, and systems misalignment across divisions/geographies. Establishes systems and processes that promote the seamless sharing of knowledge and data across the organization. Continuously strives to simplify organizational structure and operations as much as possible.
Manager of managers	Develops own and others' objectives by leveraging key stakeholder perspectives and own expertise. Identifies strategic opportunities in the value chain that will expand and sustain competitive advantage over time. Presents clear and compelling business cases, influencing others to align resources with the strategy.	Eliminates obstacles/barriers to, and ensures sufficient resources for, change. Creatively integrates different perspectives or contradictory information to solve problems. Encourages innovative thinking in others by asking challenging questions and proposing novel alternatives.	Proactively asks employees, customers, and stakeholders for their perceptions of the workflow, operations, and systems to get fresh, diverse perspectives. Ensures that work teams systematically review process flow, operations, and systems on a regular basis. Holds self and others accountable for driving continuous improvement in organizational processes, operations, and systems.
Individual contributor	Prioritizes own work activities to help team or work group meet its objectives. Effectively handles uncertainty, risk, and conflicting priorities in planning and managing own work and projects. Demonstrates understanding of company strategy and how own objectives contribute to it.	Readily adjusts own ways of working to suit changing situations. Displays innovative ideas and solutions. Seeks to improve on others' ideas rather than discourage them.	Constructively challenges the standard approach to work and finds better ways to get the work done and meet customer requirements. Identifies and eliminates redundant work efforts and inefficient processes. Consistently looks for opportunities to reduce costs.

as a competency associated with three primary skills: strategic focus, sponsor change, and operational excellence. For each skill, the table also shows acceptable behavioral traits that can be integrated into your performance management system for three levels of individuals: executives, managers, and individual contributors.

Ideally, for each of the three primary skills, you will also need to identify behaviors to determine when someone is underperforming or overachieving. Doing this will greatly assist you in the annual performance review process.

Intrapreneurship is the missing corporate competency needed in the twenty-first century. If you evaluate leadership training programs, corporate university curriculums, and top talent training tracks, you will see very little focus on intrapreneurship as a topic. Why? This happens because most HR departments have not recognized the need for it or have been unsuccessful at making a business case for it.

What's worse is when we hear HR leaders say, "Businesses are not looking to build innovation skills as a priority this year," or "Leaders are focused on many other priorities," or "We are focused on a lot of basic technical skill building these days." In other words, what they are really saying is "We are trying to *survive* and cannot invest in the future."

Every business needs intrapreneurship as a core competency. It is required and cannot be built overnight. So how does an organization achieve this goal without being committed to investing for the future? Simply, it cannot be done.

If you want innovation, you need to commit to intrapreneurship and to building intrapreneurs.

Entrepreneurs and Intrapreneurs

By working with hundreds of entrepreneurs and intrapreneurs, we have learned that the primary motivation for either is not simply to accumulate great personal wealth, although they are visionary and highly confident and will succeed on all levels once they have clarity. This insight provides a huge opportunity for corporations to do everything possible to avoid losing such talented individuals and risk them becoming competitors in the future.

Entrepreneurs know that when they succeed in their independent businesses, they will generate a great amount of wealth and prestige. But for them the primary motivation is the freedom to act. If they become successful, they'll have more capital to take on larger risks with larger time horizons. This formulates a strong innovation engine that allows them to continuously conduct idea experimentations and incubations. They can make mistakes they don't need to justify to a boss.

Just like entrepreneurs, intrapreneurs are also visionary and full of energy. When it comes to innovation, however, they have several advantages over entrepreneurs:

- They do not need to personally fund their ideas.
- They can do new things but retain the friendship, expertise, and security of a large company.

- Capital is easier to access inside the firm than outside.
- They can test creating a business inside before risking it outside.
- They can take advantage of an existing large brand name and distribution channel to expedite market introduction of a new offering.
- If access to new technology is important, it is easier within the larger organization than outside.

Despite these advantages, there is one big disadvantage for intrapreneurs. Despite prior success, they have no capital of their own to start new ventures. Due to the nature of corporations, they must begin from zero every time. Unlike entrepreneurs, intrapreneurs do not have the freedom to act on their intuition and must justify every step they take. This makes it very difficult for intrapreneurs to take a strategic long-term view because they never know if their project will be killed after the next bad quarter. Also, an intrapreneur's inability to use earnings from a previous venture is one of the biggest barriers for a successful innovation program. This, however, should not be a reason for not intrapreneuring in a large corporation. By encouraging and empowering intrapreneurship, corporations can prevent the best inventors from leaving and benefit from their great ideas.

Nature of Intrapreneurs

The very best professional baseball players in Major League Baseball (MLB) didn't pursue a baseball career primarily because they wanted to accumulate wealth. They followed their passion for the sport. Of the thousands of MLB players, only a handful are admitted to the prestigious Hall of Fame. The players who receive this honor showed consistency in performance, their careers contributed to the game of baseball, and they had clean reputations.

Similarly, the greatest corporate innovators are always working on something that will improve their environment at large. To these great individuals, money is oxygen, required for living and generating new inventions, but it is not the goal. The best innovators are not motivated by greed and wealth accumulation. If they are, they usually fail soon after their first idea.

Here is what Gifford Pinchot III says about intrapreneurs in his seminal book of the same name:

> *Intrapreneurs will make all the difference between your firm's success and failure. The cost of losing entrepreneurial talent is more than just losing a skilled technologist or effective marketer. Intrapreneurs are the integrators who combine the talents of both the technologies and the marketers by establishing new products, processes, and services. Without them, innovation remains potential, or moves at the glacial pace of bureaucratic processes that no longer suffice in an environment filled with entrepreneurial competitions.*[3]

The importance of intrapreneurs becomes self-evident after they leave. Ed Roberts, a professor at Sloan School of Management, tracked 39 intrapreneurs. All of these individuals once worked for the same company in Boston, Massachusetts, on Route 128. Over a period of time, they left and started their own companies as entrepreneurs. Roberts tracked them and discovered that after five years, nearly 85% of these people were very successful and their businesses were flourishing. Most interestingly, these 33 individuals had combined revenue of two and a half times that of their previous employers combined.[4]

Indiana Jones: A Great Intrapreneur

While I was growing up, some of my favorite films were creations of Steven Spielberg and George Lucas—specifically the Star Wars and Indiana Jones series. Jones is a classic example of an intrapreneur and personifies the role of a leader supportive of budding talent. In my opinion, Jones should have been teaching a course on business and entrepreneurship instead of archeology.

Indiana Jones, portrayed by Harrison Ford, captured the thrill of being an action hero for so many of us growing up. In *Raiders of the Lost Ark*, Jones goes on a mission to save the world from the Nazis. He is focused, practical, multitasking, persistent, nimble, operationally fluid, and a destroyer of villains. He embodies all the qualities missing today in most workplaces.

Indiana Jones exemplified five core qualities we find in great intrapreneurs:

1. **Practical persistence.** Unlike the risk James Bond posed to his MI6 boss, Jones did not just go on a wild mission. He waited until his boss and academic department head and friend Marcus Brody secured a government grant to fund his travels and other expenses. His mission was to find the lost Ark of the Covenant before the Nazis, so it could be put in a museum. Throughout the story, you notice he never gives up and always comes up with a creative solution by thinking on his feet.

   Many people were after him, yet he didn't take things personally or let others' personal issues distract him. He knew they just wanted to stop him from getting the ark because they wanted it too. He knew the struggle was not about him.

   When a corporate intrapreneur moves forward, people will resist. It is an automatic human response to change. As we can become more objective about that reality, we become better innovation leaders. We can practice looking for resistance and noticing it rather than personalizing it.

2. **Generating real value.** The Nazis were blindly obsessed in their search for the ark without even knowing what they were going to do with it. They ignored the advice of Sallah, a friend of Jones, that the ark was "something that man was not meant to disturb." How many times do we see this mind-set in firms where projects are initiated without a clear purpose, albeit on a much less dramatic scale than in the movie, resulting in costly, ill-thought-out product rollouts, expenditures, and hires that fall short of expected outcomes?

   In one scene between Indy's French foe Belloq and the Nazi officer Shliemann, Belloq declares: "Archeology is not an exact science. It does not adhere to time schedules." Shliemann replies: "The Fuhrer is not a patient man. He demands constant reports and he expects progress."

I am not implying that all management is like Nazis, far from it. But Shliemann's point clearly resonates with the nonintrapreneurial and bureaucratic conditions in most firms where thousands of hours a day are spent on creating spreadsheets, calendars, or reports without knowing their value. The machinelike environment has produced many micromanaging bosses who are focused on short-term success through process plans and metrics for the bosses above. An excess of this behavior has created company cultures that limit the scope and time for creativity and innovation and has reduced the potential for achieving the very gains the documents are designed to deliver.

As a creative problem solver, Jones had clear focus: to find and preserve the integrity of an artifact of great archeological history before it was destroyed or used against humankind. Jones used every ounce of physical, mental, and emotional courage to achieve that end.

3. **Action, not activity.** In the famous street fighting scene in *Raiders of the Lost Ark*, Indiana Jones faces a sword fighter dressed all in black. The assassin performs a masterful and elaborate routine, whipping his sword around with flash and arrogance. For a split second the street crowd and the audience are convinced that Jones has met his death. Surprisingly, with a look of fatigue and disgust, Jones simply pulls out his revolver and blows the assassin away. The kill was unexpected and utterly effective in its simplistic swiftness.

   The assassin was focused on the activity and the process of killing, while Jones was focused on the "action" at that very moment. Jones did not have to plan, think, or prepare for unexpected challenges while searching for the ark. He met every challenge by thinking on his feet. By being in action, we are more spontaneous and more creative. Focusing on activity takes us away from discovering what might be possible or delivers a stretched solution. Intrapreneurs are always *in action*, not just filling the day with activities.

   Every successful intrapreneur has these kinds of inspirational off-the-cuff eureka moments (without necessarily having to kill anyone). Advance preparation is a prerequisite for a meeting or presentation, but developing a radical successful solution is often determined by a spontaneous response to an unscripted question that has to be formulated and communicated in a split second. Being one with the problem, which often means thinking on your feet, outweighs the information you've accumulated in your head.

4. **Keeping a sense of humor.** Even under the most trying of times, Jones was able to laugh, or at least smile. After being shot, dragged behind a truck, and fighting off Nazis, his friend Marian Ravenwood says, "You don't look the same as you did ten years ago." Jones replies, "It's not the years, it's the mileage!"

   Intrapreneurs are intense in their work, but they also know it takes light-heartedness to build innovative work climates. They intuitively know that the emotional quotient (EQ) is much more important than the intelligence quotient (IQ). They use EQ to strengthen their position all the time, and humor is a powerful instrument to help achieve that. Humor constructs bridges in everyday relationships while keeping sanity in an always connected, stress-driven business world. Seeing the funny side of things engages the right brain—the creative part of our brain.

5. **Breakdown before breakthrough.** Early in the movie we learn that Jones was afraid of snakes. Not surprisingly, he ended up in a pit of snakes. He had to cope with his phobia in order to survive.

The best intrapreneurs are similar. When they commit to a challenge, they inherently know to achieve extraordinary results, they will have to endure a significant breakdown—some "inner devil" or a deeply ingrained mental pattern not easy to overcome. Often it is in these personality traits in our life we are most reactive and create our biggest pitfalls. When something happens to the project or team dynamics or sponsor, and we can't see or think straight, we have a clue that there are deeper layers at work within us. Usually, if not always, these patterns come from our family upbringing, teachers, past relationships, previous managers, and coworkers. Just facing those fears and anxieties can be a lifetime of work. But as it was with Indiana Jones, the payoff can be well worth the trouble.

Some days we may wish we were racing around the desert like Indiana Jones. His adventures are very similar to what intrapreneurs must endure to be successful as innovators in today's business world.

Successful Intrapreneurs

In the course of our firm's work over the past 25 years, we have met hundreds of great intrapreneurs. To prepare for this book, we launched a research study to obtain deeper insight into how one becomes a successful intrapreneur.

During the study, we were given the freedom to explore the IQ, EQ, and spiritual quotient of the participants. I am deeply indebted to all of them for allowing us to find their unique and similar patterns by getting into their heads and hearts. You will now meet some of these great corporate innovators.

Twenty-six candidates participated, with variety of global experiences in 11 different industries. Our research team used three primary criteria to select candidates for the study:

1. Experience in successfully building or growing a new product/service or starting a new business in a listed/public company of 2,000 or more employees that has been in business for at least five years
2. Contributed to the company's top line (e.g., through product development, a new distribution channel, new markets, or new services)
3. Evidenced an exceptional knack for uncovering and seizing opportunities to help advance business growth

After evaluating the research, we discovered *six patterns* that made our intrapreneurs very successful. Armed with these new insights, we started Phase II of the project—to validate our findings in practice. We informally surveyed and watched in practice hundreds of corporate employees during workshops or consulting projects and weighed the data against our research insights.

Bob Hedinger, before he retired in 2010, was a very successful intrapreneur at Bell Laboratories and Skynet, a division of AT&T that was eventually sold to Loral Space and Communications of New York. His primary job was very technical—designing and launching telecommunication satellites in space. He eventually became part of the senior leadership team responsible for technical architecture, global strategy, and business development. Between 1997 and 2003, he helped grow the business from $70 million to $400 million.

George Castineiras is the head of Prudential Retirement's Total Retirement Solutions business. George is formerly head of sales and distribution at Prudential Retirement in Hartford, Connecticut. Prior to that, he was the senior vice president of the Institutional Income Innovations group, a team that launched the industry's first in-plan guaranteed minimum withdrawal benefit for defined contribution plans. Available on more than 7,000 defined contribution plans, IncomeFlex Target® helps participants(policy holders) accumulate assets and convert those assets into guaranteed income. The retirement insurance business in the United States had been a flat market filled with players sitting on a commodity island—everyone competing on price and service alone.

Mark Wright was a rising star at Bristol-Myers Squibb (BMS), a New York–based $21 billion global pharmaceutical conglomerate. He started in 1997, as a VP of the U.S. Consumer Medicines business and eventually was promoted to managing director for the Australia and New Zealand operation. In 2007, he was appointed president of the Japan operation and shortly after was given the responsibility to run the U.S. Cardiovascular and Metabolics business unit for BMS. He initiated numerous innovation practices in a highly consolidated, heavily regulated biopharmaceutical industry where there is very little appetite for daily innovations in non-R&D areas.

Rose Mihaly, a natural entrepreneur, started her career working for a small private business and became very successful in a short period of time. Because of her natural intrapreneurial skills, she was quickly recruited by a Fortune 100 company, the Hartford Financial Services Group, in its HR department—an "accidental" track. Soon after, her bosses realized she should be helping to drive the business, not just support it. She was promoted to chief administrative officer to run Hartford's crown jewel, the variable annuity business operation in Tokyo, Japan, a rare occurrence for any HR executive. When she returned from Japan, she was appointed leader of The Hartford's enterprise-wide onnovation, product and marketing intiative to capture retirement-products market share globally. She was later named chief marketing officer for their Group Benefits business.

Juan Andrade, since joining the ACE Group in New York in 2010, is the chief operating officer for ACE Overseas General and the Global head of Personal Lines and Small Commercial insurance. Previously, he was the president of Property and Casualty Insurance and a member of the executive leadership team with the Hartford Financial Services Group and also ran its claims and sales organizations.

Before joining the Hartford, he held numerous senior management positions with the Progressive Insurance Corporation, serving as general manager. He started his career at American International Group (AIG), where he worked with the company's international property and casualty businesses both in the United States and overseas. Prior to his positions with AIG, Andrade worked in national security and international affairs within the U.S. Federal Government's Executive Branch and the Executive Office of the President of the United States.

Hari Mahdevan is a serial intrapreneur with a Ph.D. in chemical engineering from North Carolina State University, an MBA from The Wharton School at the University of Pennsylvania and a Bachelor of Technology in Chemical Engineering from the University of Madras in Chennia, India. He did his early research work at NASA, and then moved into the healthcare industry. He received two global patents at Merck right around the time he turned 30. Starting in 1996, Hari worked at McKinsey & Company for five+ years, advising mostly healthcare Fortune 100 companies on many strategic issues. He then joined Rosetta, to build a healthcare consulting and interactive agency business. At Rosetta, he built and grew two disparate yet connected divisions from zero to over $100 million in annual revenues serving global clients in pharmaceuticals, medical devices, biotechnology, and other healthcare sectors. After selling Rosetta to The Publicis Groupe in 2011 for over $575 million, Hari is now an independent consultant and a board member at Symphony Health Solutions, a company with an approximately $250 million portfolio of health data, analytics, and insights assets.

SIX INTRAPRENEURIAL PATTERNS   By studying great intrapreneurs, such as the ones just mentioned, it became very clear why they were extremely successful.

They exhibited all the Indiana Jones qualities plus many other unique attributes important to helping build a climate and culture of innovation. We believe that such individuals exist in every organization but are most likely hiding. To accelerate your journey, it would be advantageous to search existing talent and recruit from outside for such qualities and then develop these highly talented people as quickly as possible.

Pattern #1: Money Is Not the Measurement   Why was Bob Hedinger so successful at Bell Labs and AT&T? He said, "I could have easily gone into investment banking and earned hundreds of millions of dollars a year, but it would not have motivated me the way my career in the telecommunication field did. I was never chasing a financial goal. I was successful as a corporate innovator because I loved what I did every day. Money automatically came because I was lost in my work and I had a great boss and very smart people around me."

The primary motivation for intrapreneurs is *influence with freedom*. One hundred percent of our candidates clearly demonstrated this pattern—with story after story. This doesn't mean they don't want to be rewarded fairly. It means that money is not the starting point for them. Reward and compensation are like a scorecard of how well they are playing the game of being a successful intrapreneur, but it is not *the* game.

Intrapreneurs are much more interested in the ability to help direct the business in a direction they strongly envision. Many of our interviewees exhibit strong domain expertise supported by some deep technical background in their industry. A technical person supporting a business organization can have a commanding influence. However, the challenge for most technical innovators is their inability to be included in the financial arena or the market analysis, and they often lack these business skills. Our intrapreneurs, however, showed tremendous sensitivity to this gap and consistently demonstrated their ability to bridge the gap to business executives and their teams. Hedinger, who has a Ph.D. in physics, said, "It actually excited me to take my physics, math, and technical knowledge of building satellites and look at a much broader problem of business architecture. I believe this was my unique gift to the organizations I served. It made all of us move faster as markets shifted and allowed me to shift leadership mind-set—that was a great reason to wake up every day and go to work."

Pattern #2: Strategic Scanning Intrapreneurs we met are constantly thinking about what is next. They always seem to be one step into the future— what we call the second pattern, *strategic scanning*. "I am always looking at new things to do with old things and new ideas. I am always looking for the most efficient way of doing things, no matter what it is," Hedinger commented.

These change agents are highly engaged, passionate, very clear, and visibly consistent in their work and interactions. They are not sitting around waiting for the world to change. Often they are figuring out which part of the world is about to change and arrive just in time to leverage the new insights. They love to chase the new and novel—not for the sake of new, but to make shifts in their surroundings. This makes them natural trend hunters.

Learning is like oxygen to them. When we met Hedinger, he was learning and writing about the origins of the universe. He said, "I don't plan to research anything. But I love to observe." George Castineiras of Prudential said, "My own belief is that there is not a lot that's created from scratch. In other words, there is no such thing as a completely new invention." He continued, "Almost everything can be brought from another industry to develop a new solution in your industry. So for me, it's about looking, learning, having a deliberate focus on connecting ideas, visualizing patterns in solutions, and then refining what I find to best solve a challenge in my own world, personal or professional."

Castineiras finds a fresh idea by what he explains as "active listening, then visually thinking, and then asking others for validation." For over 80% of the candidates we studied, new ideas came after they observed something visually in their surroundings—something not working, working really well, or missing. Later on, they used data to help validate and substantiate a hypothesis. "Everything starts by observing and actively listening for me," Castineiras stated. Such intrapreneurs are not just seeing things differently but finding new insights that only an idea hunter can discover.

Mahdevan said his life has always been somewhat serendipitous. This is an interesting comment and yet not unusual compared to others we talked to. They don't think they are intrapreneurs or looking to create innovations in their careers. In fact, more than 80% of our participants never thought of themselves as innovators. They don't even use the term "innovation" in regard to their work, but they exhibit all the traits of remarkable innovators.

Mahdevan commented, "I am always listening for the most strategic conversations. I tell my partners that I don't need to be a decision maker on everything, but I want to be there when decisions are being made. As an example, when I was at Merck, we were ready to launch a very important new product. It was expected to be a huge part of the pipeline. I was only 29 at the time. I was surrounded by plenty of smart people with deep expertise in various subjects. During the prelaunch process of this new product, our team and I were often in the same room with heavy industry experts. As an example, by listening to marketing experts and attorneys, I learned more about the pharmaceutical business in the United States than if I had attended school for two years. I found tremendous insights that allowed me to eventually build a marketing consulting practice at Rosetta. I have never looked for ideas, but they come to me accidentally. That is the best way I learn. I listen for deep insights between the lines in a conversation. I see and hear things that are often missed by others."

Intrapreneurs have this uncanny ability for strategic scanning. Some surround themselves with individuals to help supply domain knowledge they feel they need, others allow connections to form as they go along throughout the day. Some spend quality time with their customers to uncover unfulfilled opportunities and use their strategic relationships to test their ideas quickly. Still others spend valuable time thinking about future market and technology convergences to find new ideas to pursue before others.

What is consistently common is their ability to know the unarticulated need of their customers and also recognize their "wow" moments. They just know it!

"It was two o'clock in the morning when I decided to pursue getting an MBA. I was so sure that I had to wake up my wife and tell her about it and seek her support," Mahdevan shared. "I already had a Ph.D. and a great job paying six figures, while I was still in my early 30s. What I didn't have was the business knowledge to help drive more impactful outcomes for the healthcare industry I was interested in. Somehow I intuitively knew there was lot more I could do. I could have stayed at NASA or Merck. Both would have given me tremendous opportunities and challenges to pursue. I left both because I was 14 layers away from meaningful decisions. I needed to see my future through two critical lenses—which I only realized years later. After years of experience being an intrapreneur and listening to my own internal patterns, I feel I am best when I can answer two important questions about an opportunity that I am thinking about. If the answers to these two questions are positive, I pursue it with full vigor. It never was about personal compensation. It never occurs to me to think about monetary goals, I am actually quite terrible at it. I chase opportunities mostly for learning something remarkably new and then to actually solve it. My Ph.D. professor was a great mentor. He once told me 'Ideas are everywhere.' What gets me up every morning is that I am working on an idea that can change the world for the better."

Mahdevan continued, "The first question I ask of myself is: 'Is this passionate enough internally (meaning for me?) Does this put a smile on my face? Is it something I am willing to think about 24/7?' The second question: 'Is the organization ready for it?' I have learned the hard way that both have to coexist. I am ready to move to a next opportunity when one of the two questions becomes false."

Interestingly enough, all of our intrapreneurs have at least a few *big* ideas they are sorting out, playing with, and incubating. There are always *new* and *next* ideas they are zealously scanning for clarity. They're never done!

Pattern #3: Greenhousing   When the idea seed is formed, Castineiras commented. "I contemplate on it for days and weeks between calls, meetings, and conversation. As I shine more light on it, it becomes clearer, but not bright enough for me to share it with potential naysayers. If I share it too early, people will dismiss it without fully appreciating it. So I protect it for a while." This is the third pattern—*greenhousing* the ideas.

For Mark Wright, "The very best ideas must create volume." By "volume" he means sales growth, market share, or change in either internal or external mindset that can positively leapfrog other incremental projects, initiatives, or solutions. "Typically the newly formed idea lacks data and is often very difficult to even articulate in simple words. At this stage, I can hear the voices of critics shooting it down already," said Wright. It is at this idea-forming stage where intrapreneurs show their uniqueness. Because the idea is very green and on the surface implausible, typical employees will easily let it go. Intrapreneurs, however,, *feel* the idea and use their intuition to keep it fresh. By now, they have formulated a strategic question deeply within that no one else is asking. It is at this stage, past the stage of intrigue, that they find a deep conviction to merge themselves with their idea. In other words, they are emotionally committed to an important challenge that needs an innovative solution.

Pattern #4: Visual Thinking   Intrapreneurs grow the idea by applying visual thinking. The fourth pattern, *visual thinking*, is a combination of brainstorming, mind mapping, and design thinking. Only after an exciting insight do they seem able to formulate and visualize series of solutions in their head—not just one. They never converge on a solution the first time around. They are keenly aware of the need to honor the *discovery* phase for the new solution, giving it time to crystallize in their heads and hearts. They know that the first solution is not the best solution. They allow themselves to say "I don't know all that I need to know about this or that. So what else is possible?"

To take the idea and grow it, Castineiras takes his fresh insights and, with perspective from his past experiences, goes from there. The challenge at this stage is to protect the idea, grow it, validate it, and enroll other key individuals into it—all at the same time.

Most intrapreneurs we met seem to be balanced between being introverts and extroverts. They are very effective communicators with a strong command of language and are very effective in conversation. Being with them creates a sense of penetrating engagement and excitement.

In order to validate whether their crazy ideas are any good, intrapreneurs start having conversations and asking other people questions related to their idea and its feasibility in a stage-by-stage, purposeful fashion. For example, Castineiras said, "I never disclose the entire idea while I'm exploring its feasibility. Instead, I ask a thoughtful question about an element of my idea. With that person's input, I'll refine that aspect of the idea, and then go to someone else. The next person might say they like the element of the idea, except a specific facet of it. Then I refine it further. So, I'm asking for validation from all the right people, from different walks of life, to the point that, by the time I'm presenting it for 'buy-in,' the ideas is very refined and an easy sell."

Pattern #5: Pivoting   Once more, 100% of intrapreneurs we interviewed practiced the fifth pattern called *pivoting*.

"Pivoting" means making a courageous and significant shift from the current course of action, a shift most people would never make. For example, Apple and Steve Jobs pivoted from being an education and hobby computer company to a consumer electronics company in the late 1990s. Wipro of India pivoted from being a small vegetable oil manufacturer to a software outsourcing powerhouse because of the vision and courage of their CEO, Azim Premji. When Zappos started in 1997, it wanted to sell shoes without touching shoes. The company almost went bankrupt. The now-famous founder and CEO Tony Hsieh pivoted to only selling shoes that were in the Zappos warehouse. Zappos shifted from being an online shoe company to an online *customer experience* company. In 2009, Amazon bought Zappos for $1.2 billion. Speaking of Amazon, Jeff Bezos pivoted Amazon from being the world's largest online megamall that sold everybody else's stuff (books, music, apparel, computers, electronics and DVDs) to selling its own hardware—the Kindle line of readers. Bezos knew that e-books would not sell without e-readers. This strategy has paid off well—as of this writing, Amazon owns about 60% of the e-reader market share, and its market capitalization value is north of $100 billion.

These entrepreneurial leaders embody pattern 5—pivoting.

Pivoting means making a strategic change from the current path you have chosen. For high-tech venture capital–funded start-ups, it is a badge of honor. It is expected. For others, it is an admission of failure. The period leading to making a pivot decision is filled with tremendous pressure to change—by the management and the investment body. It often creates a feeling of desperation and often crumbles teams. Pivoting can force people to leave a project and sometimes even the firm they work for. Pivoting sounds scary and unfathomable to most mature organizations, although it's often what is needed to resuscitate a dying company.

Pivoting has three attributes:

1. Discontent—the current path is not working and change is needed
2. Ability to see when it is time for a new direction (not a destination)
3. Courage to let go of the current path and swiftly move toward a new one

To our intrapreneurs, finding and knowing when to pivot is like finding a hidden treasure. The people we studied consistently demonstrated all three attributes just mentioned.

Rose Mihaly described intrapreneurs as "intellectually very curious people. They are reading things, exposing themselves to information, interacting with many people at many levels within and outside the organization. And they take bits and pieces of information and come up with a hypothesis. Then they pursue their hunch. This is when they *feel* a modification to a strategy or tactic or might even change a direction entirely. I could think of a variety of situations, whether it would be with product design or with distribution methodology or product placement. I can think of a couple examples and situations around acquisitions where those things occurred."

Before pivoting, intrapreneurs are very participatory and very self-directive. They take in a lot of information from a wide variety of sources. Ultimately they make decisions on their own. There is no single individual or source of influence leading them to make a pivot decision. They just know what they need to do. They may not know when that will occur, but it always does.

Once they *see* the pivot and the new direction, they act fast to test their hypothesis. At this stage, the new pivoted direction is more important than destination. So if you ask them at this point to define the final goal and what outcomes can be expected from the new pivoted strategy, they will not yet be able to tell you.

As a leader, this is the time to back off asking for new ROI numbers. Instead, provide more open space and fast experimentation support so these intrapreneurs can test their hunches as fast as possible. In most cases, you will win with them—often with remarkable innovations.

To turn an average intrapreneur into a great business leader who can build your next S-Curve, find the pivot they are seeing. As an executive, help them bring it to reality by removing as many internal barriers as possible. The result will be acceleration toward a new direction and most often will bring new profits and new knowledge.

Pattern #6: Authenticity and Integrity   The intrapreneurs we studied demonstrated the attributes of confidence and humbleness at the same time. They did not exhibit the mavericklike behavior often associated with successful corporate innovators. They all, however, exuded high self-awareness and sense of purpose. None of these individuals was handed a silver platter. Each earned their way up the ladder and carved out their own future through hard work and tenacity.

The sixth pattern we observed in the intrepreneurs we studied was the premium they placed on *authenticity and integrity,* both in their work and in the work of others around them. These corporate innovators see their work and workplace as a playground for much more than earning a living. Since they already have self-confidence, to them the *means* are as important as the *end*. The means have to do with the quality of relationships and quality of the effort they expect of themselves, people around them, and the firm they work for.

Instead, often there is turf protection going on or departments looking down at other departments as less important. For example, R&D feels neglected by marketing, or the IT department receives cold treatment by the finance area. The technical folks are usually the first people Finance calls when they need something, but try to get them to listen to IT's ideas, and it's usually an unsatisfying exchange.

Most intradepartmental wars start because there is lack of authenticity and integrity on at least one side, if not both. This is because a significant mind-set variance exists between departments when it comes to new ideas and new products and their implementations.

Typically, specific business plans must adhere to budget cycles, and marketers' plan initiatives to correspond. These departments therefore think and plan for the short term. R&D by its definition, however, needs to take a much longer-term view.

By no means are we suggesting that intracompany competition should not exist. What I am suggesting is that the style of work must not create toxicity in how the work gets done.

Intrapreneurs are at their very best when organizations provide opportunities for them to work from a place of integrity and to achieve aspirational objectives, often beyond making money. Gold-medal intrapreneurs innately realize that nothing happens without deep integrity in the people involved. They believe that within that integrity lies a respect that must be conveyed for those relationships and that those relationships are seen as a privilege, not as an entitlement.

As Mihaly aptly described, "When there is integrity, there is a candor in the *why* things are being done, and *how* things are being done. There should be respect for the relationships that exist, which necessitates communication. If an organization is going to be successful amidst the array of relationships amongst all stakeholders, they have to be listening. Every leader and aspiring leader must role-model and demonstrate clarity in them and what they believe in. There has to be a discipline about why you exist, why you do what you do, and there should be a thread of evidence that the integrity of it prevails."

Lack of integrity and authenticity is a significant barrier for intrapreneurs. Mihaly says, "A showstopper for me is when actions and words don't match. That's probably the most common symptom that is seen in most workplaces today. People will say what people want to hear or say things in a way that are palatable. The lack of integrity in that is that they are aware that what they are saying is easy for the listener to hear. The words may be true, but the underlying intent may not. When one becomes what is being commonly heard, that is where everything starts to come unglued for them and the firm."

Mark Wright commented, "I have worked for organizations that criticize themselves too often. It takes a tremendous amount of hard work to be clear about the future and get everyone to focus on it every day. In 2003, at BMS, our executive leadership team agreed not to seek new product opportunities unless they fell in one of the ten disease areas. That was bold. At a time when people were diversifying, for us to go pure play, that's courageous. Such courage is difficult to find in senior teams. Whether such clarity and integrity will work or not, almost doesn't matter. What is more important is they have created an environment where if we have conviction earlier than everyone else, we are going to make significant progress. Why is that exciting? Because such focus demands innovation in every part of the organization, and I want to be part of such success."

Juan Andrade concurred: "I want to be surrounded by people whom I trust and are trustworthy. Trust shows up as transparency and openness in your thoughts, words, and action. In my relationships, I want trust in the fact that what they are telling me is the truth and trust that they are speaking up and telling me their point of view. The second part of being a successful strategic growth contributor is action orientation. The best intrapreneurs I have worked with are those who are the antithesis of complacency. They are passionate about what they do; they are into it. They are team oriented and collaborative. They are never done. They are winners."

If you lack integrity and authenticity, it basically guarantees that you will not be able to build a climate and culture of innovation. It will be impossible to attract the very best intrapreneurs.

If I had to choose one word to describe the hundreds of great men and women we interviewed in our research, it would be *jazzed*.

These intrapreneurs have disproportionately high IQs. They are curious about nature. They have an excessively high success rate in diagnosing problems, making decisions, and being correct. If you were to take ten business decisions and evaluate their rate of the correct decision being made, they tend to have a high hit rate. Such success occurs for them because they possess combination of high IQ and high EQ. They have the ability to diagnose issues that don't always travel together. Their curiosity and the desire to enroll themselves in new experiences are extremely high, while the degree of personal risk they feel in trying new things is disproportionately low.

Finally, they carry a bit of a carefree confidence that says "If I fail, I will go innovate somewhere else."

Supportive Environment for Intrapreneurs

In the *Raiders of the Lost Ark*, Indiana Jones was a great action hero as well as a great problem solver. But he would not have succeeded without a supporting environment. The same is true for the intrapreneurs we just met. They all agreed it was the supportive environment that allowed them to bring their A game to the forefront every day.

Once leaders find an intrapreneur in your organization, what can be done to support him or her?

Jones was successful because of four core qualities that existed in his professional surroundings at the college (see Figure 8.1):

1. **Extreme challenges to solve.** His boss helped him identify the project of finding and saving the treasures of the lost ark while protecting the world from villains.
2. **Freedom to find solutions.** No matter what, fight to the end until the ark is recovered.
3. **Supportive environment.** His boss was like a partner—on the same side. Additionally, the university supported him by providing the grants he needed to pursue his passion for research in archeology.

FIGURE 8.1 Supporting Intrapreneur

4. **Rewards and motivation.** He didn't accept the adventure to find the ark for money. Instead, he was pursuing it for the sake of writing new history in the field of archeology and to shape the young minds of his students to encourage them to pursue careers in historical preservation.

In our research and field experience, these are the same four factors that attract and retain your best intrapreneurs.

EXTREME CHALLENGES TO SOLVE   Ambition. In our experience when organizations have large ambition, they tend to create significant value. Intrapreneurs are very motivated to solve ambitious challenges. Extremely exceptional engineers live for tackling difficult challenges.

Sundara Nagarajan has been a successful intrapreneur in various firms over the last three decades. He was part of the team that developed the early multi-user minicomputer in India while working for Wipro in the 1980s. As Wipro moved into the global product engineering service business, he pioneered some of the early process innovations while supporting global customers such as Intel, Xerox, and Tandem. He then moved to Phillips Consumer electronics to start its embedded software innovation center in India. He also worked with a number of Silicon Valley companies, such as HP, IPValue and NetApp, to help produce a variety of new products and services. As a resident of Bangalore, India, he is also a visiting professor at the International Institute of Information Technology, Bangalore (IIT-B).

When Nagarajan began his career at Wipro Technologies in the mid-1983, the company only had about 200 employees within the IT business unit. He described *ambition* this way, "In the early days when the employees worked at Wipro, the company was not known for pay compared to its peers. Most employees didn't have stock options, or any of those monetary rewards which one would consider as the best practices for fostering innovation. But I think the biggest strength of Wipro was that it created a very ambitious organization with standards of business ethics. Mr. Azim Hasham Premji, the CEO, led the company with sharp business acumen while venturing into several diverse business lines. The leadership would declare large ambitious business problems to solve and selected the best to solve them. They gave *freedom to fail fast* or win with personal pride."

"They selected the best people that they could find, put them together, and gave them the opportunity to innovate and take risk. Mr. Premji, personally interviewed the first few hundred selected into the company. He personally interviewed me for an hour as a new college graduate aspirant to an entry-level R&D position. He didn't need to. He personally took time to spot leadership talent at all levels who are practical problem-solvers, entrepreneurial and ambitious. He had a keen eye to find innovative thinkers and put them together in teams to deal with a large ambition that he had created for the organization."

"We worked among friends in a non-political environment. Those early days within R&D at Wipro were unique and not often seen in many organizations now. It was agile in the true sense of the word: self-organizing and self-driven teams that created individual innovations together. Many colleagues became life-long friends even after they had left the company to purse their dreams in life."

Bill Hewlett and Dave Packard are also examples of entrepreneurs who created a solid environment for intrapreneurs. Both founders had a system to recognize people who took risks and had a knack to directly face an ambitious challenge. They built an organization that encouraged people to go into uncharted areas.

The software industry regularly uses hackathons as a way to solve difficult challenges. These events first started in 1999. By 2005, every major software firm was using the process to energize their best technical engineers. Typically, hackathons are organized around a theme or a well-defined problem that needs to be solved through software. Participants form teams based on individual interests and skills. Then the hackathon, which can last anywhere from several hours to several days, begins. For hackathons that last 24 hours or longer or especially competitive ones, eating, and sleeping are often very informal, and organizers will provide an unlimited amount of snacks, pizza, and energy drinks.

At the end of hackathons, each team demonstrates its results. Very often, a panel of judges selects the winning teams, and prizes are given. Such prizes are sometimes a substantial amount of money. At a social gaming hackathon at the TechCrunch Disrupt, the conference offered $250,000 in funding to the winners.

FREEDOM TO FIND SOLUTIONS The venture capital system is very effective because it empowers entrepreneurs to act swiftly and decisively based on their idea before the market closes up. Intrapreneurs and entrepreneurs are hands-on people who like to get their hands dirty. Their decisions are informed not only by weekly or monthly reports but by daily interactions with customers, suppliers, and/or partners. They are at their very best when they can take the internal data and reports and experiment using their intuitive style of decision making—especially during early stages of idea formulation and design. A structure of operating within four hard walls will kill these individuals.

Seasoned senior *leader-investors* have learned to get the best of intrapreneurs' intuition by choosing outstanding talent and letting them run their own idea experiments. As a leader-investor, your job is to look at intrapreneurs who are so deeply— even irrationally—committed to making their ideas succeed that almost no amount of surprise and setbacks will stop them. Once you find them, give them the time, resources, and team members to succeed.

In the West, there is game called rock, paper, scissors played by two people. The game is a choosing method similar to a coin-flip, drawing straws, or throwing dice. Players thrust their hands into one of three gestures simultaneously by extending the hand toward their opponent. A fist (rock), flat hand (paper), or two fingers (scissors) represents the player's selection. The objective is to select a gesture that beats the opponent. Rock beats scissors (i.e., a fist wins over two fingers), paper covers rock, and scissors cut paper.

The freedom to act for intrapreneuring can serve as scissors that cut away the excessive paper, data, and analytical controls in today's corporations. There should be the freedom to allow a group of trusted intrapreneurs to look at problems from the bottom up, not always from the top down. It is the bottom half of the organizational pyramid that is closest to the customers and partners, and that is where intrapreneurs can make a significant difference—if they have the freedom to act.

SUPPORTIVE ENVIRONMENT   As already mentioned, intrapreneurs know that if they want to, they can easily start their own businesses outside the company. But they have decided to stay with your company. They are with you because they can see a faster path for bringing their dreams to life. At some point they realized that they are willing to commit to their boss and the organization for a successful journey together. The best intrapreneurs are not in it for themselves alone. They see a much broader opportunity to impact the organization. The intrapreneurs are looking to work on critically important financial performance growth challenges. They have confidence they can make it, but they also know they need a supportive environment to reach it. These intrapreneurs are not interested in an administrative job role. They would not tolerate being in a division that is just harvesting a market. They want volume and growth—growth for the biggest opportunity the company has decided to face. They desperately want to be with others who want the same. As a leader, how can you create a nurturing environment for them?

Here are few powerful ideas to help as you build a climate conducive to developing intrapreneurs:

1. At the right time and in the right situation, avoid rules and avoid order. Throughout the day, most employees conform to systems and policies.

But there are times when you must create little bit of chaos in your team and allow the intrapreneurs to help you do it. Managers should embrace constant change. It keeps people nimble and flexible (and shows that you want constant change). If you hate change, you will not be able to attract great intrapreneurs to your team.

2. Give yourself and your team permission to be creative—permission to try something new, permission to fail, permission to embarrass yourself, permission to have crazy ideas. Ask one important question every day of yourself and of your direct staff: "What did you fail in today?" If you didn't fail at something, you didn't try anything new and you were not curious enough.

3. Hire weird people—not necessarily the tattooed and pierced-in-strange-places kind, but people from outside your industry who would approach problems in different ways from you and your normal competitors.

4. Meetings are a necessary evil, but avoid the conference room and meet people in the halls, by the water cooler, or at their desks. Make meetings less about delegation and task management and more about cross-pollination of ideas (especially the weird ideas). This is a lot harder than centralized, top-down meetings. As a manager supporting innovation, this is your job; deal with it.

5. Structure your company and unit to be flexible. Creativity is often spontaneous and brings surprises. If it had to, can your business, teams, and individuals pivot in a new direction quickly? I am not saying you should ignore specific operating procedures for parts of your business, such as the assembly line or customer service centers. What is most needed is flexibility to deal with surprises or unplanned situations. Teams that lack flexibility and nimbleness often become rigid and promote the status quo—the nemesis of innovation.

In order to create intrapreneurial environment, managers must engender followership. Hari Mahdevan says, "I've been lucky to be around very good bosses who demonstrated this quality. I have done my best to replicate that in my work, my management style and with my expectations for my teams. The best way to do that is to be a positive shield for them. When I can manage their issues upwards, and they know that I genuinely believe in and care about their work, they give me and the organization tremendous creative output and grow as leaders themselves."

Followership cannot be taught. It has to be lived by managers. Only then will the intrapreneurs in hiding believe you.

REWARDS AND MOTIVATIONS   To a large degree, a culture of innovation is created based on the actions of managers along with a thoughtful program that recognizes and rewards those behaviors that support innovation outcomes. A reward scheme can easily make or break your innovation initiative.

In his opinion, Nagarajan shared, "One common factor in all the companies that I worked with is they have a large ambition and a mechanism that motivates individuals who are willing to take risks, within their set frameworks of business models. The rewards are not necessarily monetary in nature; often they are emotional. In my case

I had a chance to directly interact with the most senior-level executives as a young fresh college graduate at Wipro. That was critical motivation for me and many others at that time."

Mark Wright emphasized: "I never took an intrapreneurial business challenge during my assignments in Australia, Venezuela, Japan, or here in U.S. for rewards or recognition. First and foremost I asked: Does the assignment have a critical enterprise financial performance element that was aligned to my skill set? Does it allow me the freedom to innovate and run the P&L as I wish to? Does the opportunity have some huge unconstrained opportunity for growth of the business and myself? If the answers were yes, I knew rewards would be there if I performed. In fact, just being considered for such an opportunity was rewarding enough. I have always worked for bosses that compensated me well for the results I produced. Being recognized by seniors that I am the guy who can solve most difficult business growth and performance challenges is more important than money. Money is always down the list."

Working with your HR department, here are some guidelines to help you design an appropriate rewards and recognition policy for building a pipeline of intrapreneurs:

1. Keep your rewards and recognition (R&R) program as simple as possible in the beginning.
2. Integrate innovation R&R into existing practices first. For example, consider rewarding individuals for demonstrating innovation success as an extension of the current annual bonus program you might already have. In the beginning, it is not necessary to treat innovation as a separate reward process, especially if it involves money.
3. There are two types of R&R to consider: transparent and translucent. Transparent rewards are publicized and everyone knows what they are before the innovation program is launched. Translucent rewards are given based on an individual's unique contribution and are privately announced on an as-needed basis, such as a promotion or new position in the company. Nevertheless, it is made clear that the person's ideas and commitment to the innovation activities produced the rewards.
4. Be clear on the proper behaviors you want to promote and how you will measure those behaviors.
5. Recognition is a much better tool than a financial reward. Make all recognitions public, top down (from CEO/managing director or other top-level executives), and frequent in the beginning. Overcommunicate recognition. All recognitions can be accompanied by small gifts, such as dinner for two or a paid day off.
6. Intrapreneurs love challenges and being challenged. Cultivate this by developing case studies from their successes on projects.
7. In the beginning, acknowledge *all* participation by anyone and everyone. Over time, recognize *only* those who are actively participating in the innovation activities.

8. Big rewards versus small rewards. Be careful. Never turn intrapreneurs against one another. It is very hard to know which team member did what. Do not promote the unhealthy values of jealousy and greed. Promote unity, diversity, and equality.
9. Reward "good tries." Focus on recognition for lessons learned from failure. Have the person/team develop a two-page case study and share it with others. The best intrapreneurs are hiding because they do not want others to know they have crazy but possibly great ideas. Give them a path to try the ideas out, and recognize them for trying.

Recognizing innovation by filing patents or giving kudos is far more effective than any kind of cash reward or stock. People who innovate do so because they are given an innovative environment and are recognized for their creativity.

Conclusion

For Managers Concerning Intrapreneurs

During this stage of planning to build your innovation engine, the most consistent question we find in most organizations is this: How do we find intrapreneurs within our company?

While intrapreneurs exist everywhere in each organization, they cannot be identified easily. Here is how you can quickly find real intrapreneurs rather than just idea promoters. Intrapreneurs:

- Believe it is too difficult to ask for permission now and easier to ask for forgiveness later.
- Come to work ready to get fired each day.
- Get the job done, whatever the costs. Achieving project results regardless of title or job description is very important.
- Think freedom to execute ideas is more important than money.
- Never tolerate a bad apple on the team. We are in this together.
- Forget pride of authorship and spread credit to the team.
- Collaborate freely. It is never my idea alone. It cannot be done without collaboration.
- Ask for advice before sponsorship. What I don't know, I don't know.
- Love to underpromise and overdeliver.
- Are always true to their goals and practical in the change effort to achieve them.
- Feel growth and challenging projects are more important than money when it comes to retaining their services.
- Love to build and scale rather than to administer.
- Dislike professional managers and a bureaucratic management mind-set.

This list is not a scientifically formulated one to find and select your intrapreneurs but rather a good starting guide that has worked well in our fieldwork.

For Aspiring Intrapreneurs

So, you want to be an intrapreneur. How sure are you? Here are five questions to assist in your thinking and planning to become an intrapreneur:

1. Am I ready and committed to be an intrapreneur?
2. What do I need to unlearn to be successful?
3. What is my magic sauce—my hidden gifts?
4. Is my company ready for innovation and intrapreneurship?
5. What do I need to do next? What are my options to proceed?

Here are some more questions you should ask yourself to create an appropriate amount of clarity and commitment toward intrapreneurship:

1. Do I get excited about what I am doing at work?
2. Do I think about new business ideas while driving to work or taking a shower?
3. Do I get into trouble from time to time for doing things that exceed my authority?
4. Am I able to keep my ideas under cover, suppressing the urge to tell everybody about them until I have tested them and produced a plan for implementation?
5. Have I successfully pushed through bleak times, when something on which I was working looked as if it might fail?
6. Do I have more than my share of both fans and critics?
7. Can I consider trying to overcome a natural perfectionist tendency to do all the work myself and share responsibility for my ideas with a team?
8. Would I be willing to give up some of my salary in exchange for the chance to try out my business idea if the rewards for success were adequate?

If the answers to these questions are positive, you are a good candidate for becoming a corporate intrapreneur.

For Human Resource Leaders

If you are an HR consultant or a manager desiring to develop intrapreneurs, here is a list of skills and competencies (previously mentioned in Chapter 4) required for building a pipeline of world-class intrapreneurs:

1. High degree of self-knowledge
   - Clear idea of their strengths and weaknesses
   - Know how to leverage their strengths and compensate for their weaknesses
2. Knowledge of the business and culture of the organization
   - Good command of the business including the financials (how we make money)
   - Understand the culture, the values of the organization and their implications for getting things done

3. Excellent communication skills
   - Able to persuade and influence others
   - Present ideas clearly, can speak coherently in front of a group
   - Good networking skills (internally and externally)
   - Clear and concise business writing skills
   - Have evangelized successful ideas in the past
4. Moderate risk taker
   - Not afraid to fail
   - Are neither timid nor overly aggressive about taking risks
   - Take personal responsibility for their actions, don't blame others or the system
5. Team building and collaboration skills
   - Know how to leverage differences to form a winning team
   - Are seen as credible and trustworthy by others
6. Are forward thinking and opportunity oriented
7. Persevere in the face of obstacles and setbacks
8. Demonstrate passion and enthusiasm for their work
9. Open to new ideas; eager to learn

Teach to Think Small and Fast

Many world-class companies have designed their innovation engine to stay small, nimble, and fast just like a start-up.

Here are some specific examples of how they run their innovation engines to speed up the success hit rate of innovation teams and intrapreneurs:

- IBM has become the world's technology leader because of its commitment to innovation through collaboration. Its innovation philosophy is "Fail Many, but Fail Cheap." It uses "Single Portal" (one of world's top 10 intranets), innovation incubator (technology adoption process), IBM Connections (formerly Lotus Connections) (for fast information sharing), innovation jams (worldwide online ideation sessions), BluePedia (one of the largest internal Wikipedias), Sametime (for instant online meetings).
- India's Tata Group uses Tata Group Innovation Forum (TGIF), a 12-member panel of senior Tata Group executives and some CEOs of the independently run companies. "TGIF's main objective is to inspire and share best practices," says Sunil Sinha, CEO of Tata Quality Management Services and a member of the forum. At Tata Consulting Group, managers are trained in how to direct an employee's idea: Incremental innovations are handled and funded by the business unit in which the idea originated; platform-level innovations that might extend an existing offering are directed to one of the company's 19 global innovation labs, leading-edge research centers focused on specific technology areas or business sectors. Disruptive ideas tend to originate in the labs, but if one emerges from a business unit, it would be

directed to a lab or funded through an incubator fund run by the chief technology officer's office.

- Whirlpool has an innovation college–like program that creates innovation mentors, who are trained in structured innovation tools. These mentors are the primary innovation consultants for business teams to achieve their respective execution strategies.

- Intuit conducts multiday "lean start-ins" for trained intrapreneurs to teach them how to conduct rapid experimentation for their products and services.

- Kimberly-Clark conducts "expert acceleration sessions" where it brings external thought leaders (domain experts, industry analysts, scientists, leading edge technologists) face to face with business teams to help identify game-changing opportunities.

- 3M mandates internal sharing of all new innovations across product lines, markets, and R&D centers. It also has 30 customer technical centers across the world designed to better understand unique market needs and to accelerate global product introductions.

- Cognizant has idea champions, innovation champions, and igniters. Over 2,000 idea champions are active and trained in the company. Each champion must complete an Innovation Capability Building Program. There is one trained idea champion for every 100 employees. Idea champions assist building an innovation culture using the systems and process created to inculcate an environment for innovation. These champions are responsible for delivering the end result—their area's innovation portfolio. An innovation champion is a nominated individual for each client account. Often the person is the head of delivery. He or she is responsible for implementing the innovation charter and strategy for the client account. Doing this includes setting innovation objectives, interacting with customers, driving culture, and delivering the desired outcomes for the account. Igniters are everyone else who completes an innovation awareness training program. This training workshop is about 90 minutes long and is delivered through classroom and online formats. As of 2012, over 80,000 associates have completed this course and are designated igniters.

These companies are successful because they understand how to grow big but with a Silicon Valley mind-set. They have nurtured a small start-up environment within a large organizational structure. They have embraced how to continually experiment with what might be next. Most important, they have realized that they cannot survive just by relying on the knowledge and expertise within the walls of the company. In other words, they deliberately utilize outside-in (looking for emerging needs of the customers and markets) and inside-in (collaboration across internal business areas) perspectives as a standard practice.

Notes

1. Gifford Pinchot III, *Intrapreneuring: Why You Don't Have to Leave the Corporation to Become an Entrepreneur* (New York: Harper & Row, 1986).
2. Tomas Chamorro-Premuzic, "How Bad Leadership Spurs Entrepreneurship," *Harvard Business Review*, September 10, 2012. http://blogs.hbr.org/cs/2012/09/how_bad_leadership_spurs_entrepreneurship.html
3. Pinchot, *Intrapreneuring*, p. xiii.
4. Ibid.

CHAPTER 9

Sourcing Radical Ideas

At some point, you will have exhausted all the good ideas from within your company. For sustainable growth, you will need to access radical fresh ideas that can catapult you to the next business model. This effort requires deliberate reimagination. By looking at trends and convergences, you can put new ideas into your innovation pipeline. Here are important resources, ideas, and methods to help you create disruption in various industries and some important macro trends that may impact your business within the next five years.

Ideas, ideas, ideas!

Ideas are the starting point for all innovations. The bigger the idea, the more radical the innovation.

In our experience, whenever we begin to work with an organization, we see it has plenty of ideas. The issue is that the organization can't find them, or don't know which to select, or have no clear method to materialize them for results. Finding small and safe ideas is somewhat easier than large radical ideas.

As described step by step in earlier chapters, let's say you begin to install your innovation engine. In the first year, you will find plenty of ideas, both small and big. If you find 500 ideas to fill your pipeline, there should be at least 100 worthy of exploring. Of these, at least 25 will be very interesting and worthy of experimentation. Of those, two or three ideas should be extremely large. Most everyone at the senior level will like these but will be hesitant to jump in. (If you've implemented your innovation engine correctly, there should be at least 25 teams working on exploring these ideas and some starting to see successful results within six months or less.)

When our global clients work with us and pursue the path of implementing the innovation engine, they typically yield 250% ROI within the first ten months. This happens because the innovation engine method allows strategic sponsorships from leaders, commitment of resources toward the innovation program, clear processes to move ideas to execution, proper innovation tools, and clear governance and management of your program.

What about after the first year? Your real challenge then is to keep that momentum going.

After the first year, you will need a process to source *radical ideas*. This process to find big ideas that can catapult your business to new heights, open up new markets, or bring in completely unfamiliar profits will be much more difficult.

In this chapter, we address two critical strategies to help fill your innovation pipeline beyond the first year:

1. Allow ideas to travel and grow in your organization
2. Leaders and managers: Learn five power skills to help find uncontested ideas

The Path: How Ideas Travel

To help create and keep a culture of innovation, many world-class companies have designed their business innovation engine to be small, nimble, and fast, just like a start-up. As a result, they are able to outcompete their rivals much more often.

As we discussed in earlier chapters, intrapreneurs have a crucial role to play in the organizational innovation journey. But this doesn't mean that only intrapreneurs can innovate. Everyone in the firm should be encouraged and motivated to be creative and innovative—every day. To build a culture of innovations across the entire organizations, it all starts with new and novel ideas. Help everyone find ideas, small or large, and then assist them on a journey toward execution.

How do ideas travel from inside the person to outside in the environment?

As shown in Figure 9.1, all ideas travel through four steps before they become innovations.

1. **Creativity.** Being creative generates ideas. Everyone has creative capacity. Some people are able to tap into their creative side more often and with more frequency than others. Everyone has been very creative at least once in their life. Since the act of being creative lies within people, ideas always come from people. The question you might ask is: What stimulates creativity itself? We'll look at this little later.
2. **Design.** Every idea selected must then go through a design process. Depending on the industry or type of idea, the design process varies. A toy manufacturer has a very specific design process for taking new toy ideas into working models. A manufacturer of industrial electrical components has a design department that follows the electrical standards and regulations of that country to build custom solutions for customers. A software company has a design process for taking a business requirement software application and turning it into a working solution. The quality of your design capability is dependent on two critical factors:
   a. The quality and quantity of total knowledge in the firm
   b. Access to new technologies during the design process

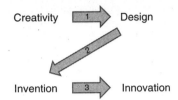

FIGURE 9.1   Four Steps: From Ideas to Innovation

3. **Invention.** A design process applied to an idea produces a working model, a prototype, or a pilot. If the idea is completely new to the person or the company, it is called invention—to that person or company. It may not be an invention to the market, but it may be an invention to the firm.

4. **Innovation.** When an invention is brought to a group of customers and to market (internal or external), and the user/buyer ascribes a value to the invention, it can be called *innovation*. In other words, innovation is innovation when your customer says so, not when you do. If the same invention changes the consumer behavior of the majority of the market being served, it can be called a *disruptive/radical/breakthrough innovation*.

As we discovered in Chapter 7, not all ideas are worthy of going through each step. Doing so would consume a lot of time and resources. Companies that have years of experience in the game of innovation or that have successful innovation engines are able to step through the path much faster. Because of that, they have new insights or new knowledge about the market, technology, customers, business model, or various other competitive elements, often resulting in a clear advantage over the competition.

Source of Creativity

If creativity gives rise to ideas and, ultimately, ideas give rise to innovation, then what gives rise to ideas? In other words, what stimulates creativity?

This is a very significant and arguably the most fundamental question regarding innovation that has not been fully addressed by the innovation gurus. The secret to innovation lies within the answer to this question. We have attempted to answer this question based on 25 years of working in the field. See Chapter 10 to find the *one* secret of creativity and innovation.

Quality of Ideas

When it comes to innovation, the most frequent complaint we hear from senior executives is that there are "not enough good ideas."

What constitutes a good idea? Saying "ideas are worthless and only execution matters" misses the point. Instead, if ideas were viewed more in terms of path direction, then good execution would help either to refine them or to reveal the need to abandon them as you move forward.

Good ideas depend on the accumulated context, knowledge, and technologies available within your organization. Most large organizations have a wealth of all of these. So why aren't there more *good ideas*?

Critical Thinking and Creative Thinking

What is missing is the combination of critical thinking and creative thinking to help find great ideas.

Creative thinking alone is not sufficient, because all creativity is based on your current understanding of a topic. You can be very creative, but only within your own total sphere—your skills, values, beliefs, knowledge, and experiences. A radical idea might lie outside of that sphere. This is one of the reasons why in ideation sessions, we promote diverse perspectives by inviting a variety of people for brainstorming. Yet even that does not fully work for breakthrough thinking. How many times have you been invited to an innovation session where most ideas the teams found were all safe? None pushed the envelope. Thus, creative thinking alone is not good enough to compete in today's markets.

Critical thinking is the missing step in most innovation initiatives.

Critical thinking may look like the opposite of creative thinking, but it is as essential. Critical thinking gives you direction, defines large problems to be solved, and identifies the emerging unmet needs of your customer base. Creative thinking initially will give you fresh ideas, but both it and critical thinking are essential to find *good* and *great ideas*.

If ideas were better designed to be actionable in the first place (e.g., as a testable hypothesis), your execution would not only be more efficient but would yield better insights for future iterations. To say that (all) ideas are worthless does not serve anyone, especially intrapreneurs. Operationalize both types of thinking, critical and creative, to help find an outstanding pipeline of ideas.

Case Study: Energy Market

When it comes to energy and our carbon footprint, the utility industry has invested heavily in a complex web of technologies, business models, regulations, and processes over the past few decades. Large industrial companies have taken advanced steps to make their plants and facilities smarter, especially within the last ten years. Many service providers, such as Siemens, ABB, Schneider, GE, Tata, and IBM, are helping to make our planet smarter.

This leading-edge clean web, as it's called, is technology that controls energy use in buildings (such as lighting, heating, ventilation, and air conditioning) in a way that responds to real-time conditions in the electric utility grid. As the costs for generating and delivering power go up during times of community peak usage, minimizing facility use reduces the strains on business and community budgets and reduces climate impacts. At least in the United States, companies that commit to making their buildings smarter can receive significant incentives from their utilities and make the electric grid much more efficient.

This innovation is rapidly advancing, given its great benefits to all stakeholders, especially our planet. It's an indispensable innovation that helps avert climate change, which would otherwise lead to much more severe weather, flooding, drought, food insecurity, conflict, and migration.

One of the first instances of this dynamic facility management was created in 1996, at Connecticut-based Northeast Utilities (NU), under the leadership of Tim Maurer, director of market management and an intrapreneur in the making. Maurer had been hired to help the utility transform from a regulated entity to a competitive energy marketer in the nation's first open market.

During Maurer's preparation for his job interview with NU's president, he conducted exhaustive research and noticed in the trade press that General Motors had entered into a contract with its Michigan-based utilities to conduct spot "sub metering" to help the company learn how much electricity it used, where, and when. To help GM identify and control electric usage, the utility companies needed to visit each GM facility and plug in monitors, outlet by outlet and panel by panel.

Maurer's hypothesis was that "there was an opportunity in the GM example that NU could replicate regarding helping clients know and manage loads."

Back then, Maurer was familiar with the financial services industry only and had no previous knowledge of the utility industry, although he had natural instincts and a frame of reference for knowing if an idea was good. He pondered whether what GM was requesting fulfilled one of four strategic business value propositions: customer intimacy, price superiority, operational excellence, or product leadership.

Maurer had built his career on the *heartfelt quest* for customer intimacy, seeking to solve issues and to meet unmet needs that would yield either consumer lifestyle contributions, or total-lower-cost solutions for businesses.

He used this very nascent idea of helping clients know and manage their usage in his meeting with NU's president, Hugh MacKenzie. The interview went well, and Maurer got the job to help NU's transformation toward a market leadership position.

The *inspiration* to take this customer intimacy concept further as an innovation took some time to happen. In fact, Maurer faced many challenges that might have impeded turning this into an innovation: These included the need to build a market-centric organization, assess fast-evolving regulatory frameworks, develop research-based strategies to support all market sectors and types of clients with sound products and pricing, and market the new NU brand.

As Maurer describes, "One day it struck. The inspiration occurred. It was like a *divine intervention*. I wasn't even thinking or focused on it. I had stored it in my subconscious."

It turned out that the HR manager Maurer worked with to build his department was married to a manager of Rockwell Automation, a company that served both the industrial and commercial customers. With help of the HR manager, Maurer learned about how Rockwell was just releasing its Power Monitor device that could monitor usage real time rather than simply going from panel to panel and outlet to outlet to identify electric usage data (loads).

At this point, Maurer intuitively figured out that by creating a new portal that, with a bit of ingenuity, could be integrated with Rockwell's process control systems and energy management systems, NU could do more than just monitor and quantify usage of a building—NU could actually monitor and affect real-time electrical usage and reduce costly peak usage. This would be a game-changing solution.

Maurer began leading a collaborative interaction with Rockwell. The idea was solidified and execution issues were solved. Maurer credits this idea to divine intervention, and it would not be his last one.

This innovation was acknowledged in the awards Maurer received from NU for successfully leading its transformation—which resulted in the company securing over 35% share of load among 30 of the nation's top competitors, all of which were fiercely gunning for load share to make a mark in this new deregulated industry.

Maurer continued to evolve this innovation. However, in mid 2007 he left the industry to run a refugee resettlement organization. Later he returned to the business world to lead product and marketing for a unit of the global payment processing giant First Data. There Maurer learned more about information technology informatics, database management, rules engines, account portfolio optimization, straight-through processing, and financial settlement.

A decade later, Maurer returned to the electricity industry as vice president of product and marketing for a municipal utility cooperative, just as the industry was evaluating smart meter deployments that were to be fueled with federal stimulus funds. While small utilities couldn't afford the costs of meter change-outs or the effort to secure federal funds, Maurer knew that by working with the latest in monitoring and control technology and insights from both NU and First Data, he could innovate again to help clients and utilities lower their peak use and cut overall costs within the entire supply-chain.

This time inspiration and what Maurer views as divine intervention struck again. Maurer's company was housed in the same building that housed corporate offices for a software company that helped control heating, ventilation, and air-conditioning at facilities such as Heathrow Airport, Disney, and the Pentagon. Maurer attended a trade show to explore the latest technologies and discovered a wireless energy management system deployed by GE that could be tapped for behind-the-meter control.

This gave rise to a new idea—for a wireless system to support smaller, underserved commercial and industrial clients. Maurer would get all parties to see the new white space necessary to meet the unmet needs and to integrate municipal utility power supply and facility management via a "building area network" as the next generation of electric smart-grid innovation.

Maurer would later build a third generation of the solution and demonstrate it in California and to federal and state regulators. This led to the U.S. Chairman of the Federal Energy Regulatory Commission (FERC), Jon Wellinghoff, proclaiming "I think the traditional utilities are either going to have to change or die. With the building systems that are now available, and with the ability to allow those systems to participate in the grid, we now have the ability to have everyone be, in essence, their own mini utility."[1]

More than a decade later, when most intrapreneurs would have given up on their vision, Maurer kept pushing the idea as high as possible all the way up to FERC's innovation department to underscore that this is a people–process–technology issue rather than just a simple technology innovation. He noted that success would require a new business model innovation with critical and creative thinking each step of the way. He envisioned a new ecosystem across utilities, energy service companies, device manufacturers, and demand response providers—a herculean but truly disruptive idea.

Today, Maurer has successfully built the new business model and is incubating fourth-generation innovation offerings for the U.S. multibillion-dollar smart-grid and smart-building markets for DS Energy Innoventures, a small start-up in Hartford, Connecticut. He is doing this by co-creating with companies offering wireless energy management system, open IT protocols, and facility visualization of water, gas, and electric usage as a best-in-class sustainability solution.

Five Power Skills to Source Uncontested Ideas

The next sections present five power skills (see Figure 9.2) that can be taught to your leaders and intrapreneurs to improve both critical and creative thinking. Based on your industry, these skills are not easy to learn and may require customization. Some skills may be more important to your organization than others. When implemented well, they can be a great source of game-changing opportunities for your organization.

Skill #1: Develop Discontent

When the times are tough, many companies become restless, but when everything is going well, they sit back and enjoy the profits.

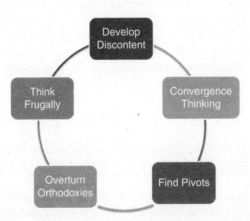

FIGURE 9.2   Five Power Skills to Source Uncontested Ideas

In contrast, when good times are rolling, real intrapreneurs are restless. All successful companies and individuals are highly discontented during peak periods. They know that past success does not guarantee future glory. They know they can become the next Kodak, Digital Equipment, or Novell—companies that enjoyed huge success for decades but too easily stumbled and died. How today's darlings, such as Google, Apple, Cognizant, and Facebook, will fare in the future remains to be seen, but what is known is that the fundamentals of business—the climbing and jumping of S-Curves—will continue separating those businesses that lead their industries from those that lag.

Creative discontent is not about anger, unhappiness, or any type of negative emotional state of mind regarding your subordinates or peers. Instead, it means discomfort with your current state of mind. While humanity's inner quest is to be peaceful, peace is elusive when you know there is something much better around the corner, even though current conditions do not suggest that change is necessary. Discontent, in this context, is like an undercurrent in the ocean bringing a feeling of uncertainty to even the best of swimmers.

All of our intrapreneurial candidates seemed to be somewhat restless like the undercurrent. As we learned in Chapter 8, they always had two or three large-vision questions (and ideas) brewing even though they were getting continuous growth opportunities or working on a critical business challenge. They are never done. They are most unhappy when everyone else is happy. If you have a few really great intrapreneurs around you, you know this for a fact.

A very effective way to create discontent is to ask questions that shake people up. For example, let's say your business is in the energy sector. Your business may be doing fabulous, but my guess is that it is making just an incremental difference relative to the size of the world's energy problem. Many argue that since we already have some alternative energy technology available, we should quickly deploy it, but this won't solve the problems we face today. Any time focused on short-term, incremental solutions will only detract from working on the home runs that could change the assumptions around energy and society's resources. Ask home run questions such as these:

- What are the next-generation technologies (very risky investments that stand a high chance of failure but, if successful, enable larger technological leaps that promise earthshaking impact)?
- How can we make solar power cheaper than coal or viable without subsidies?
- How can we economically making lighting and air conditioning 80% more efficient?
- What will it take to make vehicle engines 100% more efficient?
- What technologies can give ultra-cheap energy storage?

The goal is not to find the silver bullet within next quarter. But even one Facebook-like disruption out of 100 attempts can upend all internal conventional wisdom, strategic forecasts, and, most important, our energy future.

For you as a business leader, the issue is not to motivate the intrapreneurs. Instead, your challenge is to promote creative discontent for everyone else in your organization—before the business slows down or goes south.

TIM MAURER   Tim Maurer is a good example of a leader innovator who generated creative discontent everywhere he went. He had a huge vision—to fundamentally change the game being played by the energy sector in the United States, to move the sector focus from energy generation and utilization to energy optimization. As of today, hardly anyone is working on this complex challenge. There is a multibillion-dollar market out there, and virtually no one is looking for solutions. Tim Maurer is.

Successful companies exhibit high discontent during peak periods. They know that past success does not guarantee future glory.

CHESTER CARLSON   In the early 1930s, U.S. patent lawyer Chester Carlson was dissatisfied with existing methods of making copies of patents. He was determined to find a better method than the existing photographic methods, which were slow and inefficient.

After an extensive search through patents and other literature, Carlson finally had a promising idea. He began experimenting and in 1938 produced the first print using a process that eventually would become the basis of the modern photocopier. Static electricity was the key to his invention. In his 1939 patent, Carlson called this process electrophotography. But he soon came to call it xerography—from the Greek *xeros*, meaning dry, and *graphein*, meaning to write.

His invention was a radical departure from existing technology, however, and it took many years both to develop and improve it and to persuade a company to invest in it.

Now it is impossible to imagine a modern office without photocopying facilities. Xerox also took advantage of the increasing use of computing in the office to diversify into computer printers, scanners, fax machines, and multifunction machines. Many people predicted that the spread of computers would lead to the paperless office. However, recent estimates suggest people are making 500 billion photocopies each year and that there are 15 trillion (15,000,000,000,000) copies on photocopiers, computer printers, and multifunction machines combined in the United States alone.[2]

"Creativity is predicted on some sort of dissatisfaction with the current state of things; otherwise, the impetus for creativity would be absent," says Harvard University researcher Shelley Carson, author of *Your Creative Brain: Seven Steps to Maximize Imagination, Productivity, and Innovation in Your Life*.[3]

SERGEY BRIN AND LARRY PAGE   Since 2004 in their IPO letter and once a year since then, the founders of Google, Sergey Brin and Larry Page, write a letter to all their employees and shareholders. They were inspired by reading Warren Buffett's essays in his annual reports to Berkshire Hathaway shareholders titled "An Owner's Manual." Google's 4,000-word compositions are classic examples of messages that create excitement and discontent for everyone. Each letter is articulate, edgy, personally engaging, and an example of what makes Google tick. No wonder that Google continues to outpace the competition.

Skill #2: Convergence Thinking

What two or more areas are merging?

In today's dynamic and complex business environment, we need to create organizations capable of operating with urgency, multidimensionality, flexibility, creativity, and in context, providing complex solutions. One of the primary missing ingredients is the ability for convergence thinking among executives and leaders. In our opinion, this is an important factor for today's corporations.

The business game is changing due to convergence—a process by which the boundaries across industries, businesses, markets, geographies, and/or customer experiences become blurred, resulting in new business opportunities for serving customer needs and improving customer value.

CONVERGENT ECONOMY   We are now in a convergent economy. This does not refer to basic partnerships between, say, NGOs and businesses—occasional cooperation or arm's-length agreements. Convergence is not about one-time projects and programs. It is about global development, as the convergence of issues and interests and, most important, solutions continues to grow with an unwavering emphasis on outputs and impact rather than on organizational structures and stereotypical roles.

Convergence of solutions means that all participants pivot continually around the same sets of requirements for those in need. Those living in poor communities clearly *do* care about obtaining access to clean water, healthcare, and education—but exactly how these services are delivered and paid for makes little difference, provided they meet the needs of the communities themselves.

For successful growth through innovation, executives must understand the key drivers of a broader concept of convergence as well as how to detect and manage convergence. By using a multidimensional framework with changing customer needs as the anchor, they can better position their firms for the increasingly convergent economy.

EXAMPLES OF CONVERGENCE   Digital and analog have been converging for over three decades, facilitated by advances in digital technology. Several goods and services are being reshaped by changes in the mix of digital and analog elements. A growing number of goods and services are emerging in the middle of this continuum. This middle area is represented by a balanced proportion of analog and digital elements in the choice and consumption of the offering. For example, air travel reservations, which before the advent of the Internet used to be characterized primarily by analog elements, are now increasingly made online, leading to a substantial influence of digital elements. Such convergence has fundamentally altered managerial thinking in many markets.

Cosmeceuticals is the new industry emerging from the convergence of the personal care/cosmetic and pharmaceutical industries. This industry is fueled by advances in chemistry and biotechnology that allow the use of pharmacological and cosmetic therapies in areas where, earlier, surgical intervention was needed.

Nutraceuticals is the new industry emerging from the convergence of food and pharmaceutical industries. The new products in this industry are sometimes known as functional foods and are strategic answers to consumers' growing sensitivity to health and wellness in everyday consumption.

Nutricosmetics is an industry generated by the fusion of food and beauty products. These convergent industries are big and are growing substantially. For example, the global nutricosmetic product market for 2010 was $2.4 billion, up from $1.9 billion in 2005.

We are also seeing evidence of some tech markets converging with some "touch" markets as some tech products are increasingly incorporating "touch" fashion attributes.

Vertu, the jewelry mobile phone from Nokia, is a luxury phone brand touting the aspirational position as the "Rolex of the mobile communication world." Vertu's offering, like fine jewelry, is available in silver, gold, or platinum finishes. Other high-tech offerings incorporate strong aesthetic design elements—for example, the Serene fashion phone is a product of a joint venture between Samsung and Bang & Olufsen.

High-touch products are also embracing greater high-tech attributes. Some textile companies, for instance, are incorporating micro-encapsulation technology into their products and cultivating a new breed of products—cosmetotextiles. This technology allows for the slow release of desirable cosmetic properties into the fabric. There are fast emerging markets for new fabrics and clothes being introduced that have medicinal properties such as anti-diabetic and anti-asthmatic properties. For example, cellulite affects nearly all women and some men for most of their lives. In the past few decades, the personal care industry has responded by designing anticellulite gels and lotions to topically reduce its appearance. Lytess, a French company, has developed more than 20 shape-wear products. One line of their micro-massaging garments includes sleeves, shorts, capris, a top and leggings that are designed to target cellulite with a double-knit fiber of 92% polyamide and 8% elastane. These special innovative fibers are engineered to stimulate blood flow and are dosed with actives before being spun and dyed. This process binds the ingredients to the fibers in a similar way to glue.

Convergence is not simply about combining ideas and technology; it is a primary leadership competency that allows organizations to design the right future.

Does your organization nurture such a competency and/or a method for building and nurturing it?

CONVERGENCE LEVERS   Three major factors drive convergence: technology, competition, and customer. Each factor directly influences convergence, and the three are interdependent in that they may indirectly influence each other. Technology is only one of the contributors to convergence, which may stem from the interaction of many forces, including growing intra-industry competition and the needs of the customer. The essence of convergence is that it is driven by new forms of competition—growing interindustry and cross-industry competition—and the collapsing boundaries between industries.

Teach convergence thinking to all your top talent and the executive team.

Skill #3: Find Pivots

One definition of the word "chaos" is the uncertainty sparked by uncharted territory, economic recession, and bubbles of opportunity. Chaos often makes organizations retreat.

But not always. Disney, CNN, MTV, Hyatt, Burger King, FedEx, Microsoft, Apple, Gillette, AT&T, Texas Instruments, 20th Century Fox, IBM, Merck, Hershey's, IHOP, Eli Lilly, Coors, Bristol-Myers Squibb, Sun, Amgen, the Jim Henson Company, LexisNexis, Autodesk, Adobe, Symantec, Electronic Arts, Fortune, GE, and Hewlett-Packard are all iconic companies that were founded during periods of economic recession.[4]

The wonderful thing about our world is that everything, everyone, and every system evolves over time. Where there is evolution, change exists. Change creates opportunities for innovation. And if the amount of change is disproportionate in size, there is chaos. Chaos causes movement in a completely new direction—we call this a pivot. For world-class intrapreneurs, a pivot is similar to Nirvana, a heavenly abode for growth and opportunity.

Table 9.1 shows some examples of pivots that have changed our world in the last five years.

TABLE 9.1   Examples of Pivots

From	To
Broadcast television	Viral videos
Newspapers	Blogs
Album sales	Concert tours
Physical stores	Online e-commerce
United States and G7	China and India
E-mail	Social media
Voice calls	Text messaging
Phone calls	Facebook status updates
Public libraries	Wikipedia
Classroom method	Virtual learning
Recruiting	Offshore outsourcing
Medical doctors	Nurse practitioners
Accountants	Online filing
Lawyers	Online legal forms
Loan officers	Automated lending
Oil on canvas	Digital Imagery

The good news about pivots is that they don't occur overnight, yet they can be seen, if you have the eyes for it. You can teach people how to find pivots.

SMITH CORONA   For many reasons, in 1992, executives at Smith Corona, a typewriter and word processing company, founded in Syracuse, NY, and later with headquarters in New York City,, decided to relocate part of its production to Mexico after a partnership that was started with Acer, a Taiwanese computer hardware and electronics manufacturer. There was very little support for this move at the top ranks—for obvious reasons. This sort of project created a sense of urgency and distraction. The organization was entering a period of chaos, and it was not clear that computer word processors, instead of their core business in mechanical type-writers, could save the company.

The decision to move became the single biggest initiative for the $500 million company. The relocation was expected to slash the company's costs by nearly 12%, a single best strategic choice at the time.

Smith Corona was going through a change that required organizational alignment and focus. When the world became chaotic, the company did what most organizations do: It retreated to its comfort zone. After only one year, the board killed the Acer partnership.

In a trade interview, the CEO, G. Lee Thompson, defended his dying industry, saying: "Many people believe that the typewriter and word-processor business is a buggy-whip industry, which is far from true. There is still a strong market for our products in the United States and the world."[5]

Three years later, Smith Corona declared bankruptcy. Acer went on to become the fourth-largest PC company in the world. Mike Chernago, former Smith Corona VP of operations, noted, "People screamed like crazy when they killed that deal. But at the time, the executives thought that Smith Corona was never going to be put out of business. It was hard to imagine that the typewriter would be annihilated."[6]

Even as late as 1992, Smith Corona did not see the pivot: typewriter to software-based word processing computers.

DISRUPTION CREATES PIVOTS   In an article titled "Disruption Is a Moving Target," Scott Anthony reports that disruption is a three-step process:[7]

1. "Disruptors enter a market incumbents don't care about." Protected by their unattractively small markets, entrants build skills and acquire market insight that big companies don't have. By servicing unwanted customers, they build maverick brands.
2. "Entrants grow as incumbents flee." Growing in popularity and success, entrants begin to creep up the value chain. The "old school" incumbents respond by shifting focus away from their full customer base and instead toward "high-value customers."
3. "The incumbent hits a ceiling." Once new entrants reach a critical mass, they create partnerships that enable them to "go for the kill." The incumbents get pushed past their ability to compete and crisis ensues. Sneaky.

Intrapreneurs can see disruptive technologies ahead of others. As an example, Steve Jobs and his team at Apple disrupted Sony's music and the Walkman business because they were able to see that compact discs would be disrupted by downloadable music files. In 1999, Marc Randolph and Reed Hastings of Netflix were able to see VHS- and CD-based entertainment move quickly to an online and on-demand format and completely disrupted Blockbuster's business model. Sam Walton was able to see an untapped market for consumers looking for low cost and high convenience with a large variety of products, and disrupted JCPenney, Sears, and Kmart by opening Wal-Mart stores all over the country—the key innovation being a just-in-time inventory management and technology system.

Many organizations that do not have a process to see fundamental disruptive technologies that create pivots in their industry will lose. Kodak could not see that digital photography would disrupt chemical photography. Smith Corona did not comprehend the power of personal computers. Facit AB used to dominate the European market for mechanical calculators but did not adapt digital technology and failed to compete with digital competitors.

PIVOTS: NEXT FIVE YEARS   Where can you find the future pivots? Here are some good sources to help you find pivots for your industry:

Books
- *Beyond the Obvious: Killer Questions That Spark Game-Changing Innovation* by Phil McKinney
- *Microtrends* by Mark J. Penn
- *Minitrends: How Innovators & Entrepreneurs Discover & Profit* by John H. Vanston
- *The Next Big Thing: Spotting and Forecasting Consumer Trends for Profit* by William Higham
- *Outrageous Fortunes* by Daniel Altman
- *The Secrets of Economic Indicators* by Bernard Baumohl

Web Sites Worth Exploring:
- Trend Hunter: www.trendhunter.com
- Now and Next: www.nowandnext.com
- World Future Society: www.wfs.org
- Database of upcoming innovations: www.moreinspirations.com
- Network of 15,000 spotters across the world: www.springwise.com
- Innovation and insights scanning network: community.iknowfutures.eu
- Global trends: www.globaltrends.com
- Macro- and microtrends: www.trendone.com

These lists are in no way comprehensive, but they should give you a good start in finding pivots that will impact your business, markets, and industry in the near future. The faster you identify the pivots, the quicker your ability to make strategic choices for your next big innovations.

Another good way to find pivots is to monitor the institutional flow of money. Two great sources to monitor this are the venture capital and the private equity community and Silicon Valley and other similar ecosystems across the global.

Pivots are influenced, and sometimes created, by very smart people in the world. Find where they are making personal and institutional investments, and you will find emerging pivots.

Skill #4: Overturn Orthodoxies

To find radical ideas, most organizations promote "learning" new tools, techniques, and methods. The more important barrier to innovation is the inability to *forget* things that prevent innovations from arising. *Unlearning* is just as important, if not more so, than learning in regard to innovation. Teach everyone to *forget* things—in other words, remove orthodoxies in the systems.

The term "orthodox" has been defined as adhering to what is commonly accepted, customary, or traditional. Orthodoxies are self-imposed boundaries on how a company operates and competes. Orthodoxies are invisible patterns, never fully articulated, but always driving daily decisions. When left unchallenged, they prevent individuals and teams from taking advantage of new opportunities.

Identifying and overturning old organizational conventions or boundaries enables breakthrough applications to be born; in so doing, they frequently push companies with deeply held conventions out of the marketplace.

Every organization has a plethora of orthodoxies, in every corner. A new employee often can see them immediately, but the tenured staff may not. Orthodoxies show up as internal issues holding things back.

Challenging orthodoxies can provide clarity on existing paradigms worth changing to improve your business model, products, services, processes, customer experience, or brand.

SIGNS OF ORTHODOXIES Once we identify orthodoxies, they need to be overturned. Challenging orthodoxies allows you to redefine the rules of competition and invariably develop new opportunities. Doing so quickly opens up thinking within the group to dissolve arguments that "That's the way we've always done it." Challenging them does not require us to overturn the laws of nature; rather, it allows us to redefine the perceived constraints and boundaries regarding:

- The industry business model
- Identifying consumers/customers
- The delivery and service model vis-à-vis customers
- How the value is delivered to customers
- How product/service is designed, manufactured, and supported
- The economic engine: target costs, margins, and profits

- The operation model for service and monitoring
- Operational flexibility and compliance within a regulatory structure
- "The way things are done here"
- "This is the way we have always done it"
- "This is expected by (customers, management, our shareholders)"

EXAMPLES OF ORTHODOXIES   Entrepreneurs and intrapreneurs are very good at finding *industry* orthodoxies. Overturning orthodoxies leads to huge new opportunities for growth and disruption. Examples of young start-ups that challenged industry orthodoxies, thereby creating some of the world's biggest brands:

- Starbucks: "No consumer will pay more than $2 for a cup of coffee."
- University of Phoenix: "College or university education must occur in a physical place" (not online via the Internet).
- Dell: "Computers can be sold only through retail outlets" (not through catalogs).
- Apple: "A personal computer must have a separate CPU, screen, and DVD player" (unlike a screen with a built-in CPU and DVD player).
- Fresh Express: "Consumers want a fresh head of lettuce" (and will not buy pre-packaged in a plastic bag).
- Federal Express: "All goods can travel only in a linear transportation system" (not a hub-and-spoke system).

When we are helping our clients build a systematic innovation engine, we uncover plenty of industry orthodoxies as well as internal ones. Often orthodoxies have a negative or limiting connotation. Here are some specific examples of orthodoxies that may reside within your organization.

Concerning Competition
- "Our primary competition is (*company name*); others are not big enough." (This can create a limited, biased view of market players. Sony dominated the portable music player and music businesses. It viewed Panasonic, Samsung, and Sanyo as competitors. Then Apple arrived, a computer manufacturer.)
- "We have the best technologies to outcompete anyone in our markets." (No technologies are permanent. Every technology evolves, and new ones can be bought or built using open innovation, sometimes overnight by a young start-up.)
- "XYZ company is more innovative than us."
- "Our competition is outsourcing to bring price down."
- "We differentiate ourselves on the breadth of our offerings."

Concerning Culture
- "We can't take risks because of the nature of our business."
- "We can grow only through acquisition."
- "Our leaders have many years of industry experience; we should never challenge them."

- "Savings don't matter unless they are clear-cut and quantifiable."
- "We don't have resources for that."
- "We can't use your idea because it isn't our standard."
- "We have so much work, we have no time to think."
- "We don't have time to come up with new ideas."
- "Working from home doesn't allow enough *face time*."
- "Employees working from home are less productive."

Concerning Customers
- "It takes months to train someone on our applications; they are very complex."
- "Our strong customers love us because we are very flexible."
- "We are very customer-centric, which is why we are the industry leader."
- "Vertical business units are our primary customers."

Concerning Industry
- "We are not cutting-edge due to our industry needs."
- "Our industry is limited by current legislation."
- "We have to comply with regulations."

Concerning Products and Product Development
- "All products must comply with our standard product development process."
- "We invested in a platform/vendor so we have to use it."
- "All of our products use the best components."
- "It will be too costly to sunset legacy product/applications."
- "Mobile technology is too cost prohibitive to give to all our employees."
- "Open systems (e.g., Facebook, Twitter) will cause security issues."
- "We need to make this run faster."

Concerning Processes
- "Our IT best practice is to deliver three releases per year."
- "We can't bring on a person/contractor quicker than three weeks."
- "Our systems are too large for us to move quickly."
- "You need a ticket for that; anything can be done with a ticket."
- "Business must provide us the requirement first."
- "Compliance will not let us do it."
- "We must keep our data safe, so we must lock down our environment tightly."
- "We need formal approval for that."

If you look hard enough, you will find similar orthodoxies concerning brand, service, employee benefits, community involvement, and partnerships. Not all orthodoxies are bad, but when they are not examined, challenged, and validated, they can harm the organization. When the right ones are overturned, you can transform the organizational culture.

All of the intrapreneurs we met, knowingly or unknowing, have a natural talent for finding and challenging orthodoxies. Teach and develop this skill as part of all executive development programs.

Skill #5: Think Frugally

With a revered history of innovations, the developed nations have become the engine for all economies. Dominant logic says that the emerging (some might say already *emerged*) rivals, such as India and China, will never be able to create the next 3M, Hewlett-Packard, Apple, Google or Facebook because those countries lack the ecosystems for innovation readily available in Silicon Valley and Route 128 in Boston. In fact, proper analysis may show validity of such arguments.

However, Professor Clay Christensen, in his seminal book, *Disruptive Innovation*, clearly shows that chasing only high-margin solutions can displace any business very quickly.[8] He argues that most incumbents have already lost their market leadership to new entrants attacking the low-end markets first; the U.S. steel and automotive giants of the 1970s are two good examples. Incumbents use the ideology of primarily investing in higher-margin markets and overtly leaving low-end businesses open to smaller players. Over time, these so-called small competitors move up the value chain by increasing quality and service. Soon after, customers cannot see any large difference between a large and a smaller player. This drives intense price competition. When firms compete on price alone, products and services become commoditized. Due to inherently higher overhead, incumbents eventually find it difficult to survive and often go out of business. This happens because of the incumbent's lack of focus on their low-end, or, frugal, markets.

Besides hard work, start-ups become successful because they were frugal in their origins. Such fast-growing companies have been resourceful and flexible during their growth stages. This same innate ability exists in our intrapreneurs. Even if the company is large, successful corporate innovators have a natural ability to think on their feet, tap into just the right internal and external resources, and convince others to follow their ideas. In other words, the are very resourceful, they will exhaust all the free resources available to them first, before spending resource (time and money) too early in the idea development process.

Our firm has been working with some of the leading brands in India, such as Coromandel International—one of the largest fertilizer manufacturers; Larsen & Toubro—one of the top five multinational national, multi-sector company; and Cognizant—the world's second largest IT services company. We are on the ground closely working with these companies to make them more innovative.

As described in Chapter 8, intrapreneurs in India are not different much from intrapreneurs anywhere else, except they have one noticeable attribute. Due to India's history as an underdeveloped nation, intrapreneurs there often find fixes, shortcuts, and workarounds to every daily activity. It is the way of life, part of every individual's DNA and so deeply ingrained that it has a slang name: *jugaad,* which means a creative, just-in-time solution that will make do. Such solutions can be called *frugal innovation* practices.

Frugal innovations require *frugal thinking*—an ability to engineer cost-conscious solutions to address large unmet needs of internal and external customers. This does not happen just in India, but it is most visible in a country like India. The primary driver of frugal thinking is scarcity of time and resources.

Frugal thinking forces individuals to be highly creative just to accomplish routine jobs. It is not about being cheap. With the daily pressures of limited time, resources, and money, it is crucial to help everyone find more creative ways to innovate. India is one destination where this can be observed.

In India, you are exposed to the role of "culture" as a system for solving life problems; it is a holistic approach very different from the technocratic, optimizing, fast, growth-oriented strategies that tend to rule in the West. If you look hard enough into the eyes of a vibrant young software engineer, electrical engineer, or mechanical engineer, you will be able to observe an intrapreneur in making who is already equipped with the frugal thinking skill.

Frugal thinking is now pervasive elsewhere, thanks to a groundbreaking book written by Dr. Vijay Govindarajan of Tuck Business School at Dartmouth College and General Electric's boss, Jeff Immelt. Two other new books are influencing the C suites. The first, written by Govindarajan and Chris Trimble, is called *Reverse Innovation*,[9] and the second, *Jugaad Innovation*, is by Navi Radjou, Jaideep Prabhu, and Simone Ahuja.[10] Both sources are filled with frugal innovation stories from companies such as General Electric, Harman, Toyota, Mahindra & Mahindra, Haier, Logitech, John Deer, Pepsi, Renault-Nissan, and many others.

Many Western firms have self-imposed boundaries on what a product should be, how it should be sold, or how it should be packaged and delivered. Intrapreneurs are very good at identifying such assumptions and challenging them, especially in the context of a given issue or product. For example, if you are a product manager for a shampoo brand, the cost of a bottle of shampoo for the consumer in the United States is $3 to $5. You can succeed at selling the same brand in India by setting up a plant there, making smaller bottles, and using low-cost manufacturing labor. You might be able to get the price down to about $2. Unfortunately, over 500 million people in India live on an income of less than $1 a day; they still cannot afford your shampoo. A clever frugal solution would be to have street vendors in every city and village sell shampoo in small sachets. To build this solution, you must deploy frugal thinking for product strategy, pricing, engineering, manufacturing, delivery, and service.

Expect frugal thinking to accelerate in the West. With over 50 million Americans lacking medical insurance and 60 million lacking regular bank accounts, it is obvious the Western world has ignored frugal markets and, therefore, frugal thinking for too long. Such people are crying out for new ways to save money.

Expect frugal markets in every nation to grow more quickly in the next five years. According to an article in *The Economist*, a "growing number of Western universities are taking the frugal message to heart. Santa Clara University has a Frugal Innovation Lab. Stanford University has an (unfrugally named)

Entrepreneurial Design for Extreme Affordability program. Cambridge University has an Inclusive Design program. Even the Obama administration has an Office of Social Innovation and Civic Participation, to encourage grassroots entrepreneurs in health care and energy."[11]

Remember, true innovation loves constraints. By deploying frugal thinking, world-class innovators and intrapreneurs are able to keep the new entrants at bay and also stay competitive with the existing product portfolio. We believe this approach is going to become more popular in Western businesses in the near future.

Conclusion

If your company is like many other organizations that have embarked on an innovation journey, finding ideas in the first year is not the problem. Finding intrapreneurs is also not that difficult. The challenge is in the second and third years. You will need a solid innovation engine to source radical ideas then. In this chapter, we explored proceeding once you find the ideas, the road the ideas travel, and how to keep them alive. Ideas come from people who feel safe in a climate that promotes discovery, exploration, and experimentation.

We also learned about five power skills that every organization must practice in order to keep the idea pipeline full. Teach these to your leaders and intrapreneurs to improve their critical *and* creative thinking. When implemented well, these skills can lead you to many game-changing opportunities for your organization. To recap, the skills are listed next.

Skill #1: Develop Discontent
Skill #2: Convergence Thinking
Skill #3: Find Pivots
Skill #4: Overturn Orthodoxies
Skill #5: Think Frugally

Here is a stretch suggestion: Embed these five power skills in your HR system, especially for top talent, key managers, and certified intrapreneurs.

Notes

1. Comments on a new energy business model from FERC Chairman Jon Wellinghoff at the 2012 Green Biz VERGE Conference, March 15, 2012 "VERGE: Converging Energy, Information, Buildings and Transportation." www.greenbiz.com/video/2012/03/27/jon-wellinghoff-conversation-joel-makower.
2. Peter Lyman and Hal R. Varian, "How Much Information." *School of Information Management at University of California at Berkley*, 2000.

3. Shelley Carson, *Your Creative Brain: Seven Steps to Maximize Imagination, Productivity, and Innovation in Your Life* (San Francisco: Jossey-Bass, 2012), p. 215

4. Sarah Caron, "14 Big Businesses that Started in a Recession," InsideCRM.com, www.insidecrm.com/features/businesses-started-slump-111108

5. Kris Frieswick, "The Turning Point—What Options Do Companies Have when Their Industries Are Dying?" *CFO Magazine*, April 1, 2005, www.cfo.com/article.cfm/3786531

6. Ibid.

7. Scott D. Anthony, "Disruption Is a Moving Target," *Harvard Business Review* (July 15, 2004): page no..

8. Clayton M. Christensen, *The Innovator's Dilemma: When New Technologies Cause Great Firms to Fail* (Boston: Harvard Business Review Press, 1997).

9. Vijay Govindarajan and Chris Trimble, *Reverse Innovation: Create Far from Home, Win Everywhere* (Boston: Harvard Business Review Press, 2012).

10. Navi Radjou, Jaideep Prabhu, and Simone Ahuja, *Jugaad Innovation: Think Frugal, Be Flexible, Generate Breakthrough Growth* (San Francisco: Jossey-Bass, 2012).

11. "Asian Innovation: Frugal Ideas Are Spreading from East to West," *The Economist*, March 24, 2012. www.economist.com/node/21551028

CHAPTER 10

The *One* Secret about Innovation

Embrace the *one* secret. Everyone can innovate or contribute to innovation efforts. But can they do it year after year? Organizations can identify and launch an unending pipeline of great innovations if they embrace this one secret that will continually produce streams of innovation success. What is the secret?

It is true that milk contains butter; corn seeds contain oil; and cane yields sugar. But by merely holding milk in the hand, you cannot get butter; burning corn cannot yield oil; shaking the cane will not result in a shower of sugar. Merely knowing that your company needs to be innovative does not create innovations. Reading books and sending employees to creativity and innovation workshops alone won't yield the optimum results from innovation-related activities.

The cycle of investment–effort–management–results is no longer modern or sufficient enough for growth. It may work for a little while, but don't bet on it for continuous growth. The world of commerce is very different today from what it was like yesterday. The factors driving change are too numerous and invisible.

There is *one* secret that can help you outcompete. This secret is within your grasp. You already have it. You don't need to buy it. You just need to discover it for yourself and for everyone around you, at all levels.

If you activate this hidden secret, it will enable a tremendous number of innovations. You will still need to support this secret with a good innovation strategy, a playbook, and an execution methodology, as explained in the earlier chapters.

Many organizations have been successful without enabling this secret, but eventually they stagnate. The world-class innovators know this secret and are using it to outpace their competitors. Inherently you know it also but are not able to operationalize it easily and continuously.

This secret will turn milk into butter and take an average company to great heights. It cannot be fully harnessed overnight. But every company can find it and use it to grow their business.

Let's explore it together.

Story of Silicon Valley

What is the formula for success behind Silicon Valley?

According to authors Arun Rao and Piero Scaruffi, in *A History of Silicon Valley*:

> *The microprocessor that runs your smart phone in 2012 is a million times cheaper, a hundred thousand times smaller and thousands of times more powerful than a mainframe of the 1970s. In less than four decades the computing power that one can buy with the same amount of money has increased a billion times. The amount of data that one can store for $50 has also multiplied astronomically (one teradata for less than $100 in 2012 versus 28 megabytes for $115,500 on the IBM 1301 Model 1 of 1961, whereas one tera is one million megas). The number of documents that one can print and mail has also increased by several orders of magnitude. The speed at which a document is transmitted has decreased from days to milliseconds, down nine orders of magnitude. The amount of free information available to the user of a computer has escalated from the documents of an office in the 1960s to the 30 billion webpages of the Web in 2010.[1]*

Silicon Valley has been very successful over the last four decades. Every leadership training program and management book cites it as the source of digital revolution and computing inventions.

However, that is not the case. Computers were *not* invented in Silicon Valley and it has never been home to the largest hardware or software companies. It did not invent the personal computer, the transistor, integrated chips, the Internet, the World Wide Web, browsers, search engines, e-commerce technologies, or social networking. It did not even invent the telephone, cellular phone, or the smartphone. Then why does everyone hail Silicon Valley as a technological marvel: The reason is, at some point, Silicon Valley figured out how to *bring in the best inventions* and turn them into the *game-changing innovations* the world's markets were waiting for. More important, it has mastered the skills on how to "viral" new inventions.

It started with the focus on infotech—hardware, software, and the convergence of telecommunications domains. Today, there is renewed focus on biotech and greentech also. Silicon Valley entrepreneurs and intrapreneurs have mastered the game of exploiting inventions coming out of the East Coast of the United States. For example, AT&T Bell Labs (New Jersey) invented the semiconductor electronics technology that powers every computer in the world—of any size. IBM (New York) created data storage. Xerox (Connecticut) perfected graphical and human user interfaces, such as Mac and Windows, mouse, and touch-screen technologies. The U.S. government invented the Internet and used the Stanford Research Institute as a node. In Europe, the European

Organization for Nuclear Research (CERN) invented the World Wide Web, but it was first tested in collaboration with Stanford University's SLAC National Accelerator Laboratory, formally known as Stanford Linear Accelerator Center (SLAC).

In the early years, many smart engineers (with intrapreneurial qualities) disliked working for large companies because their employers did not allow them to start new projects that would exploit the research coming from the East Coast. So they started their own ventures, using the core research from the East. Silicon Valley has never housed the likes of AT&T's Bell Labs or IBM's Watson Lab that churn out Nobel laureates. Most of the valley focuses on the D in R&D

You may think that we should never look to Silicon Valley for the next big thing but instead look elsewhere. Based on history, that is partially correct. We will continue to look elsewhere for extraordinary game-changing *inventions* in fields such as energy, biosciences, material sciences, transportation, and so on. But when it comes to personal computing, Internet services, mobile phones, and, in the near future, biotechnology and environmentally friendly green technology, we should be able to turn to Silicon Valley for answers.

"In a sense, Silicon Valley *loves* socially destabilizing technologies. It has a unique (almost evil) knack for understanding the socially destabilizing potential of an invention and then making lots of money out of it,"[2] says Scaruffi. Fundamentally, that is why people define Silicon Valley as an engine for innovations. We can conclude that Silicon Valley is not where inventions occur but where uncontested innovations arise. In today's complex and sophisticated world, it is more important to positively impact human society rather than just create an original invention for the sake of invention.

When you assess the roots of Silicon Valley companies and their culture, you discover three mantras they live by:

1. Challenge the status quo, especially the authoritarian spine
2. Think new and novel
3. Improve the lives of everyone on Earth

Silicon Valley developed after important sociopolitical unrest that started in the San Francisco Bay Area and then spread all over the world, such as the free speech movement and the hippie movement. New Age lifestyles and countercultures have always been in the genes of the Bay Area, starting with the early gold miners of the 1800s. This culture of independence and individualism is inherent in the DNA of the Bay Area and predates Silicon Valley's start-ups.

It is this do-it-yourself ideology of the maverick that began Silicon Valley. Then the notable engineering schools arrived, along with government investments, university–industry partnerships, and, finally, the explosion of private investments in the form of venture capital and private equity. All of this would not have happened without the *creative independence spirit* that propelled the Bay Area to be the new destination for high-tech growth.

Another insight concerns the location. Could Silicon Valley have started somewhere else in the world, such as the East Coast of the United States, London, or Germany? The answer is no. What propelled Silicon Valley was the high regard for ultra-freedom combined with abundant youthful spirit. At the core of Silicon Valley, we find the concurrent evolutions of both the youth culture and the high-tech industry. Both are akin to the two sides of a coin and, therefore, difficult to separate. Both represented the power of youth and zeal for high tech.

In London, young Isaac Tigret opened the first Hard Rock Café because he saw the unfair class system that gave privileges to the best dressed and affluent in society, leaving out the "low-class" citizens. He was a rebel and wanted to change such notions. He invited anyone and everyone to come. Very quickly the Beatles, Eric Clapton, and Jimi Hendrix started to hang out there. As they say, the rest is history. Like many other cultural attributes, this European upper-class system had been exported to the East Coast of the United States. Even today, if you work for an East Coast company, invariably you will run into a corporate culture where promotions are directly correlated to an Ivy League education and the way you look and dress. Silicon Valley could not have started on the East Coast or in Europe for the same reasons the hippie and freedom of speech movements could not—a lack of free-spirited *playful independence.*

Historically with East Coast company cultures, especially in Europe, the corporate rewards systems promoted strictly from within even if the candidate did not have the skills, although it is somewhat different now. This often meant that excellent engineering talent from outside was ignored. This mind-set also encouraged good engineers to become complacent and move upward into nontechnical careers, completely shutting down any creative/innovative engineering ideas within the company. This is the negative side effect of knowledge sharing confined within company walls.

In huge contrast, Silicon Valley engineers continuously refine their technical skills *as they move* from company to company while at the same time facilitating a flow of knowledge from company to company. On the East Coast and in Europe, you are valued by how many years you have remained with one company or in one industry and the degree of power conferred by your job title. In Silicon Valley, you earn a premium for working with numerous companies in a short period of time.

This may be why, in Europe, engineering positions were considered inferior to market-facing positions, such as sales and marketing jobs, while in Silicon Valley, being an engineer is a status symbol only second to being an entrepreneur. In Europe, customer-facing positions made more money and had better prospects than highly talented engineers. Europe forced thousands of bright engineers into mediocre bureaucratic or sales positions (suit and tie); Silicon Valley converted them into advisors to the board or founders of companies (blue jeans and T-shirts).

Another big lesson we can learn from Silicon Valley is the diverse global talent it attracts. It is a dreamland for the smartest technocrats on the planet. It is the cool place to be for education and turning dreams into reality. The Bay Area had been underpopulated before the Silicon Valley boom. Today immigrants are the majority there. Most came to the United States with low or no professional status, but when they arrived in Silicon Valley, they automatically became part of the majority over-night—first-class citizens.

The antiestablishment spirit acted like a magnet drawing those highly educated immigrants to the Bay Area. It made work feel like it wasn't work but a way to fully express oneself.

Finally, the venture capital industry began to take shape. It was originally established because of U.S. and European governments. The political prowess of these two giants funded the development of the first computer. NASA, the U.S. space agency, was the first customer for integrated circuits. The Internet was invented for government projects and to connect various agencies together. When it was successful, the government turned it into a business. Silicon Valley's history shows that governments invested in high-risk long-term projects while private investment and venture capitalists invested in near-term less risky endeavors. The U.S. government was the largest venture capitalist and was the most influential strategist while the venture capitalists were responsible for creating the story of valuation and creating markets for new innovations.

There is one other element that has been very important to the success of Silicon Valley that is hard to quantify in an Excel Worksheet. It is the role of creativity. Because of its social tapestry, lifestyle, diversity, and global values, Silicon Valley operates with a unique undercurrent of creativity: a degree of chance. Work is often viewed as play, not as a duty or a job. Fun and human ideals prevail over money and status. This is the one secret of Silicon Valley—to tolerate *playful chance*.

The eccentric independence and creativity of the years from the 1970s to 2000 cannot be forgotten and will always drive Silicon Valley to continue to produce global brands, such as Google (the global leader in search), Apple (the dominant force in handheld devices), and Oracle (the behemoth of business software). These brands show us that one thing about innovation: Involved in innovation are a durable culture of play, risk taking, and early adoption of new inventions.

This *one thing* is the *playful mind-set* that is the very fabric of Silicon Valley. It is its soul and its DNA. It pervades the entire infrastructure and is designed to promote, assist, and reward risk takers in new technologies. That infrastructure consists not only of laboratories and plants but also of corporate law firms, marketing agencies, employment agencies – headhunters and, of course, investors.

Remember, the culture of inventing was never the mission; the culture of turning an invention into a viral innovation has always been the specialty of Silicon Valley.

The perfect ecosystem for building your innovation engines is the story of Silicon Valley itself. It teaches the power of the ingenuity, passions, and motivations of thousands of bright engineers and businesspeople. These entrepreneurs and intra-preneurs carry a vision: to make Silicon Valley the engine available to the people of the world via the Web because of a smartphone; a search for information—Google; socialization—Facebook; shopping the Web—eBay; and paying remotely—PayPal.

Soon that same engine will try to solve the deepest challenges facing humanity, such as energy, water, oil, poverty, and meaning.

Hang on for the ride!

The *One* Thing

Therefore, I offer *one* important lesson about innovation from the story of Silicon Valley to build a climate and culture for playful independence in every corner of your organization. Promote playful independence as the daily behavior for every employee.

Rao and Scaruffi's research shows that

> Many places in the world have tried to "build their own Silicon Valley," such as Malaysia's Multimedia Super Corridor, Dubai's Internet City, Bangalore's eCity, and China's Zhongguancun Science Park. None has succeeded. The closest has been Singapore, whose GDP of $182 billion (2008) is less than half of the Bay Area's GDP of $427 billion. However, venture capitalists invested $1,370 per capita in the Bay Area (2006) versus $180 in Singapore (nonetheless ahead of New York's $107).[3]

Why have these other areas failed? Was it because of location? Or lack of sustained-sponsorship by the governments? Or lack of great engineering minds? Or lack of a venture capital community? The answer is none of the above. Please allow me to propose that the main reason for failure is that the organizational cultures of the companies established in these locations lack playful independence.

Silicon Valley was not launched with a vision of creating a playful independence in the DNA of each company there. But that doesn't mean today's corporations should not be.

Playful Independence

"Play" means to act "for the fun of it." Fun comes as an adrenaline rush, a feeling of euphoria—mild or wild. We play to have fun. We play to develop relationships. We love our hobbies because we are playful in them. We lose track of time and sometimes even forget to eat or drink when we are having fun. When we play, we become one with the activity. Some people might call it a flow or a live meditation. When we play, we lose our self-consciousness and sometimes even our body consciousness. Such oneness with our favorite activity is exhilarating and stress-free. It generates a feeling of deep accomplishment.

"Independence" is the freedom to think, speak, and act in harmony with one's belief, values, and assumptions. When such independence exists, the person feels open-hearted and not constrained. She feels safe in her speech and actions, without worrying "Will I get fired?" or "Will I be judged by others?" She also is open to transparent conversations both ways, like it or not. If she is wrong, she welcomes constructive feedback, and if she is right, she wills everyone around her to take the credit. She knows that such independence is not given but earned. There is a feeling of loyalty to her work. To her, the yardstick of success is the freedom to accumulate new skills, competencies, and knowledge, not the next job title up the ladder.

Silicon Valley operates with this unique employee engagement model. It has a different view of failure. It operates on the unique key value of collectivism, which is the opposite of the East Coast company culture. Silicon Valley seems to despise the East Coast mind-set. Not overtly, but the fathers of Silicon Valley wanted to show the world how to deliver Picasso-like engineering success stories. They were never satisfied with current and as-is. Today, every company in Silicon Valley is continually, if not exclusively, focused on answering "What if?" not "Why it?"

Different View of Failure

Most managers struggle with the concept of failure not only with their own actions, but also that of their subordinates, especially when they perceive such actions of others reflect back upon them. Bernd Kriegesmann, Thomas Kley, and Markus G. Schwering discovered a preference within companies to develop "zero error cultures" as managers strive to reach business excellence standards in a hypercompetitive environment.[4] When zero-error performance standards are combined with the dogma of short-term positive contributions, most managers will always prefer to skew toward tried and tested behavior patterns.

When we meet with senior executives, they tell us that they want their managers to be creative and take risks, but those managers are actually being rewarded for predictable, fault-free, well-proven, tried and trusted methods for delivering results. It is not uncommon for companies to create a culture of imitation and plagiarism. Often they promote safe action and antipathy toward making errors.

At Google, the cofounders have established a cleanup day, where they sunset products no longer marketable. These are celebration events that promote failure and new knowledge acquired through those projects. No one gets fired. At BMW, one of its factories gives out a flop-of-the-month award to honor employees who champion innovative ideas that fail during rollout. The award is given to the senior executive in charge and is called "successful failure."[5] These firms recognize that failures, learning, and innovating are inextricable. If failures do not occur once in a while, one is probably not curious enough to try something new. Yet in most companies, failure is greatly avoided at all costs; instead, something safer in the middle route is chosen. Fear of failure, however, promotes mediocrity.

With such a mind-set, employees attach certain costs to failing. They don't want their names associated with any failed projects. These *perceived* costs are what create organizational gravity – feeling of stagnation and lack of forward movement towards growth. As an example, consider bankruptcy. Clearly it is a type of failure. But it is a benefit also. The liberal laws of the United States reduce the perceived cost of failure for any start-up company. Therefore, bankruptcy actually promotes more innovation by new firms.

In a large company, a good exercise is to ask people to cite people they know who have attempted something entrepreneurial, then failed, and then paid a clear price in terms of job loss, a smaller pay raise, a missed promotion, a blemished record, loss of autonomy, personal embarrassment, loss of stature, or something else. They will have difficulty recalling such examples. This proves that failure is mostly a *perceptual phenomenon* in large organizations. In other words, the perceived cost of failure is psychological. These costs can easily be reduced by an open and trusted climate between managers and subordinates. R. W. Johnson, Jr., the former CEO of Johnson & Johnson, once said that "failure is our most important product."

In the early days of 3M, it was operating in the mining business and almost went bankrupt before it became the company it is today. Eventually it gave up the mining business and completely changed its structure to manufacture other products, such as sandpaper. The management and employees of 3M believed that it could become a large company someday. During the bankruptcy era, employees worked for free sometimes to keep the company operating. The mining business died but 3M lived. The people of 3M succeeded because they understood one of the most important success concepts worthy of teaching all managers: Products may die but companies live. Failure is required to create a successful future; sponsor it, promote it, embrace it, celebrate it.

Key Value of Teams

Neither entrepreneuring nor intrapreneuring happens without teams. Creating inventions and innovations in a large company is a team business. Someone may be an idea owner, someone else may be the champion who sponsors it, and someone else may help persevere in the face of resistance and rejection, make adaptations, and keep the idea alive. A motivated coordinated group of coworkers, each with unique gifts, skills, and methods, can contribute to make the idea move down the innovation funnel. Innovations just don't happen without a villagelike effort.

This positive pattern, which exists in every organization, is called an I versus We culture.

"I" refers to an individualistic focus with self-orientation. It implies a motivation for one's own control and success for power and fame. This attitude is rooted in self-preservation and promotion at the cost of others on the team. Pride is derived from one's own personal achievements. "We," however, promotes the goals of the larger group, with an emphasis on sharing, respect for the group's success, and concern for the group's welfare.

According to research by Michael H. Morris, Ramon A. Avila, and Jeffrey Alien, the I culture may nurture an individual's self-confidence, accountability, competitive spirit, and risk taking and can generate new breakthrough innovations. It can, however, also produce higher levels of stress, interpersonal conflicts, and selfishness. A We culture promotes consensus building, create harmonious relationships, fosters collaboration, and creates synergies for social support and can result in a continuous flow of incremental innovations. A downside to the We culture could be losing a competitive edge, relying on others often, too much group thinking, greater emotionally dependency, or compromising rather than optimizing behaviors. We-ism can create a closed-minded singular view of how to deal with challenges within a team or a department.

In order to create your innovation engine, you will need to create a culture that is a balance of both I and We attributes. Innovation success will come when there are individuals who can take it upon themselves to initiate new ideas, rely on the spirit of cooperation among others, and be supported by group ownership to take nascent ideas forward. Innovation teams must master the skill between both. Within such teams, there should be tolerance for the idea owner to champion the idea in the early stages of development. As ideas move along the innovation pipeline, other team members must be able to collaborate, meet deadlines, and overcome unanticipated barriers and be open to redefining original ideas and solutions. Sometimes it is the intrapreneur who keeps the team in line; other times the team is the voice of reason.[6]

Playful independence means having a tolerance for risk taking, fear is removed from failure, and there is a balance between individualism and collectivism. To create a climate and culture of innovation, promote it. If you do, what would your company look like?

At this time, there are four important questions you might ask about playful independence.

1. What is the source for playful independence?
2. How can it help find disruptive opportunities?
3. What are the hidden benefits of it?
4. How do you cultivate it?

The Source

The source of playful independence is *within* people, not outside them. It is invisible because it shows up based on a person's values, beliefs, and assumptions. Everyone has the ability to be playful within their own context. People's view of the world is an expression of their current life design: a summation of past experiences and cultivated values. We can say that playful independence directly arises from a person's character.

Finding Disruptive Opportunities

Innovation helps migrate companies and markets from an existing business model to another. In that journey, innovation requires a bit of luck, some preparation, hard work, and immersion. Invariably, this effort leads to uncovering new insights and opportunities. When you discover new insights, they are like what Geoffrey Moore describes as the first bowling pin. In a ten-pin bowling game, the highest points are given to the person who knocks down all ten pins with the first roll, called a strike. The best strategy for winning is to knock down the lead pin with a precision angle. If you roll the ball perfectly, all ten pins will come down.

Market disruptions occur when something similar happens to your new product or a service. Moore suggests that not everyone can find the lead pin and not everyone can knock it down, even if they see it. But if you want disruptive innovation, you must:

- Have a desire to play the game.
- Find the lead pin.

- Prepare to knock it down.
- Roll the ball.
- If you don't succeed the first time, try it multiple times until you win. (In bowling, there are ten frames per game, which means you have up to ten chances to beat your opponent.)

Facebook executed the bowling pin strategy brilliantly by starting at Harvard and then spreading out to other colleges and eventually to the general public. If Facebook started out with, say, 1,000 users spread randomly across the world, it wouldn't have demonstrated its usefulness so clearly to anyone. But since the first 1,000 users were at Harvard, Facebook became extremely useful to the Harvard student body. Those students in turn had friends at other colleges, which allowed Facebook to hop from one school to another. Amazon started with books first, then diversified into CDs, DVDs, MP3 downloads, software, video games, electronics, apparel, furniture, food, toys, jewelry, and now even wine.

The key point here is that in order to win the game of business innovation, playful independence must be a cultural attribute practiced daily in your company.

Benefits of Playful Independence

Playful independence is not about a human resource competency that you ask your head of HR to go out and buy or build. It is a mind-set attribute. It is a business filter through which you envision the future of your company. It is an act of daily habit as simple as breathing in and breathing out.

When it exists, besides the obvious benefits of possibly developing disruptive innovations for your firm, playful independence can also expand organizational learning and knowledge base.

Learning, in relation to the organization, should focus on a broad range of innovation research. Both the content of the material knowledge gained and the style in which the material is learned are cited as crucial to developing intrapreneurs. Unorthodox learning techniques through playlike experiences can provoke learners into using innovative methods of problem solving in future situations, which tends to arouse curiosity and provide new knowledge.

Individual learning and intrapreneurship are deeply related, as they combine to create the culture and processes of organizational learning. Intrapreneurs, in turn, help increase performance and renew organizational structures and strategies for the purpose of better adapting to new demands.[7] Intrapreneurs influence organizational learning particularly as it relates to opportunity assessment and the creation and/or commercialization of new knowledge-intensive products, processes, or services.[8]

Intrapreneurs use their individual and organizational learning to turn innovative ideas into profitable products. Carlos Molina and Jaime L. Callahan[9] summarize the process succinctly: "Intrapreneurs learn as individuals first, and then share this knowledge with their teams. Teams enable intrapreneurs to engage their particular backgrounds or specializations under a strategic perspective to support a firm's goals." Therefore, we can say that playful independence can make employees and teams more intrapreneurial. It enables individuals to bounce ideas off one another and openly experiment, in turn giving them the possibility to create new knowledge they can use to cope with constantly changing environmental demands. They are then able to use that knowledge to evaluate their organization's position versus other organizations. Because individual learning can produce team members with different perspectives and skill sets, each person learns from the others, helping to improve the organization's position among its competitors by striving toward innovation.[10]

Benson Honig, a researcher, performed a longitudinal survey of 283 Swedish intrapreneurs and entrepreneurs regarding their preferred learning techniques. The study revealed that these innovators continually reexamined knowledge for additional uses and applications. Learning was a dynamic process with strategic means, usually governed by a cycle of discovery, diffusion of knowledge, and informed action. Therefore, organizations that explicitly push learning, specifically through playful independence as a core value, can also increase the overall level of creativity among employees.[11]

Because expert intrapreneurs pride themselves on finding innovation in every aspect of their work, they possess the ability to problem-solve through various scenarios. Interpretation is also seen as a way to learn how to think critically and see the world in a different perspective. In people, this learning process develops new mental maps and behavioral changes that can be linked to intrapreneurial activities. In turn, the interpretation process facilitates a more conceptual approach to learning. Conceptual learning happens through know-how, meaning employees have a critical vision for interpreting existing procedures or conditions.[12] Ultimately, the knowledge and context expands both the learner and the company at large.

The other large benefit of playful independence is the social capital generated in the culture, which plays a critical role in effective intrapreneurship. According to studies by Abbas Monnavarian and Mostafa Ashena, the most important characteristic for successful intrapreneurship is not a person's current capabilities, knowledge, or intellectual proficiency but rather his or her relationships with others who support the use and understanding of knowledge. The researchers claim that employees are no longer selected simply for their knowledge; today's organizations increasingly require contributions too great for any one person to handle on their own. Instead, effective workers build a network of relationships that allow them to take advantage of a vast array of resources they would not be able to generate without others.[13]

How to Cultivate It?

There are hundreds of ways to move from a why-it to a what-if culture. As we have discussed throughout the book, when it comes to building an intrapreneurial spirit, one of the best methods is to attract and retain intrapreneurs skewed toward achieving innovation. Doing this includes developing an evolving organizational design that fosters freedom and ownership of work, and advertising it to potential employees. This builds value within their work and enhances their stake in creating a successful product. John Zimmerman cites GE as an ideal example of this practice. It creates strategic business units that work on specific services/products while remaining free from the majority of corporate bureaucracy and still being supplemented with reporting and training. These units are semiautonomous and report to the CEO to enhance their visibility, which allows employees to develop personal projects that benefit the company.[14]

Leaders can stimulate learning processes that promote intrapreneurship among individual employees through training and development. Organizations can also foster an environment that encourages incidental learning by incorporating learning-to-learn formal learning experiences (training, workshops, and special projects) and by expanding the way employees see their roles within the organization.[15]

Finally, it is no surprise that the best way to cultivate playful independence and intrapreneurship is through nurturing trust, reciprocity, and open, high-quality communication. Intrapreneurial organizations engage in new business venturing, are innovative, continuously renew themselves, and are proactive. In transitional economies that are moving toward becoming more developed economies, social capital can be particularly crucial for a company's survival.[16]

Final Thoughts

According to Chuck Palus and David Horth, authors of *The Leader's Edge: Six Creative Competencies for Navigating Complex Challenges*, there is a need to "see with new eyes."[17] Human beings are magnificent, imperfect, and predictable and do not like change. That is why the entire change management field was born: to help organizations adapt to a constantly changing world. Since the days of Adam and Eve, humans have learned to lead life through habits, looking at things with the same eyes, analyzing using the same logic and creating the same perceptions. It is easy to get used to this routine. Most managers act the same way. According to the authors, most managers "act on what they expect to see," take shortcuts, and do not spend enough time analyzing information to make sound judgments. It's as if the managers are walking around blindfolded since they have already created built-in perceptions of what they see.

What is needed is the ability to *see* something new, especially on a daily basis. What we need to do is build a new lens for ourselves and others. We must teach people to see something new every day—although seeing alone is not enough.

The only way humankind really changes is through the emotions of love or fear. "Love" means passion, to desire, to achieve, and to give. "Fear" means a feeling of failure, loss, negative judgment by others, and demise. These two emotions are at the center of all human motivations. They make the world go around. Love is expansive. Fear is contractive. Fear can generate short-term creative solutions. Love can create lasting momentum. Teach people to play with what they love. At the end of their play lies your next innovative idea.

Cognitive Role of Innovation

We live in the supposedly bone-dry world of hypothesis testing, mathematical constraints, and data-dependent empiricism. In the world of science, innovation stretches the mind to find an explanation when the universe wants to hold on to its secrets just a little longer. This can-do attitude has been a boon to solve the world's most constrained challenges, such as the continuity of mass and energy, absolute zero, and the Higgs boson, the supposedly last subatomic particle waiting to be roped into the fold. Innovation is a critical enabler of discovery. It is the occasional architect of that rare, wonderful breakthrough even when the tide of scientific opinion is against you.

Looking through the scientific lens reminds us of the extreme power of innovation as a cognitive tool, one that every human being already possesses. Through innovation, we all can transcend social, professional, political, scientific, and, most important, personal limits. If only we all put it to better and more frequent use!

For Young Intrapreneurs in the Making

People ask me, "How did you do it, Jatin?" or "How have you become so successful as an entrepreneur with so many businesses launched?"

Joining my father, while I was still in my last year of college at University of Connecticut, to become an entrepreneur was the most natural and obvious and most joyful and energizing decision of my life: to fully commit 100% to my life's work.

I've spent every day falling more madly in love with how I live my life, spend my time, with the contributions I'm making to society, and with the discontent and growth that I feel each day.

My journey getting here was both arduous and enthralling. It was not at all straightforward. I had numerous experiences that collectively brought me here, teaching me what I'm capable of and showing me what does and does not resonate.

Though I've known for many years that my purpose is to unlock human potential, it took me some time to fully embrace my intuition, to figure out how to actualize this vision, and to build the courage to lean into my fears. And it's still, and always will be, an ongoing learning process.

I've made enough so-called mistakes to realize none was an error. It was just a lesson I had not learned previously. Now I can easily sense the right directions to move toward to find what we are all searching for: a feeling of deep fulfillment and meaning. Though I would relive my mistakes all over again in a second, and I believe making more mistakes helps you grow and gain confidence, I'd love to save you some time and energy along your journey.

Inspired by all the great masters who have shaped my being today and based on my own experiences and conversations with friends who are in love with how they work, live, and play, here are some final pearls of wisdom that I have kept close to me. I offer them with deep conviction and best wishes to help you make your life a true playground.

1. **Work should be worship.** If it is *just* work, it is not play. If it is not play, it is not a *playground* for living. Work shouldn't feel like work. Envision the lifestyle you want to live, and design your career to enable the lifestyle you want for yourself—and your lifestyle includes your work. Ask yourself, "Wait, am I seriously working right now, or am I living my purpose?" You can hardly distinguish among work, play, and life, as they are all intertwined. A great grand master from the East, Sri Sathya Sai Baba, once said, "Life is a challenge, meet it. Life is a dream, realize it. Life is a game, play it. Life is Love, enjoy it."

2. **Live a life of integrity.** Align personal and human values. Everything we think, see, speak, and do is a reflection of our inner values. Is the cup half full or half empty? We seem to attract what we think. Our thoughts are shaped by our inner belief system. Therefore, our worldview is shaped by our inner thought patterns and habits. Human values are universal, the same in all human beings, and are never changing—truth, love, peace, right action, and nonviolence. Integrity is when personal values are aligned to human values. This alignment will inspire you to move mountains, if that's what you have to do to realize your vision.

3. **Be willing to unlearn.** Unlearning is more important than learning. Everyone around you will tell you what you need to learn. But hardly anyone will tell you what you need to forget permanently. This is because they don't know what to unlearn themselves. The best way to unlearn is to look at your image in the mirror and be honest with yourself. You know your strengths and weaknesses, and what hinders you from operating at maximum levels of daily performance. Listen to yourself making excuses for everything in your life. Become a witness, and you will see all the silly things you do every day: speaking before thinking, not listening to a conversation fully, forgetting people's names, judging people on how they look when you don't even know them, and so on. Mountains of mental patterns shape your beliefs today. Most were given to you by your parents, teachers, and bosses. Inside you, there exists patterns about how you should dress going to work, how you should get a job, how to deal with tough bosses, how to get a promotion, and thousands of others. Ask how you got those patterns and whether you wanted them in the first place. These patterns are the very source of boxed thinking that limits your creative and critical thinking every day. They are holding you back and you don't even know it. Bring these patterns to the surface so you can see their attributes—good or bad. Unlearn your negative mental patterns. Doing so will create new space for more important lessons in life.

4. **Welcome painful lessons.** Pleasure is an interval between two pains. Joy and sorrow are parts of life. Only through pain will the best growth occur. Welcome pain and be willing to suffer. In some ways, your life's work is less about following a passion and more about your willingness to suffer along the way. The

best innovators and memorable leaders went through immensely challenging tests. You'll be exposed to unexpected challenges and setbacks, and you may endure hardship, rejection, and sacrifice. These roadblocks will motivate you. You are not alone but in the company of the best change agents in the world. Embrace short-term pain and discomfort as opportunities for learning, growth, and depth; they're critical to finding beautiful and joyous moments of pleasure just around the corner.

5. **Commitment is the highest virtue.** When you honor your thoughts and words, you discover your life's highest work. Then the question of commitment is easy. There is no pause, hesitation, or afterthought. When your mind and heart say yes, your body automatically says yes. Commitment to your work feels as natural as breathing in and breathing out. You cannot imagine spending your time dedicated to any other purpose. If you cannot follow through on your commitments, you must proactively manage them so the other party is not impacted negatively. As you mature, you are able to recognize how to manage the expectations of others. The virtue of commitment brings others to develop a deeper faith and trust in their relationship with you.

6. **It is all about the art of living.** Your career and work make up just one of many commitments in your life. To fully enjoy the pleasures of creation and the beauty of nature, live fully and enjoy life. Though you may be captivated and enthralled by the project at work, make room for healthy routines, such as fitness, connection, spontaneity, and play. These activities reenergize and enable you to live a holistically fulfilling life.

7. **Don't be a hero, be a zero.** It is easy to take credit for good work. But it is unlikely you did it on your own. Numerous people around you helped you become "great" at something—parents, friends, teachers, old bosses, and customers. Be humble, be grateful to them in your heart. Walk away from praise. Your ego probably doesn't need it; it is probably big enough as is (as mine is).

Many days you will come home from a challenging day, fall asleep exhausted, somewhat fulfilled, and ready for tomorrow. But you go to sleep each night grateful for the day, because you happen to be doing what you love to do. You are physically tired but mentally and spiritually happy. That is when you know you're on the right path. You gave the day your all, and you can't wait to do it all over again tomorrow. This is your life, and you cannot imagine living it any other way.

Namaste, and best wishes—always!

Notes

1. Arun Rao and Piero Scaruffi, *A History of Silicon Valley: The Greatest Creation of Wealth in the History of the Planet* (Omniware Group, 2011). www.scaruffi.com/politics/sil18.html
2. Ibid.

3. Ibid.
4. Bernd Kriegesmann, Thomas Kley, and Markus G. Schwering, "Creative Errors and Heroic Failures: Capturing Their Innovative Potential," *Journal of Business Strategy* 26, No. 3 (2005): 57–64.
5. Ibid.
6. Michael H. Morris, Ramon A. Avila, and Jeffrey Alien, "Individualism and Modern Corporation: Implications for Innovation and Entrepreneurship," *Journal of Management* 19, No. 3 (1993): 595–612.
7. K. S. Davis, "Design Criteria in the Evaluation of Potential Intrapreneurs," *Journal of Engineering and Technology Management* 16, No. 3 (1999): 295–327.
8. Mark Robinson, "The Ten Commandments of Intrapreneurs," *New Zealand Management* 48, No. 11 (2001): 95–98.
9. Carlos Molina and Jaime L. Callahan, "Fostering Organizational Performance: The Role of Learning and Intrapreneurship," *Journal of European Industrial Training* 33, No. 5 (2009): 392.
10. David R. Schwandt, "When Managers Become Philosophers: Integrating Learning with Sensemaking," *Academy of Management Learning & Education* 4, No. 2 (2005): 176–192.
11. Benson Honig, "Learning Strategies and Resources for Entrepreneurs and Intrapreneurs," *Entrepreneurship Theory and Practice* 26, No. 1 (2001): 21–35.
12. Molina and Callahan, "Fostering Organizational Performance."
13. Abbas Monnavarian and Mostafa Ashena, "Intrapreneurship: The Role of Social Capital—Empirical Evidence and Proposal of a New Model of Intrapreneurship and Its Relationship with Social Capital," *Business Strategies Series* 10, No. 6 (2009): 383–389.
14. John Zimmerman, "Corporate Entrepreneurship at GE and Intel," *Journal of Business Case Studies* 6, No. 5 (2010): 77.
15. P. M. Silva and J. L. Callahan, "The Epistemology of Learning," *Proceedings of the Academy of Human Resource Development* (Cambridge, MA, Emerald: 2009).
16. Monnavarian and Ashena, "Intrapreneurship."
17. Charles J. Palus and David M. Horth, *The Leader's Edge: Six Creative Competencies for Navigating Complex Challenges* (San Francisco, 2002, Jossey-Bass), p.182.

About the Author

Jatin H. Desai, cofounder and chief executive officer, The DeSai Group, is a seasoned business executive, strategic advisor, and coach for senior leadership teams. He has extensive field experience in the areas of strategy alignment, corporate innovation, talent management, large-scale change, culture transformation, and information technology.

Jatin has been active in leadership and operating roles since 1983, when he cofounded The DeSai Group, which offers solutions for strategy, innovation, and leadership development and provides innovation execution and management services to Fortune 1000 and Global 2000 companies.

Jatin has helped address and manage the complex issues of worldwide market strategies, positioning, market expansion, development of innovative applications, mergers and acquisitions, joint venture management, cross-border outsourcing, new product introductions, human resource development, sales and marketing, and manufacturing.

His firm's clients in United States include: The Hartford Insurance, Bristol-Myers, Cigna, Merck, Macy's, Atkins, Wal-Mart, Vistage, Ketchum, BIC, Pitney Bowes, Prudential, ESPN, Duracell, United Technologies Corporation, Pratt & Whitney, Carrier Corporation, Sikorsky Aircraft, Hamilton Sundstrand, Vistage International, and many more. In India, the firm's clients include: 3M, ABB, Aditya Birla Group, Bangalore Airport, Bosch, Coromandel International, Cognizant, JRF, Infosys, Infotech, Larsen & Toubro, Siemens, Titan Industries, UPL, and many more.

Jatin has written papers, regularly speaks at conferences, lectures at colleges and universities, and delivers educational workshops.

In India, he has given speeches at IIT-Bombay, IIM-Bangalore, University of Mysore, Sri Sathya Sai University in AP, Alliance Business School in Bangalore, MS Ramaiah Institute of Technology in Bangalore, and CII–Bangalore. He chaired a session at CII's Fifth Annual Innovation Summit in Bangalore in June 2009 and lectured at the CII Innovation Forum in Bangalore in July 2009.

Jatin was born and raised in Gujarat, India, and immigrated to the United States at a young age in 1973. He holds B.S. degrees in electrical engineering and computer science from the University of Connecticut. He currently lives with his wife and three children near Hartford, Connecticut.

Jatin can be reached at jdesai@desai.com.

Index